FIGURATIONS OF THE FUTURE

Ethnography, Theory, Experiment

Series Editors:
Martin Holbraad, Department of Anthropology, University College London
Morten Axel Pedersen, Department of Anthropology, University of Copenhagen
Rane Willerslev, Museum of Cultural History, University of Oslo

In recent years, ethnography has been increasingly recognized as a core method for generating qualitative data within the social sciences and humanities. This series explores a more radical, methodological potential of ethnography: its role as an arena of theoretical experimentation. It includes volumes that call for a rethinking of the relationship between ethnography and theory in order to question, and experimentally transform, existing understandings of the contemporary world.

Volume 1
AN ANTHROPOLOGICAL TROMPE L'OEIL FOR A COMMON WORLD
AN ESSAY ON THE ECONOMY OF KNOWLEDGE
By Alberto Corsín Jiménez

Volume 2
FIGURATIONS OF THE FUTURE
FORMS AND TEMPORALITIES OF LEFT RADICAL POLITICS
IN NORTHERN EUROPE
By Stine Krøijer

FIGURATIONS OF THE FUTURE
Forms and Temporalities of Left Radical Politics in Northern Europe

By Stine Krøijer

berghahn
NEW YORK · OXFORD
www.berghahnbooks.com

First published in 2015 by
Berghahn Books
www.berghahnbooks.com

© 2015, 2020 Stine Krøijer
First paperback edition published in 2020

All rights reserved.
Except for the quotation of short passages for the purposes
of criticism and review, no part of this book may be reproduced
in any form or by any means, electronic or mechanical,
including photocopying, recording, or any information
storage and retrieval system now known or to be invented,
without written permission of the publisher.

Library of Congress Cataloging-in-Publication Data

A C.I.P. cataloging record is available from the Library of Congress

British Library Cataloguing in Publication Data

A catalogue record for this book is available from the British Library

Printed on acid-free paper

ISBN 978-1-78238-736-7 (hardback)
ISBN 978-1-78920-753-8 (paperback)
ISBN 978-1-78238-737-4 (ebook)

CONTENTS

Acknowledgements … vi

Introduction … 1

Chapter 1. 'Other Worlds Are Possible': A Political Cosmology of Capitalism … 37

A DUMPSTER DIVE … 62

Chapter 2. Becoming Absorbed: Youth and the Interstices of Active Time in Ungdomshuset … 67

NAMING AND RAISING A CHILD … 96

Chapter 3. 'A Common Choreography of Action': Preparations and Intentions … 101

Chapter 4. 'We Are Humans, What Are You?': Securitization, Unpredictability and Enemy-Becoming … 138

A STREET DANCE IN HYSKENSTRÆDE … 162

Chapter 5. 'I Used to Run as the Black Bloc': Style and Perspectivist Time in Protests and Direct Actions … 165

Conclusion: The Collective Body as a Theory of Politics … 207

References … 219

Index … 233

ACKNOWLEDGEMENTS

This book was made possible by all the people who shared their experiences of political activism with me, who allowed me to attend their meetings, housed and fed me and gave me access to their lives, hopes and concerns. I would like to thank all my friends and informants in Ungdomshuset in Copenhagen, those working around the European Social Forum in Malmö, the Revolt Network in Berlin and Strasbourg, and the many activists in Copenhagen who permitted me to follow their activities. I am grateful for their openness, and their genuine interest in discussing and analysing the meaning and range of their practices. I sincerely hope I have done them justice.

I would like to thank Inger Sjørslev for her careful and generous encouragement and thoughtful reading of various drafts. Martin Holbraad, Elizabeth Povinelli, Morten Axel Petersen, Heiko Henkel and the three reviewers at Berghahn Books have contributed greatly to developing my thoughts, and have made whatever insights are expressed in this book more coherent. I have benefited from the exchange of ideas with my many colleagues at the Department of Anthropology at the University of Copenhagen, particularly within the Forum on Political Anthropology, the Scandinavia 'reading group' and the Spectacular Disorder research project. Individual chapters have received the considered comments and critique of many friends and colleagues – Ida Sofie Matzen, Dan Hirslund, Maja Hojer Bruun, Birgitte Romme Larsen, Regnar Kristensen and Helene Risør among others. I have had stimulating discussions on youth, mobilization and violence with researchers at Dignity (the Danish Institute against Torture), and fellow anthropologists at Aarhus University working on ethnographies of youth and the future. I also thank my students Mark,

Ea, Julie and Jacob who acted as my affinity group and field assistants in Strasbourg.

Last but not least, I thank my family for all their love and support. Special thoughts go to my mother – my first encounter with a person of anarchist sensibilities – who unfortunately did not live to see this project through.

The personal names of people who make an appearance in this book are pseudonyms, and in some cases the names of activist networks, or other details, have been altered in order to protect interlocutors against legal prosecution. A version of Chapter 2 appeared in *Social Analysis* 55, 2 (2011), and a version of Chapter 4 in Martin Holbraad and Morten Axel Pedersen (eds), *Times of Security* (Routledge, 2013). Some of the ethnographic passages in Chapters 1 and 5 first appeared in articles in *Social Analysis* 54, 3 (2010) and in Anne Line Dalsgård, Martin Demant Frederiksen, Lotte Meinert and Susanne Højlund (eds), *Ethnographies of Youth and Temporality* (Temple University Press, 2014). My research has been made possible by funding from the Danish Council for Independent Research. The Council has also generously funded a new project, which enabled me to set aside time to write this book. I thank Menaka Roy and the editors at Berghahn Books for careful language editing.

Introduction

'Argh! I need a beer – that meeting just went on forever', says Aske with a deep sigh as we walk along a snowy street in Copenhagen looking for a pub. For the past three hours, we have been sitting, together with some 200 climate activists, on a cold floor in an abandoned municipal building in order to evaluate a mass action known as Reclaim Power, which produced a spectacular confrontation between activists and the police during the Copenhagen Climate Summit in 2009. Nevertheless, most people, including Aske and I, had left the meeting when the agenda moved from shared reflections on the successes and failures of the action to 'future movement building'.

Aske, a 24-year-old activist from Copenhagen, has fallen behind a group of activists from Climate Justice Action (CJA). He shivers slightly in his big coat and confesses to have been kind of depressed for the past few months, that is, ever since the eviction and deportation of a group of Iraqi refugees from a squatted church in the neighbourhood. Aske had been involved in this action for several months as an organizer, but then he disappeared, saying he was depressed and burned out. 'So, it was nice to be back on the streets', he says now, with a boyish smile. The aim of the Reclaim Power action had been to push our way through a fence and an imposing line of riot police around the official summit venue in order to hold a 'people's assembly' on climate issues somewhere inside. Aske had followed the front line from the sound truck, which was accompanying the action, and comments: 'It was actually amazing how close we were. They [the police] were overwhelmed by that first push, and we were so close to getting through. I could see it from the truck: it was just like one big body acting together. All this talk about forming a new movement: in these situations, you *are* the movement'. I nod and make a mental note of this recurrent theme, namely the emergence of a collective body in the moment of confrontation with the police – an issue that has figured repeatedly during my research on the form politics takes among Left radical activists. We reach the door of a typical local pub: 'Push! Push!' we laugh, mimicking the battle cry of the action, while trying to open the heavy wooden door. In the bar, the exchange of views about tactics continues over cheap beers after all those assembled have aired their frustration with the poor facilitation of the evaluation meeting. Iza, an experienced action trainer from the US gets our full attention when she argues: 'I know that you Danes have good experiences with this tactic of pushing, but we were too few for it to work in a summit context. Swarming is better. People move faster in smaller groups, so it is much less predictable'.

My thoughts wander off. There had been a moment of hesitation when the so-called blue bloc[1] reached the perimeter of the Bella Centre summit venue. Nobody took immediate initiative to storm the police line. People were urged to move left of the truck accompanying the action, which was decorated with an oversize bolt cutter. From the truck there is a countdown: '10, 9, 8 ... Push! Push!' a woman cried. There was some serious chaos, screaming and pushing for around twenty minutes as activists used their bodies to push their way into the summit area. As a consequence, a tight pack – of rebel clowns, Italian Ya Basta activists, British climate-campers and Swedish, German and Danish Left radical activists – was created between the truck and the police line. Some participants had padded up their bodies to endure the beating of the riot police who had formed a ring around the fence. Only a few activists from the so-called bike bloc, who had transformed discarded bikes into elaborate 'machines of resistance', had made it across a muddy stream into the summit area on air mattresses. Another group had pressed themselves against the police line with a big inflatable rubber dingy while chanting, 'This is not a riot!' Sitting in the pub, I was still puzzled about what kind of statement this was. In the end, the protesters had settled for holding the peoples' assembly on climate change right there in the snowy street.

Back in the nicotine-stained bar, somebody fetches another round of beer while Iza concludes: 'What I have been most concerned about is the level of infiltration. The surveillance has a very negative effect; people get scared, and you cannot talk or plan together. Instead, we should try to be radically open'. We continue exchanging stories, mixed with exhilarated planning of a street party, practical concerns about what to do with the leftover vegetables from the soup kitchens and whether the climate assembly on the street could qualify 'as a new thing', as well as the legal perspectives of the charges against the arrested spokespersons, even though we are exhausted after months of preparation.

* * *

This situation from the Climate Summit in 2009 speaks to the main concern addressed in the following pages, namely the forms that politics takes among Left radical activists in Northern Europe. This book sets out to describe how activists perceive the possibilities of radical change in the context of the emerging economic crisis that peaked between 2007 and 2009, as well as the different forms of political action in daily life and during larger actions, such as the one described above. I describe the troubled relationship between activists and the police, highlighting the importance of bodily confrontation for the success of an action.

The central argument is that the forms of action must be understood within an analytical perspective relating to time and the future. I argue that the various forms of action have effects of their own, insofar as they often succeed in giving determinate form to an indeterminate future. This is what I will call 'figurations of the future'. In this book I espouse a perspectivist model of time inspired by the theorization of Amerindian perspectivism (Viveiros de Castro 1992, 1998) and more recent anthropological theory on time (Guyer 2007; Hodges 2008; Miyazaki 2004; Robbins 2001, 2007a), which implies that the future is not conceptualized as a future point in linear time, but as a co-present bodily perspective. This stems from the way activists associate their activism with bodily vitality and absorption in common activity. The collective body that often emerges during actions and confrontations with the police momentarily becomes the site of such a bodily perspective – a state of active time – which is 'at a right angle' (see Viveiros de Castro 1998: 476) of what we conventionally think of as a continuum between the past, the present and the future. By taking its point of departure in the body, time becomes a question of simultaneous angle or perspective rather than continuum or sequence.

The empirical centre of gravity for my work is Copenhagen in Denmark, and southern Sweden, with excursions to other northern European cities such as Berlin and Strasbourg. The abstract question about the relationship between form and time is investigated through a number of ethnographic cases: the struggle over a local social centre known as Ungdomshuset (the Youth House), and summit protests and other direct action in Copenhagen and Strasbourg, in addition to more mundane food practices such as 'dumpster diving' (collecting food discarded in supermarket containers) and eating vegan food. Finally, the European Social Forum in Malmö, Sweden, is also examined. The European Social Forum is an offspring of the World Social Forum; the latter was established as a supplement to summit protesting and focuses on formulating concrete alternatives to capitalism under the slogan 'Another World is Possible' (De Angelis 2006; De Soosa Santos 2006; Juris 2008; Leite et al. 2007; Osterweil 2004; Sen 2004a, 2004b).

'Left radical' is an umbrella term used by activists in Northern Europe to refer to people on the extra-parliamentarian Left of an anarchist, autonomist and anti-capitalist bent. In Denmark, they were previously referred to as squatters or *autonome* (autonomous activists). After the protests against the summit of the World Trade Organization (WTO) in Seattle in 1999, the same tendencies have also been characterized as the radical strain of the alterglobalization movement (see also Graeber 2002, 2009; Juris 2008; Maeckelbergh 2009; Sullivan 2005).[2] In recent years this has taken a new turn, resulting in expressions such as the Indignados in Spain and other southern European countries (Castañada 2012; Della Porta and Andretta 2013) and the Occupy movement across the US and 951 cities in 82 countries (Della Porta and Andretta 2013: 24; Juris 2012; Razsa and Kurnik 2012), which pivot on the exercise of direct democracy in public space, thereby turning the logic of previous protest practices inside out. Radical in the emic sense refers here to someone who advocates radical change, or in other words, a change from the roots of capitalist society. How this is envisioned and practised is, as I shall return to in a more detailed discussion below, strikingly different from most other Marxist-inspired revolutionary movements in Europe. I show that the radicalism of northern European activists is as much related to a second, albeit related, sense of radicalism: the 'going to the origin' of widespread values about equality, autonomy, popular participation in democracy and social 'spaciousness'.

In anthropology, the study of social movements and so-called everyday resistance has revealed valuable insights into how people create meaning and come together to form collective actors (Alvarez et al. 1998; Della Porta 2006, 2007; Melucci 2003; Scott 1985; Starn 1992). However, the alterglobalization movement, and Left radical activists in particular, does not work on the basis of a shared identity or a single vision of social change (Maeckelbergh 2009: 6–7; see also Eschle 2011). One of the key contributions of the present work is to offer a way of thinking about activism, which does not rely on the constitutive power of an intentional agent, their prior motives or ideologies. Instead, the approach will highlight the unchosen quality of activism. By this, I do not mean that activists are forced or lured into participating in actions, but rather that what we conventionally think of as intentionality and political ideologies are possible effects of participation, not the motivating factors. Activists tend to describe themselves as people 'engaged in' or 'absorbed by' common activity, and I believe that this should have ramifications for how action and activism are conceptualized. In this book, the attention is, therefore, on political action *as* form, and what the form engenders.

In the media, Left radical activists are often associated with pictures of youth wearing black, hurling stones at the police and burning cars, and protesters pushing against police lines inside a cloud of tear gas. Several anthropologists have analysed this representation and its effects (de Jong, Shaw and Stammers 2005; Graeber 2009; Juris 2008; Sullivan 2005), and found that the public are seldom offered much of an explanation as to why the protests play out the way they do. On the contrary, it is often concluded that these actions are entirely devoid of content and not worthy of being recognized as reasonable in public. Hence, what concerns me here is the need to understand the logic of this particular way of protesting, and to illuminate why politics takes on this particular form.

In Chapter 1, I describe the European Social Forum in Malmö, and instead of ideology I use the concept of cosmology heuristically to denote both how capitalism is a world inhabited by different forces, and how activists experience their place within it. Through an activist optic, capitalism has nothing 'outside' or 'after' it, but may potentially embody and offer interstices of other times and worlds. The political cosmology of activists hence lacks the holism usually associated with the concept of cosmology (Handelman 2008; Schrempp 1992). Towards the end of the book, I show how it is the forms of action that engender a political cosmology rather than the other way around (cf. Sneath et al. 2009; Willerslev and Pedersen 2010) which entail that cosmology is understood as a kind of secondary effect.

Activists' acute interest in forms and choreographies of action, tactics of confronting the police and elaborate ideas about style is one of the characteristics of Left radical protesting that has puzzled me the most while being in the field. Here I describe the logics and effects of the various forms of action, and argue that style is a 'native' concept that encompasses and is used to assess the appropriateness, effectiveness and persuasiveness of form. This concept of style hence points to the inseparability of form and content in Left radical politics. Building on this concept of style for theoretical purposes, I argue that it neither makes sense to uphold a division between form and content in politics, nor to tie the political to individual plans and intentions. I propose instead to think of politics as mediated manifestations of intentionality, which means that it is the forms that materialize intentions and produce time. I show that a good style – that is, an appropriate form for the situation at hand – calls forth particular figurations of time. These figurations, different patterns of active time and dead time, repeat themselves across different scales, from the exceptional to the mundane, and what we, for lack of better options, tend to call the local and the global.

Transient Fields and Landscapes of Activism

A few years ago, an acquaintance of mine, who was involved in launching the Danish activist network Globale Rødder,[3] tried to explain the difference between Left radical activists and the traditional Marxist Left in Europe to me by comparing the former's view of the future with Islam's aniconism (prohibition against images). 'By avoiding painting pictures of the future, we want to avoid the idolatry and sectarianism that has characterized the Marxist Left, and which inevitably follow from defining one's endpoint', he explained at a meeting in a study circle where we were reading Michael Hardt and Antonio Negri's work *Empire* (2000), which describes the emergence of a new global regime without temporal boundaries. My acquaintance believed that the future must remain 'an open question'. Our conversation, which became the point of departure for the present project and its particular focus on the relationship between form and future, sparked my initial puzzlement: How is it possible to do politics without stating one's intentions, let alone formulating ideological programmes? And how can this particular relationship between form and future be made sense of?

Whereas the strategy in revolutionary Marxist movements is historically based on a linear mobilization of the masses and accumulation of revolutionary force in mass movements until the awaiting workers and soldiers could finally 'storm the Winter Palace' (Maeckelbergh 2009), Left radical activists are preoccupied by revolts and direct actions in relation to a diversity of issues, and as much by the politicization of the routines of daily life like eating and other living habits, modelling social and gender relations, as by so-called 'do-it-yourself' practices.[4]

Whereas all ethnographic fieldwork is marked by temporality and transience, this is, in my experience, particularly true when it comes to this field: demonstrations, direct actions and meetings are phenomena of a relatively short duration, and the provisional protest camps set up in the context of summit protests often only stand for a couple of weeks.

Likewise, organizational 'identities' such as Globale Rødder seldom exist for more than a few years, whereas some, like the international activist network Revolt, only crops up temporarily around summit mobilizations. Even apparently durable social centres are evicted, whereby activities are displaced onto the street. The organizational anchorage of Left radical activism seemingly consisted of a loose network of activists stretched across the globe, which led me to experience an initial doubt about how to 'cut the network', as Strathern (1996; see also 2004) puts it. Instead of focusing on how relationships are created in a world of seemingly unbounded networks, Strathern seeks, in an implicit critique of actor–network theory, to illuminate how some phenomena – for example, relations of power and control such as property ownership – create a break or a cut in the network. Among activists it is the ability to become involved and endure that may sever social relations, and which from an analytical point of view served as a way to delimit the field. When I started working on this book, the Left radical scene in Copenhagen was locked into a struggle for the maintenance of a local social centre known as Ungdomshuset. At the same time, the sense of renewal and energy associated with the Social Forum process seemed to be coming to an end, while summit mobilizations were expected to abate, becoming replaced by more 'sustained' forms of activism, for example around social centres and other local struggles (Eschle 2005: 1767–68; Juris 2008: 158–59). Traversing the landscape of Left radical activism in Nørrebro highlights all the issues of transience and continuities inherent to the scene.

Nørrebro is the most densely populated neighbourhood in Denmark, being located just outside the ramparts of the historical centre of Copenhagen. Apart from Freetown Christiania,[5] located in the opposite direction from the city centre, Nørrebro is the part of Copenhagen with the largest concentration of relatively durable activist spaces such as social centres, activist-driven cafés and co-ops, collectives and other 'amicable places', like community centres and friendly churches. Every street is steeped in activist history, while the backyards and alleyways open themselves up as escape routes that allow one to evade an arrest or a pincer movement by the police during an action or demonstration.

Cruising from the inner city down Nørrebrogade, the main street in the neighbourhood, one passes Queen Louise's Bridge, the site of innumerable clashes between activists and the police, and the place where the tradition of street parties on New Year's eve was started by Left radical activists. After passing buildings housing several large co-operatives, one reaches a side street named Ravnsborggade that runs into Ryesgade, where squatters in 1986 took the defence of a squatted house to the streets. This event was the culmination of a wave of evictions of squatted houses in the area (such as Allotria, Den Lille Fjer and Bazooka), as activists blocked the street with massive homemade barricades and beat off police attacks over nine days (Heinemann 1995).[6]

Continuing along Nørrebrogade, one crosses Blågårdsgade, the centre of what in the 1970s and 1980s was known as *den sorte firkant* (the black rectangle) – a popular name deriving from the black demarcation around the area in the municipality's slum clearance plan of 1971. At the time, this traditional working-class area was scruffy and run down, and many inhabitants lived in poverty or suffered from other social problems. As a result, it became the focus of the city council's large-scale and, in the view of many, heavy-handed reconstruction while local inhabitants, organized as the Nørrebro Beboeraktion (Nørrebro Tenants' Action Group), vainly argued for their increased involvement in decision-making and implementation (see Heinemann 1995).

Inspired by young squatters in other European cities, particularly Amsterdam and Zurich, a group of young socialists, including youngsters from Christiania and students from the Free Gymnasium,[7] started squatting empty buildings that were ripe for demolition (Mikkelsen and Karpantschof 2001: 615). Their demands were twofold: the provision of accommodation for young people that would allow collective dwelling, and a self-managed social centre for cultural and political activities. The Ini'tive (*sic*) Group for a Youth House was formed, but negotiations with the municipality about the provision of a space of their own were at first fruitless. After several occupations and evictions, which turned increasingly violent, the municipality signed an agreement with 'the users' on the running of Ungdomshuset in 1982.[8]

In recent years, the area around Blågårdsgade and the adjacent Blågårds Plads has received intense media coverage due to the activities of 'young troublemakers of immigrant descent', many of whom moved into the new public housing that was constructed during the demolition of the area. Several clashes between these young adults and the police have taken place in the area, most heatedly in February 2008, triggered by the police's body search of an elderly citizen of immigrant descent. After the attempted 'normalization' and clearance of Pusher Street in Christiania in 2004,[9] this part of the city has become the object of a struggle over the control of the marijuana market, and many activists feel that the police guard in a particularly zealous manner the so-called visitation zones, where people living in or passing through a particular zone can be searched without prior suspicion of a criminal offence. Along Blågårdsgade there is also a 'hack lab' – used by a community of hackers and computer activists – as well as an activist art space and a community centre, which was used as a convergence space during the Climate Summit in Copenhagen in 2009, as well as an anti-fascist café and information shop.

The next street on the right-hand side is Fælledvej, and several Left radical collectives are (still) located here, despite the sky-rocketing real-estate prices that have occurred since the mid 1990s (something that in activist circles is referred to as the second wave of gentrification), which led to an inflow of more well-off middle-class families and young professionals.[10] Fælledvej was the site of violent clashes between activists and the police after a second Danish referendum about the ratification of the Maastricht Treaty on 18 May 1993. The police lost control of the street, allegedly because they could not find the key for the locker holding tear gas canisters. They ended up firing 113 shots at the protesters, who had blocked the street near the Sankt Hans Square and were hurling stones at the police, who were approaching in an insecure shield formation in order to support a colleague who had called for back-up (Heinemann 1995: 217–24).

The night resulted in eleven activists being wounded from live ammunition, more than 100 police officers with greater or lesser wounds, and public critique of the police's handling of the event. As a consequence, the police changed the tactics of their interception force, and particularly their strategy for crowd control (Vittrup 2002). The new mobile concept of engagement (*indsatskoncept*), which I shall return to in Chapter 4, also required the acquisition of new uniforms, weaponry and armoured vehicles, whereby the force could give up the defensive use of shields as a means of riot control. After this, it has proved more difficult for activists to enter into the near-symmetrical conflicts with the police that had characterized the 1980s, and large-scale confrontations in the streets of Copenhagen became less frequent (Karpantschof and Mikkelsen 2009: 33–34) until the conflict over Ungdomshuset. That said, the events on 18 May 1993 led to a dawning recognition among activists of the expediency of entering into near-symmetrical confrontations with the police.

If one continues a bit further along Nørrebrogade, the street Griffenfeldsgade follows on the left, where the former activist-driven co-op Spidsroden was located, as well as an underground music venue and the premises of the Front of Socialist Youth and International Forum. In between Griffenfeldsgade and Stengade streets lie Folkets Park and Folkets Hus (People's Park and People's House). Folkets Hus was squatted in 1971, shortly after the more famous squatting of Christiania, and it still continues as a self-managed social centre. The house was revitalized after the eviction from Ungdomshuset in 2007, and now counts on a well-attended café named Café Under Construction, with frequent, popular soup kitchens and meeting spaces. Folkets Park outside the house has a playground and is used for music sessions, meetings and general hanging around. The present day park is what is left of what was known as Byggeren (slang for 'a place to build'), an activity playground established by local inhabitants and activists in 1973. In 1980, the clearance of Byggeren was the object of the first major clashes between activists and police in the area. Folkets Park Initiativet (People's Park Initiative), a group consisting of local inhabitants and activists, has re-emerged several times since then to reconstruct and defend this green space.

Following Nørrebrogade, one passes by Assistens Kirkegården (Assistant Graveyard), established in 1790 where a number of national luminaries are buried, such as Hans Christian Andersen, Søren Kirkegaard and Niels Bohr. Due to there being few green spaces in the neighbourhood, local inhabitants use the graveyard in the same way as they would any other public park, and the graffiti on the long yellow wall surrounding it is the place to take 'the temperature' of the activist scene in Copenhagen. On the next corner of Jagtvej, one can still see the empty hole in the block where the social centre Ungdomshuset was located until its demolition in March 2007.

In the eyes of the Danish public, Left radical activists have been associated with Ungdomshuset, although several other activist spaces, as we have seen, are located in the area. Ungdomshuset was the most unequivocally anarchist-inspired place, and was frequented by people with a strong interest in punk music, and/or a propensity for alternative lifestyles. The café known as Kafax has in some periods been a base for anti-fascist groups, while the planning of large actions has taken place at Folkets Hus, which is popular with activists inspired by the autonomist movement in Italy. However, all these activists have a shared anti-capitalist platform, and it would be wrong to confine particular groups and individuals to particular places, and thereby understand place-based belonging as the underlying logic. Instead, the places are the framework for a variety of activities that activists are (temporarily) absorbed by. Activists think of these places as autonomous spaces where it is possible to experiment with norms, values and forms of being together at a (internal) distance from the surrounding society (cf. Chritchley 2007: 113).

The activist scene in Copenhagen can best be understood as a complex network of people involved for stretches of time in more or less stable affinity groups and in temporary organizational structures. The term 'affinity group' is thought to have its origin in the *grupos de afinidad* of the Spanish Civil War, which were characterized as groups of friends that simultaneously made up the basic organizational units of the anarchist federation (Graeber 2009: 288). Affinity groups are still usually thought of as groups of friends who remain connected for a long period of time, and are engaged in politics together and/or have a social life outside political action, for example by living together in a collective.

In addition to the above meaning, the term affinity group is also used to refer to ad hoc groups (alliances) organized for shorter periods around a common task, for example during an action. Either way, the groups are expected to be based on mutual trust and to look out for each other during actions. Affinity groups are brought together during the planning of a large action, or across several actions, in temporary organizational structures.

The best way to describe the form of organization found among Left radical activists is probably with reference to Evans-Prichard's idea of ordered anarchy among the Nuer, who were organized in egalitarian segmentary groups (Evans-Prichard 1940: 147), that is, a system of relatively equal and small autonomous groups, which periodically come together to form larger communities. Along similar lines, the activist milieu does not have a central authority or organization, and the size of the political community depends to a large extent on the activity, the nature of the conflict and the power to mobilize peer affinity groups and network relations around particular events or causes. Activists identify themselves more with the activities they are or have been engaged in than with ideological identities such as anarchist, autonomist or Left radical. In this sense, it is the activity of 'doing something together' that delimits the seemingly unbound network (Strathern 1996), and the question about how many Left radical activists there are in Denmark, Northern Europe or elsewhere does not really make sense in absolute terms or outside the context of specific actions. In spite of all this, relatively stable social relations exist in the context of affinity groups, and around the so-called autonomous spaces, which can be understood here as particular, temporal configurations of social relations (Jiménez 2003: 140).

Becoming involved in Left radical activism transforms one's view of the neighbourhood; one begins to move within a different landscape, recognizing the large number of activist spaces, the virtual pasts and the unactualized futures embedded in the urban topography. The temporary and transient quality of the phenomenon under study significantly contributed to my insight about the importance of time for understanding the logic of this particular form of politics. In Chapter 2 I will return to how autonomy is configured in these spaces, something which serves to illuminate how what I call figurations of the future always have a spatial dimension, even if of varying durability.

Willingly or not, my work has come to resonate with the prominent trend of multi-sited fieldwork which, from the mid 1990s, has seen anthropologists move beyond the bounded field site in order to come to terms with the interconnected and unbounded world system (Marcus 1995). In practice, this demanded recurrent requests for access and repeated attempts at establishing close relations with various activist groups. While in the field, I came to realize that my initial research was characterized by what Matei Candea has called 'a problematic reconfiguration of holism' (Candea 2007: 169): I was seeking to uncover the totality, or at least a representative sample, of Left radical forms of action, while feeling haunted by a sense of incompleteness. I became acutely aware that the strategy pursued, which implied an imaginary ability to increase the complexity of the phenomenon via magnification, also entailed a loss of detail. In other words, the amount of data actually remained the same (Strathern 2004: xiv–xv).

Along the way, my attention was drawn to a figure that seemed to replicate itself through all the changes of scale (cf. Wagner 1991: 166). This self-scaling figure is what I call the figuration of the future. It operates across different scales, where each moment or figure of time mirrors all other such moments, in such a way that they come to serve as contexts for each other. In this mirroring, the relation between the figures harbours powers of digression, which sometimes contributes to a horizontal reinvention of form without relying on a master plan or ideological programme (Krøijer 2015; Massumi 2002: 16–17). One of the most desired objects of activism being newness, activists are continuously involved in planning new actions, which build on and adapt previous activities. In Chapter 5 I return to the concept of style that is deeply embedded in this reinvention of form, and I attend to how a figure is repeated, which momentarily gives determinate form to the indeterminate.

It is fair to say, therefore, that my primary field became these actually existing moments and figures that gathered the 'whole' network of relations into themselves. In principle, had I studied only one such brief moment it would be as complex as what would have been revealed through an attempt at enfolding the whole through a multi-sited approach. This realization has guided my form of writing and the structure of the book; different events and situations come to mirror and replicate each other, hopefully letting 'meaning' emerge along the way.

Form as Object

By 1990, the Danish police had evicted almost all squatted houses in Copenhagen, which led to a weakening of the squatters' movement and a reorientation among activists towards new causes, such as the fight against anti-racism and anti-fascism in the cities of Kollund and Kværs in southern Denmark. Moreover, the period saw a turn toward environmental issues, which was played out in the protests against the building of Øresundsbroen, a bridge connecting Denmark and southern Sweden, and in the upsurge of Critical Mass and Reclaim the Street actions, inspired by anti-road protests in Britain (Jordan 1998; McKay 1998), as well as in the initiation of urban guerrilla gardening, a kind of political gardening where activists take over a plot of land or even cracks in the pavement to grow their own food or flowers, and co-op shops, selling cheap, locally produced and organic foods and linking farmers and consumers. While Ungdomshuset had relatively slack years in the 1990s, the mobilizations around international summits and the upsurge of the so-called alterglobalization movement at the dawn of the twenty-first century provided a new impetus, in Denmark as elsewhere. Not only did Danish activists participate in summit protests, particularly in Prague in 2000 and at the EU summit protest in Göteborg in 2001, but the activist network, Globale Rødder, was also formed, becoming the Danish expression of the radical strain of the alterglobalization movement. Inspiration was drawn from the new forms of actions employed by the Tute Bianche (White Overalls) in Italy, and from the Zapatista rebellion in Chiapas, to mention a few.

During the EU summit in Copenhagen in 2002, a division within the Left radical scene in Copenhagen became evident. While there was agreement on opposing and confronting the meeting of ministers at the Bella Centre, there was disagreement about the tactics. A Danish Anarchist Federation was formed in the context of the summit, which favoured black bloc demonstrations – a form of action developed by German Left radicals in the 1980s, where people attending a protest give the demonstration a militant expression by wearing black clothes and masks and forming a tight bloc by locking arms to avoid identification and arrest. The tactic sometimes includes vandalism and street riots (see also Katsiaficas 2006; Graeber 2009). Globale Rødder, on the other hand, organized what was supposed to be a confrontational action of civil disobedience inspired by the Italian Tute Bianche, who also participated in the action at the Bella Centre in 2002, but under their later identity as the Disobedienti (the Disobedient). Activists who were involved in Globale Rødder consider this action to be a first attempt at adapting Tute Bianche's confrontational style of civil disobedience to a Danish context in order to move beyond the violence/non-violence dichotomy that continues to characterize the public debate about street protests. Many found that the action at the Bella Centre in Copenhagen was too 'symbolic', as they called it, and failed to 'expose the conflicts' underlying the European project.

Jumping ahead in time to the protests following the evictions from Ungdomshuset (2007–8), the contradictions there were partly overcome by adopting a new, 'diversity of tactics' approach to protesting. Diversity of tactics had been a successful way of agglutinating the different tendencies on the extra-parliamentarian Left when employed to block the G8 meeting in Heiligendamm in Germany, in summer 2007. Groups with different tactical preferences could work together in a common 'choreography of action' via a division into different colour-coded blocs, each developing its own tactics in pursuing the common goal of blockading the entrances to the summit area.

Danish activists participated in the protests in Rostock and Heiligendamm where the large blockade of the G8 summit was organized in five strands or 'fingers'. They later adapted the diversity of tactics in order to swarm a building in Copenhagen in October 2007, which they had picked out as their new social centre. Following this, new ways of combining forms of action and modes of entering into confrontation with the police have continued to develop in Copenhagen, which have allowed for the participation of activists with different tactical preferences. An example of this is Shut Down the Camp, a direct action against a retention centre for refugees outside Copenhagen, which I shall return to in Chapters 3 and 5.

From this discussion it becomes evident that forms of action travel – from the squatters' movement to the protests against the economic politics of the G8, the WTO and the World Bank; similarly, agendas change, from environmental and anti-racist agendas to a concern for global climate change. Along the way, the forms of action are adapted and altered, and new forms are invented. The newly invented bike bloc during the Climate Summit protests in Copenhagen is a fine example of this: not only did the British climate activists add a new kind of bloc to the protest choreography, but a fraction of the bloc also echoed the Danish action theatre group Solvognen's Santa Claus Army of 1974 when, all dressed as Santa Claus, they swarmed the summit venue on homemade 'warrior bikes', which are discarded bikes welded together with inventive features such as loudspeakers playing the sound of a marching crowd or with catapults that allow bikers to jump over a fence.

Taking the forms of the political among Left radical activists as the object of study also compels a broader attention to the significance of form. Contrary to older meaning-centred approaches, where bodily postures, costumes and material objects are legible objects full of symbolic meaning, newer approaches have highlighted how the relation between signs and their possible objects of signification is both complex and subject to change. Things and forms of action are not just passive transporters of human intentions, agency or identity, because not only is meaning almost inevitably transformed along the way, but things also have qualities of their own. It is key to the approach taken here that things and forms of action have effects regardless of how they are interpreted (Keane 2006: 186; Gell 1998; Henare et al. 2007). In Chapter 3 I shall return to this in an analysis of how large puppets at demonstrations (aspire to) become agentive subjects, whereas single activists seek to avoid becoming identified as instigators of action. The central issue in Chapter 4 is a concern with how activists and police alike struggle to interpret signs and assume indexicality (a connection between the sign and object of signification). What is important here, not least for my proposition about seeing activist forms of action as figurations of time, is that reality is not *pre*formed, or scripted beforehand, but *per*formed (Sjørslev 2007: 17), which, in my view, implies a constant reconfiguration of social relations.

A final point that must be made here in connection to activists' acute interest in and continuous experimentation with forms of action is that meaning does not primarily reside in one action or protest event, but relies on the internal relationship (Riles 1998) between various events.[11] Among activists, judgment about the success of an action relies more on the shrewd orchestration of a confrontation, in the light of all other such confrontations, than on actually obtaining the stated goal of an action (for example shutting down a retention centre for refugees). Piling up protests and political actions – as I will also continue to do throughout this book as part of my experiment with form – establishes relations in time. This is not only the work of historians or anthropologists, but also something activists actively engage in. It was their 'piling up' of events that led me to consider, from an analytical point of view, how time is reconfigured in activists' political practices, and how a meaningful direction seems to emerge from the relationship between them.

From Talk to Action

I already had a relationship with the Left radical scene before initiating my fieldwork. In the mid 1990s, a group of friends and I were involved in direct actions in opposition to the building of Øresundsbroen, as well as in Reclaim the Street actions and guerrilla gardening projects in Copenhagen.[12] After some years of being away, I touched base in the aforementioned study circle with friends who had been active in

Globale Rødder. This study circle, among others, became the originator of the Danish file-sharing initiative Piratgruppen (the Pirate Group), the EuroMayDay project concerned with migrant and precarious labour rights,[13] and was actively involved in importing the Social Forum process to Denmark in 2003. The first World Social Forum I attended was the one in Porto Alegre, Brazil, in 2004, and I participated in the organization and programme planning of the Danish Social Forum in 2007, this time with a view to initiating ethnographic fieldwork. It is therefore hard to determine exactly when activism ended and my ethnographic fieldwork began. In practice, my prior knowledge has been actualized as fieldwork when placed in dialogue with anthropological knowledge and modes of contextualizing experiences.

The Danish media has repeatedly represented the Left radical milieu in Copenhagen, and particularly Ungdomshuset, as closed to the public and inhospitable to newcomers. This is imprecise at best, but nevertheless influenced my own contact with activists around Ungdomshuset in the wake of the 2007 eviction. Based on activists' own stories, I have found that people have tended to get engaged in Left radical activism in one of two ways: either they are taken along by friends with whom they start hanging around a place where activists gather, whereupon they may become involved in concrete tasks; or they turn up at one of the frequent information meetings held to mobilize people for larger actions, again often in the company of friends. In accessing the field, I tried to follow analogous strategies of either getting to know people and being taken along, or attending meetings and expressing my interest in getting involved as researcher and activist. These strategies worked out fairly well in a Danish context, where it was, furthermore, also possible for activists to check up on my background.

I had planned to start fieldwork through a series of taped interviews with activists involved in the struggle around Ungdomshuset, because I expected that this would give me insights into their motivation for getting involved and perception of the political practices they were engaged in. I interviewed people who had been activists of Ungdomshuset for many years, and activists from other parts of the milieu who gathered around Ungdomshuset as the eviction approached, as well as young people who had been drawn to the struggle after the eviction. This developed into repeated conversations about getting involved, detailed descriptions of the organization of demonstrations, reflection on forms of action and tactics for dealing with the police when in the street, as well as dilemmas about how to face the municipality of Copenhagen (the former owner of the house). The interviews also served as a means of getting to know people and of making connections that I could build on later. In this sense, the interviews became a valuable way of accessing people who would later take me along to different activities.

Much to my surprise, and contrary to claims in the literature (see Rubow 2000: 21), I found that the interviews and more informal conversations (that is, language) were not the best way to get insight into topics like feelings, hopes and dreams for the future, and even less were they a means to grasp the special experiences of excitement and bodily intensity during direct actions. It is not that activists refrain from talking – talk is plentiful, for example, in the long planning meetings before actions – but their ideas about the future were not articulated in language. After trying different techniques, I realized that I had to take the activists' dictum about 'not to waste time talking' seriously (see Chapter 1) and turn to participation in actions. Through my participation in the field, I slowly came to realize that it is the forms of actions, rather than individuals, that are entities carrying motives and intentions, which also explains why it is so difficult to articulate these issues in language.

From the conflict over Ungdomshuset, my fieldwork proceeded by focusing on the European Social Forum held in Malmö in September 2008. I got in touch with the Nordic organizing committee and a couple of people working in the secretariat of the European Social Forum (ESF) in Malmö. I did not participate in the daily work, the dilemmas and conflicts, around which I had plenty of experiences from the Danish Social Forum. Instead, I undertook repeated interviews with two organizers, and followed the meetings of the European Preparatory Assembly (EPA), which is the body that follows and takes decisions on the ESF 'process' at the Europe level.[14] This was particularly insightful for coming to grips with how different people around Europe looked upon the ESF – as a process of change or as a momentary instantiation of what they were fighting for. As already hinted at, this was an occasion for stark differences of opinion to emerge between actors on the extra-parliamentarian left.

In addition, I contacted Action Network, an initiative of Swedish Left radical activists on the margins of the ESF, through which I hoped to illuminate the different ways that Left radical activists, NGOs, trade unions and the traditional Marxist left engage in the ESF. They organized a parallel and 'autonomous forum' at a newly inaugurated social centre in Malmö named Utkanten (the outskirt or margin). I interviewed three Swedish activists before and after the three-day event about their motivations, the activities they were involved in and their views of the official forum. In the beginning, they were overtly suspicious of me, or maybe of the questions I asked, thinking their answers might incriminate them, and they only agreed to meet up in public spaces such as parks and cafés. However, two of them invited me into their homes after the first encounter, which might not only be a corollary of activists' fear of police surveillance or of my having gained their confidence, but it may also, as I shall return to shortly, say something about the home as research site in Scandinavia.

During the social forum in Malmö, I followed both official and parallel activities of the autonomous forum, such as the official inauguration and the large joint demonstration aimed at displaying 'the strength' of the movement, as well as a number of workshops and talks, and attended a Reclaim the Street party organized by a loosely organized network simply called the Action Network. Few Danes were involved in planning, but many of my interlocutors involved in the Ungdomshuset case travelled to and participated in the four-day event.

Later, I followed several processes, but my focus was largely on participant observation, both in the planning and celebration of direct actions, particularly Shut Down the Camp in October 2008, planning for the NATO summit in Strasbourg in April 2009 and the preparations for the Climate Summit in Copenhagen in December 2009. This involved engaging early on in the planning of actions and logistics, participating in many meetings and taking on concrete organizational tasks together with others. After the conflict over Ungdomshuset, which was solved when the municipality of Copenhagen gave the activists a new social centre in June 2008, several of my key interlocutors started a network called Openhagen, which focused on gentrification and the privatization of public space. I followed their activities only sporadically, except for the so-called Undoing the City festival, a Reclaim the Street party in the inner city, which has found its way into these pages.

My sustained participation in the planning process around the NATO summit in Strasbourg and the Climate Summit in Copenhagen in 2009 made it possible for me to follow groups of people for stretches of time in order to penetrate the more spectacular protest performances in the street and view them from several angles. Nevertheless, it is impossible to gain a complete overview of all the preparations made for large actions; besides the large coordination meetings, a myriad of working groups crop up for taking care of action planning, media strategy and relations, alliance building and mobilization, financial management and logistics; this sometimes necessitates organizing accommodation and food for thousands of people. Several hundred can be involved during intense periods of planning in the months or weeks prior to an action, and many overlapping meetings are held each day. I have followed different routes, for example by focusing either on action planning or on logistics, which always involved participant observation in and of meetings (Jiménez 2007; Maeckelbergh 2009; Schwartzman 1987). I often found it difficult to follow the frenzied pace of the activities, in itself a reason why people sometimes 'drop out' of activism, claiming to have 'burned out'. In other words, my own experience of the exhausting tempo alerted me to both the sense of urgency and the fatigue that activists experience from time to time.

While the protests around summits or the eviction of social centres are highly visible events, sometimes involving spectacular riots or protests in the street, other modes of doing politics and forms of sociality remain invisible (or even secret), such as decision-making procedures, networking practices and the culture of security around actions, as well as the more mundane 'do-it-yourself' practices involved in concert planning or workshops on knitting and bike repair, dumpster diving and food consumption. I only became interested in the political activities that took place in activists' homes relatively late in the project, and they have, in consequence, received far less attention than they deserve. Probably because I had presented my research as focused on actions (in public space), people did not invite me to their homes, except for interviews, or when, during trips to Berlin and Strasbourg, I was considered a guest in need of a place to roll out my sleeping bag. As relationships evolved, I was more frequently invited to meetings in people's homes in Copenhagen, which sometimes allowed me to talk to people about domestic routines, eating and dwelling habits, and so on, but my access to social events in the home would have required a status as a close friend (or a different research strategy altogether).

According to Marianne Gullestad, Scandinavians tend to associate the home with closeness, intimacy, wholeness, authenticity and equality, and most social life with friends and family is home-centred (Gullestad 1992: 50–53). Yet, research in the home might not only rely on the character of the relationship, but also on the researcher's 'route' to the home. In this book I discuss a few examples of 'everyday forms of politics', not because I consider the home more real or authentic than the street, but because activists themselves consider these mundane forms of political action to be 'as important' as protesting. The practices break down the distinction between the everyday and the festive or sacred inherent to much performative theory (Gullestad 1992: 54–55; Leach 1985; Mitchell 2006), and point to the body as the site of politics.

My choosing to approach activism from different methodological angles also holds for my participation in protest events. In Shut Down the Camp and in Strasbourg, I participated without much concern about safety, being part of affinity groups with key interlocutors. This kind of participation did not only provide me with an experience of the affective side of protesting; in other circumstances, I have chosen to observe the choreography and sequencing of actions and demonstrations, or focused on talking to people about their undertakings. Finally, I have interviewed Danish police officers, supplemented with observation of the police on the street, readings on the operational tactics of the police in Denmark (Vittrup 2002) and EU policy documents concerned with security around major events. This has given me important insights into what kind of threat protests and activists are considered to be, and how the police seek to procure security via tactics of insecurity and unpredictability. Along the way, I have drawn on a number of additional sources such as YouTube videos circulating before and after protests, documentary films, an autobiography, activists' written flyers and 'zines' (small homemade publications of small circulation), accounts from protests posted on the internet and so on. I have also read through all Danish newspaper articles between 2006 and 2008 on Ungdomshuset, consulted the minutes from the municipal council of Copenhagen in relation to the case, and benefited from the booming literature on the subject (Hansen 2008; Karpantschof and Lindblom 2009; Karker 2007; Rasmussen 2008).

Access, Position, Ethics

In the Danish context, I had the experience of passing almost insensibly into the various activities I wished to study, although not having close friendships within the new generation of activists meant that I was seldom part of the more informal social gatherings where new ideas for actions are engendered. This seemingly unproblematic access was explained by one of my gatekeepers as a quality of my immediate appearance: 'People can simply tell by the way you look that you are okay', she said. I think that there is little doubt that, in a Scandinavian context, signalling equality via sameness in terms of looks, language and personal carriage (Gullestad 1992: 292) is important for being accepted. My prior experience as an activist enabled my success in this regard. But my gatekeeper's way of phrasing the idea also points to an issue that I shall return to later, namely how politics is seen as embedded in and elicited by the right form.

However, when I tried to gain access to the preparations for the NATO summit in Strasbourg, this trust proved to be insufficient, not least because my access was negotiated via e-mail. I will describe here the negotiation over access at some length because it not only illustrates the importance of personal ties, trust and knowledge of activist 'security culture' for gaining access (Robinson 2008), but also shows how the negotiations left me with only one available position within the field, namely that of a fully-fledged participant. In the early phases of my work, I registered on international listservs and frequently followed various homepages, in order to follow internal debates and activists' writings about forms of protesting, and to receive international 'calls for action' announcing, among other things, mobilizations for summit protests. Around the end of November 2008, I received the following:

> *NATO invites itself to the center of Europe in April 2009!*
> The 3rd and 4th of April, representatives of the countries members of NATO will meet again to celebrate their 60 years of domination, but also in order to develop their new plan to 'defend freedom' and quoting the terms of their own generals: 'A great strategy for an uncertain world'. From the 1st to the 5th April 2009 we will be present in Strasbourg and we'll oppose their 'globalization by force' with the creativity of our actions of resistance: direct actions, blockades, civil disobedience, demonstrations, meetings, debates, alternative village, convergence centers...

The same e-mail announced an international planning meeting to be held in Strasbourg, and I wrote to the organizers to ask if I could take part as a researcher, not failing to mention my interest in the European security architecture around major events and its consequences for the possibilities of protest as well as my prior involvement as an activist. A week later, I received an e-mail from a different quarter that recommended some readings on the subject, but when I wrote back insisting that I would like to participate, I received a brief rejection (and a possible opening) in an e-mail that only said: 'Mhm, to be honest: researcher interests are sure not welcome at the meeting. Don't know how to proceed?' The email was not signed with a name, but came from a relatively well-known network working on police repression during summits. I remembered that a person from this network had been giving a talk at a 'radical assembly' at Utkanten during the ESF in Malmö, which had been organized by one of my Swedish interlocutors. I therefore contacted her and asked if she would put in a good word for me, and subsequently wrote to my unnamed gatekeeper again trying to convince them of my good intentions with assurances of anonymity and protection of raw data, and promising not to write about the meeting until after the summit event. I received the reply: 'She wrote me already;) think you will find a way to come. Will you pass Berlin before maybe?' Later, when we were discussing my trip to Berlin, which I understood as a way to vet me before the meeting, the issue of trust was underlined together with an indication of my possible position in the field:

> I would say, I leave it up to you to decide to come to the meeting or with which 'identity' you participate. Friends say they trust you, so do I then ;) I'm just normally a bit uncomfortable with being 'watched', but if you also come to help then its fine, I think. But, if you like to come to Berlin in advance you are very welcome. Maybe we can then go with the train together. Write again if you need accommodation in Berlin.

I shall return to the particular story of my encounter with my gatekeeper, Jürgen, in Berlin, who until that point remained anonymous; what interests me here is rather how our e-mail correspondence reflects my encounter with a widespread uneasiness concerning my role as a researcher. I was usually explicitly asked to 'help out', 'lend a hand' and involve myself in practical organizing, sometimes even as a condition of my presence. When I went to Berlin, for example, it was set out explicitly that I should help facilitate the meeting, take notes and assist in the kitchen. Though I felt relatively comfortable with this, it also had ethical implications.

The particular position I was offered – together with the fact that my fieldwork was often undertaken in public spaces, or at other mass gatherings such as large meetings and protest camps (with several hundred or thousands of participants) – implied that not everyone present was aware of my role as an anthropologist. As I have described above, I was pushed in the direction of an activist role, inevitably leading to others being observed by me without their knowledge. I could with good reason have been denounced as a spy (Bulmer 1982: 3), something which was thrown into relief by two interlocutors who were revealed as undercover police agents by the press a couple of years later.[15] I handled this ethical problem about research consent (Hammersley and Atkinson 1995: 264) and the pitfalls of covert research (Scheper-Hughes 2004) by always introducing myself as an anthropologist when entering into conversations with people, following and describing only those who had been made aware of my research endeavours, and by making those not aware fade into the background in the text.

This position, along with widespread suspicions of surveillance (which are not completely unfounded) and legal actions against activists, have influenced my presentation of the ethnographic material. Generally, all names have been made up by me, and in addition I have sometimes found it necessary to alter details of people's life stories, their age, gender or occupation in the interests of anonymity. Due to court cases in the aftermath of the Climate Summit in Copenhagen, I have found it necessary to let one person appear under two different names in the text. For the same reason, a few ethnographic details have been left intentionally vague.

In the recent past, three ethnographies on the alterglobalization movement have been published, namely Jeffrey Juris's *Networking Futures: The Movements Against Corporate Globalization* (2008), Marianne Maeckelbergh's *The Will of the Many: How the Alterglobalization Movement is Changing the Face of Democracy* (2009) and David Graeber's *Direct Action: An Ethnography* (2009), which all resonate with my concern about time and take up the issue of positioning and engaged anthropology. All three authors describe themselves as different varieties of activist-researchers. Graeber positions himself first of all as an anarchist, a critical insider, who could not help writing an ethnography about his experiences with the hope of furthering the movement's goals (Graeber 2009: 12). Maeckelbergh talks of engaged anthropology, which for her implies a double role as interpreter and active participant. Taking on the role as an active participant has also been experienced by Maeckelbergh as a precondition for doing fieldwork in this area (Maeckelbergh 2009: 24). Jeffrey Juris, on the other hand, calls himself a militant ethnographer, which implies being an active participant while in the field in terms of organizing, participating in tactical debate, engaging in collective analysis and 'putting one's body on the line during direct actions' (Juris 2008: 20).

I could probably qualify as a militant ethnographer under these criteria, not least because the position I was offered while in the field was that of an active participant, but I am uncomfortable with the label. As Juris also recognizes (ibid.: 21), it does not bridge the gap between the time in the field and the time of academic writing, which is inherent in the analytical process of anthropology, nor does it address the issue of how the research is put to work, among activists, in courts or in public debate.[16] To me, there are several unanswered questions about the 'militant' label: Should one omit the 'dark side' of activism, such as experiences of fatigue or paranoia or internal hierarchies, to further movement goals? Is it a requirement that our work is a relevant tool for those we study, both while in the field and afterwards? And, in a context where many activists theorize about their own practices, should we be more than another voice in the chorus?

I do not have a final answer, but I am convinced that a position as an activist is the only one available if one wishes to undertake thorough ethnographic fieldwork in this context. As Maeckelbergh phrases it, gaining access depends on 'having engagement' (Maeckelbergh 2009: 24). Nevertheless, I prefer to think of myself as an anthropologist who keeps in mind Viveiros de Castro's words about anthropology's cardinal value, namely 'working to create the conceptual, ontological, self-determination of people' (Viveiros de Castro in Carrithers et al. 2010: 152–53). For me, this means taking seriously the claim made by some activists that a different world can emerge within this one, without trying to explain the claim away, and accepting the less spectacular talk about dead time, in order to imitate the 'native's' concepts and conceptions for theoretical purposes (Holbraad 2004). In my view, placing activists' concepts and perceptions of the world on a par with existing theoretical ideas within anthropology, understanding them as analytical insights that might challenge those of anthropology, is at least as militant as the endeavours of former generations of 'militant' anthropology (Juris 2009; Scheper-Hughes 1995). So while I am generally sympathetic to Nancy Scheper-Hughes's call for anthropologists to engage themselves in questions of power and ethics, having been called on as 'expert witness' in critical cases and debates myself, I do not share the view that theoretical abstractions are a way to keep human misery at a distance (Scheper-Hughes 1995: 416). On the contrary, I believe that theories that take their point of departure in people's own concepts and conceptions are an extension of their self-determination and can contribute to changing mainstream configurations of ethics and power.

Movement and Time

On a more theoretical note, one of the ambitions of this book is to shatter the concern for identity prevalent in contemporary studies of social movements. New Social Movement theory argues that environmental, anti-war, feminist and indigenous movements are different from the class-based movements of the past, in being preoccupied with the process of the construction of a common identity (Alvarez et al. 1998; Melucci 1996; 2003: 42). This is an expedient argument, yet a lopsided one. In *Challenging Codes: Collective Action in the Information Age*, Alberto Melucci (1996) criticizes the conceptualization of movements as analytical wholes. In his view, movements need to be understood as constituted by a multitude of different meanings, forms of organization and modes of organizing (ibid.: 13). He argues that social scientists should pay attention to how actors construct their action, and hence how unity and holism come about. For Melucci, 'the world is not just a physical location, but has become a unified social space, which is culturally and symbolically perceived' (ibid.: 8).

While Melucci rightly questions the expediency of conceptualizing a movement as 'a whole', his analysis relies on parts, that is, on primordially existing actors, who constitute, perceive and ascribe meaning to the world. As has been convincingly argued elsewhere, the alterglobalization movement, and Left radical activists in particular, do not work on the basis of a shared identity or a single vision of social change (Maeckelbergh 2009: 6–7). Even though identity does not seem to be the main organizing principle, this obviously does not entail that a shared analysis of the ills of global capitalism cannot bind people together in certain circumstances, or that some groups within the movement (women, indigenous peoples) may also pursue 'projects of collective identity' (Eschle 2011: 373). My point is that politics in the present context seems to rely far less on the constitutive power of individual actors than New Social Movement theory envisages. Therefore I have taken my point of departure in movement, that is, in the forms of action in their unfolding, implying that relations are prior to individuals and their social positions (Massumi 2002: 8–9; Strathern 2004). In so doing, I wish to come closer to understanding of how 'being movement' is also a particular way of being in and 'doing' time.

Over the years, several works in anthropology have questioned the temporal ontology underlying anthropological analysis (Fabian 1983: 10; Hodges 2008: 401; Munn 1992: 93; Robbins 2007b: 10–11). Time has been described as a chronological temporal flow, a historical flux or process, they argue, thereby implying both movement and direction. In the light of this critique, several anthropologists have in recent years developed non-chronological arguments about the working of time and the future. Here I draw on Joel Robbins's arguments about discontinuous time and moments of radical change among Protestants in Papua New Guinea and the United States (Robbins 2001, 2007a), and Jane Guyer's provocative thoughts on the punctuation of time and the near future (Guyer 2007), which resonate with activists' concerns for producing radical change while simultaneously refraining from planning for future turning points. Miyazaki's investigation of the relationship between hope and knowledge among Suvavou people in Fiji (Miyazaki 2004) is of particular relevance to my idea about figurations of the future, as he points to how time itself contains an open and indeterminate dimension. Building on Ernest Bloch's writings on hope, Miyazaki argues that hope is characterized by indeterminacy, and that the Suvavou people's orientation to the future is marked by openness (ibid.: 7). The present is conceptualized as the 'nascent state between the determinate and indeterminate' (ibid.: 4). In my view, time cannot be perceived as something which is forward moving from the past to the present and the future;

on the contrary, our attention must be on how times appear and are produced in the present. This is also where activists' work on the body/bodies comes into the picture, as it is simultaneously a work on time that gives determinate form to the indeterminate.

The three works on the alterglobalization movement mentioned above address time and activists' relation to the future in different ways, and this is where my work enters into theoretical dialogue with theirs. The three authors focus on different aspects of the movement, and engage with their subject in different geographical settings and at different points in time after the alterglobalization movement first seized the global political stage during the Seattle protests in 1999. David Graeber's extensive ethnography, *Direct Action* (2009), focused on the North America-based movement, contains detailed descriptions from the long preparations for the Summit of the Americas in Quebec, Canada, and a thorough analysis of activists' relationships with the media. Graeber argues that the movement is fundamentally about constructing new forms of democracy; he traces its anarchist underpinnings and discusses the dilemmas connected to the activists' middle-class backgrounds. He locates the transformational power of activism in what he calls 'the political ontology of the imagination', that is, in a different set of assumptions about what is really real (ibid.: 512). Citing Agamben, he defines imagination as 'the zone of passage between reality and reason' (ibid.: 512). Graeber argues that this is an immanent conception of imagination, a kind of collective creativity, which is caught up in action (ibid.: 521), and in so doing his work echoes Cornelius Castoriadis's writings on the indeterminate character of the imagination (Castoriadis 1987). The strength of the book is undoubtedly its ethnographic detail and rich description, which heightened my attention to the ubiquitous concern for creativity, newness and reinvention of forms of action within the movement. Unlike Graeber, I take point of departure in the (potential) reality of multiple worlds that temporarily emerge for example during confrontations with the police.

In *Networking Futures* (2008), Jeffrey Juris has followed Spanish-based activist networks through summit protests in Prague and Genoa with a focus on their networking practices. He argues that values such as horizontality and equality, which activists associate with their networking practices, are embodied during mass direct actions (ibid.: 5). To understand street protests, Juris draws on performance theory, and particularly Victor Turner's theorization of the ritual process, to account for the emotional response and affective solidarity that emerges among activists during protests (ibid.: 139). He concludes that the decentralized networks 'prefigure the utopian worlds they are struggling to create' (ibid.: 9). His attention to bodily techniques parallels my own work, even though our ways part at a more theoretical level, namely the extent to which a Turnerian argument about the liminality of protests is the best way to grasp public protests, which I return to below.

In *The Will of the Many* (2009), Marianne Maeckelbergh has studied the forms of consensus democracy in spaces of decision making within the movement in the context of the G8 protest in Gleneagles (2005) and the European Social Forum in London (2004). Maeckelbergh rejects talk of utopias, but argues that the forms of democracy pertaining to these spaces are 'prefigurations of process', where process is 'a practice, a fluid action, an ongoing activity' (ibid.: 21). In her view, practising prefigurations means, on the one hand, that we are 'always trying to make the process we use to achieve our immediate goals an embodiment of our ultimate goals', thereby collapsing the temporal distinction between present and future (ibid.: 66–67); on the other hand, she argues, the decision-making practices within the movement offer a 'progressive realization of future possibilities' (ibid.: 228). Her argument is subjected to more thorough analysis in Chapter 3, but in my view her use of the concept of prefiguration does not accomplish the task of grasping the non-chronological nature of time that is at play in activists' political practices. Etymologically, prefiguration is derived from *pre* ('before') and *figurare* ('to form or shape'),[17] and hence refers to making a figure of the future in its anticipation. My own argument has obvious affinities with this, but Maeckelberg ascribes the prefigurative practices to the conscious intent of human actors, and therefore her attention to the prefiguration of process arises from an ontology of linear time,[18] which does not permit us to adequately understand the radically open and indeterminate elements of activist practices. In other words, there is an underlying assumption about process as having a direction, and about time as flowing between the past, the present and the future.

While the two latter studies thus address activist epistemologies of time, they fail to make explicit their own ontology of time. In contrast, I seek to develop a non-linear argument about time that highlights how time among activists has different temporal ontologies, which hinge on the body. In developing this argument, through the empirical investigation of activist modes of being in and making time, I draw on Viveiros de Castro's theorization of Amerindian perspectivism (Viveiros de Castro 1992, 1998, 2004). Through a discussion of activists' relationship to the present and to the near and distant future, I describe how the body, and the collective body in particular, produces an oscillation between 'dead time' and 'active time'. Based on this, I advance a perspectivist model of time, the implications of which are that the future is not thought of as a point ahead in linear time, but as a coexisting bodily perspective.

Performative Appearances

According to Mitchell, the concept of performance has gained a foothold in anthropology via two routes (Mitchell 2006: 384). Goffman's work on self-representation, in which he argues that social life is essentially performative (Goffman 1959: 72), has had an impact on the work of various scholars, such as Judith Butler's theory about the performativity of the gendered body (Butler 1999) and the Birmingham School's studies of youth culture. The Birmingham School's insights about sub-cultural groups and how they express an oppositional identity via performative modification of mainstream culture (Clark 2004; Clarke et al. 2006; Hebdige 2006; Krogstad 1986) is part and parcel of how most people understand the activities of Left radical groups. The second route relates to the cross-fertilization between theatre practitioners interested in rituals, and Victor Turner, who became interested in theatre after first having studied rituals (Mitchell 2006: 384; Turner 1987).

I believe it is fair to say that it was Victor Turner who developed the anthropological concept of performance through an attention to liminoid phenomena in 'modern' societies, while simultaneously preserving a dialogue with classical studies of ritual and liminality (Sjørslev 2007: 15–16; Turner 1982: 29–32). Turner characterized his work as comparative symbology, which refers to the interpretation of symbols as well as to the study of expressions by means of symbols (Turner 1982: 20). In his early work, Turner had adopted a processual view of rites of passage from Van Gennep, according to which the ritual process was divided into three phases: separation, transition – a state of social limbo out of secular time that generates a strong sense of communitas among participants – and reincorporation (ibid.: 24; see also Turner 1987: 34). He stresses the integrative function of ritual, thereby reproducing Emile Durkheim's basic thesis about the function of symbols in ritual, namely that they first and foremost reaffirm the sentiments upon which the group is based (Durkheim 1954: 216).[19] Later on, Turner highlighted the transformative and potential quality of the liminal and liminoid phase of transition which, as he put it, 'can generate and store a plurality of alternative models for living, from utopias to programs' (Turner 1982: 33; see also Kapferer 2006: 137). Turner's allusion to the existence of such other immanent models or worlds that may appear during ritual and performance points to the heart of what is also at stake here, but the ontology of linear time underlying the ritual process, even in Turner's version, is a major stumbling block, together with his focus on single events that, as mentioned earlier, excludes the dynamics between them.

After Turner, various anthropologists have pointed to the limitations of symbolic analysis. Edward Schieffelin has argued for a move from looking at rituals as systems of representation to seeing them as processes of practice. 'When human beings come into the presence of one another they do so expressively, establishing consensus about who they are and what their situation is about through voice, gestures, facial expressions, bodily postures and action' (Schieffelin 1997: 195). Citing Bruce Kapferer, Schieffelin criticizes the idea that participants undergo a transformation just by being exposed to symbolic meaning (Schieffelin 1985: 708). Schieffelin thus proposes that the non-discursive dimensions of ritual should be studied, and argues that it is in the relationship between performers and audience that the construction of reality takes place (ibid.: 712; Schieffelin 1997: 200–2). Kapferer later amended this view, arguing that performances are not primarily expressive of meaning, but should be looked upon in terms of their effectiveness (Kapferer 2005). I build on this idea of performative effectiveness as it resonates with activists' concept of style and the distinctions they maintain between symbolic and effective direct actions.

Framing is the final aspect of the performance literature that must be considered here, particularly as it might enable us to reach a definition of 'event'. According to Bateson, the frame is a meta-communicative message, which indicates how a statement or action is to be interpreted. The most well-known examples are the statement 'This is play', as well as the more complex question 'Is this play?', which establishes a more paradoxical frame (Bateson 1972: 181–91). In the present context, the repetitive chant 'This is not a riot!' during the Reclaim Power action at the Climate Summit in Copenhagen, referred to at the outset of this introduction, can be interpreted as such a particular way of playing with the frame, and of intensifying a certain aspect of reality (see Sjørslev 2007: 18). Furthermore, one could argue that it is the framing that defines an intensified moment, or what we, in a more contemporary language, would call an event.

Yet the idea of framing, and especially the emphasis on the symbolic and communicative aspects of performance, is somewhat 'out of sync' with the approach to political protests taken here, which seeks to accentuate the effects and not the meaning of an event. This point can be further clarified with reference to Judith Butler's distinction between illocutionary and perlocutionary speech acts, which are based on J.L. Austin's philosophy of language. Perlocutionary speech acts are characterized by initiating a series of consequences, but the speech act and the consequences are temporally distinct. Illocutionary speech acts entail that what is said is considered to be an act in itself; it performs its deed in the moment of utterance (Butler 1997: 17). According to Butler, language is a form of action and not simply an expressive tool. In my view, protests are performed to have an effect, and direct actions are, furthermore, actions that aim at producing an effect without any delay in time. Following this, what would constitute an event in the present context is not so much defined by prior framing (the calling of a demonstration timed to coincide with a more formal summit event for example), as by the subsequent valuation of the situation's intensity and the form's ability to spur effects. This is reflected in the structure of the book, which is built around a selection of key ethnographic events.

In recent years the interest in performance has re-emerged in connection with the study of materiality and the agency of material objects (see Gell 1998; Keane 2006; Sjørslev 2007). The material turn in anthropology has been an inspiration, though it is the materiality of the body that is of primary interest here. In other words, I retain the concept of performance, and the particular attention to form it entails, but I aim at stripping away its constructivist legacy.

Informed and inspired by Marilyn Strathern's relational ontology, one of the implications of which is that the world is always already made up of social relations, I want to follow a somewhat different path to performative protests. In Strathern's view, performances are 'appearances' that make particular relations visible (Strathern 1988: 277–78, 324). In *The Gender of the Gift* (ibid.), it is the ceremonial exchange of pigs between male members of society that renders gendered relations visible. At the most simple level, the pig is the objectification of the unmediated exchange between men and women.[20] This objectification – that is, appearance of relations – is guided by aesthetics (ibid.: 160; Gell 1999: 37).[21] In Strathern's view, aesthetics does not refer to abstract beauty but, as I shall return to in my rethinking of the concept of style in Chapter 5, is much more closely related to appropriateness and persuasiveness (Strathern 2004: 10; see also Riles 1998). This means that only certain performances can make the relations they objectify properly appear (Strathern 1988: 181). In sum, through skilful and effective performance, otherwise invisible social relations gain a visible form. My interest here is both in the forms of these appearances – that is, the various forms politics take – and the relations that are rendered visible, for example in the moments of bodily confrontation between activists and the police. The key question is what relations the collective body, which Aske talked about on the street after the Reclaim Power action, is an appearance of?

In relation to the phenomena under study, exchanges are not gift exchanges as in Strathern's Mount Hagen but, I argue, bodily exchanges. I also argue that bodily confrontation is as much about cutting social relations as about constructing or forging them, as performative approaches inspired by Durkheim and Turner have usually held. In my writing on the body, I will draw on Marcel Mauss's classic analysis, which describes 'the way in which, from society to society, men [sic] know how to use their body' (Mauss 1992: 455). The comparative endeavour aside, Mauss is helpful in understanding how activists learn to use their bodies through action training so that synchronization of movement and a skilful performance is obtained.

Mauss's view of the body as an instrument, as both means and technical object (ibid.: 461), echoes the materiality and affect of the body in more recent contributions (Massumi 2002; Mitchell 2006). According to Massumi, affect is an experience of intensity, that is, a moment of unformed potentiality that cannot be captured in language (Massumi 2002: 30). Massumi defines affect as a 'prepersonal intensity corresponding to the passage from one experiential state of the body to another and implying an augmentation or diminution of the body's capacity to act' (Massumi 1987: xvi). What interests me in the collective body is not communitas or affective solidarity, but the intensity of the body and its synchronization, because this will enable me to illuminate, in a subsequent chapter, how the body engenders time.

Looking for politics in the body is not a new undertaking. Over the past forty years anthropologists inspired by theories of feminism and philosophy have interrogated the nature/culture and mind/body dualities, and pointed to the social and discursive production of sex, gender and bodies (Lock 1993: 135; Povinelli 2006; Vilaça 2005). According to Elizabeth Povinelli, the much-needed critique of the Western metaphysics of substance has, however, also led to the abandonment of the material aspects of the body as an unfortunate side effect.[22] As I shall discuss in greater detail later, activists' bodies are transformed through protests, but also through nutrition and abstention; however, this attention to the materiality of the body does not prevent it from being considered highly unstable (cf. Vilaça 2005).

In sum, through the study of these intensified moments of political action and protest, I show how it is the body that engenders time. Paraphrasing Povinelli, it is the body that is the source of 'the otherwise' (Povinelli 2011: 109), or, in Viveiros de Castro's words, the body is 'the site of a differentiating perspective' (Viveiros de Castro 1998: 480–82). During protests, different techniques – such as masks, colours, music, repetition or performative styles – are employed to engage participants and engender certain effects (see Mitchell 2006; Sneath et al. 2009: 12). Bodily confrontation implies, not multiple epistemologies of time, but various temporal ontologies. I therefore think of performances as acts in themselves that organize time and space; that is, as activist's temporal incarnation of another future. These moments when an indeterminate future gains determinate form is what I call 'figuration of the future'.

Outline of the Book

The chapters develop an exploration of the relationship between form and time in the context of the political practices of Left radical activists. In each chapter, I discuss recent contributions to an anthropology of the future, drawing on explanatory models of radical change, generation and prefiguration while I slowly set forth an understanding of a particular kind of body politics and settle for a perspectivist model of time.

In Chapter 1 I describe the political cosmology of Left radical activists by taking as a point of departure a description of the European Social Forum celebrated in Malmö under the slogan 'Another World is Possible' and YouTube videos circulating on the internet prior to summit protests. The aim of the chapter is to describe the activists' views of the capitalist world, its dynamics and the forces that inhabit it, as well as their experiences of temporal discontinuity and the logic of radical change.

Turning to the Scandinavian context in Chapter 2, I attempt to answer the question: Is Left radical activism an expression of young people's desire to rebel against the establishment, and therefore a 'natural' part of attaining social adulthood? Here I focus on the public debate around the eviction of Ungdomshuset in Copenhagen. I argue that the public debate surrounding this event represents activists as enmeshed in the difficult process of becoming adult, self-authoring individuals (cf. Povinelli 2006). Through a description of how Ungdomshuset was used and perceived by activists themselves, I point to a different, collective sense of autonomy embedded in how activism is about 'becoming active' and absorbed in common activities. I also argue that the body is turned into the chief realm of politics, and the site of differentiation between dead time and active time.

Chapter 3 turns to direct action planning and action training, and explores how Left radical activists deal with intentions for the near future. It is argued that intentions are considered dangerous and that, during planning meetings, they are distributed (Gell 1998) to various non-human forms, such as puppets. The question is raised about how relatively well-coordinated protest performances come about, and in answer to this, techniques of bodily synchronization are explored. Maeckelbergh's conceptualization of activist meetings as being prefigurative of the future (Maeckelbergh 2009) is discussed and, to rectify what I see as the misleading ontology of linear time that underlies her argument, I advance the idea of figuration; figuration is what gives determinate form to an indeterminate future.

The security measures around summit events, the enmity between activists and the police and the intersection of different times of security are explored in Chapter 4. I dwell on activist paranoia and fear of surveillance, and their perception of the police as slipping in and out of humanity. Inspired by Viveiros de Castro's work on Amerindian cosmology and enmity among the Arawéte (Viveiros de Castro 1992, 2004), I argue that humans, animals and police share a common culture, but they come in different 'clothes' or bodily appearances. A particular symmetry (in how they see each other) emerges from the analysis together with a set of common categories to describe the enemy that revolve around a perception of each other's unpredictability and bodily transformability. Both parties argue for a necessary play with invisibility and disguise, which is substituted by spectacular appearance in public space.

In Chapter 5 I finally turn to the appearance of activists during direct actions in Copenhagen and during international summits. The 'native' understanding of style, as integrating a concern with the appropriateness, persuasiveness and effectiveness of action, is built upon to develop an anthropological concept of style. Building on the arguments of the previous chapters, I argue that a 'good style' elicits a temporal, bodily point of view in the moment of confrontation with the police. By transposing Viveiros de Castro's theorization of Amerindian perspectivism (Viveiros de Castro 1998, 2004) to the context of Left radical politics, it is argued that the ability to create cosmological differentiation between active time and dead time, and 'see' a different world within this one, depends on the ability to establish a different corporal mode of being.

Notes

1. Summit protests are usually divided into different colour-coded blocs, which each represent a different tactic of engagement. The Reclaim Power action was organized into a Blue, Green and a newly invented Bike Bloc. Other frequently found blocs are the Black Bloc (activists wear black clothing to appear as a mass) and the Pink Bloc (activists dressed up as clowns and fairies).
2. In 1999, the mass actions in Seattle, where approximately 50,000 people blocked the summit of the World Trade Organization (WTO), marked the beginning of a storm of protests against meetings of the global political and financial institutions

such as the WTO, EU, G8, World Bank and IMF. The dynamo of the protests was a 'movement of movements', that is, a swarm of groups, organizations and ad hoc networks with different political motives, projects and forms of organizing (Graeber 2002; Katsiaficas 2006; Maeckelbergh 2009). This 'movement of movements' was known as the anti-globalization movement during the Seattle protests (Graeber 2002: 63). Other frequently used names are the 'global justice movement' and the 'alterglobalization movement' (Eschle 2005: 1767–68; Rupert 2005: 36–37), each name highlighting different characteristics of the movement as well as the political and theoretical position of the writer.

3. Globale Rødder (Global Roots/Troublemakers) is a name playing on the double meaning in Danish of *rødder* as 'root' and 'troublemaker' or 'tough'. The network was created in 2001 in view of the upcoming EU summit in 2002, hosted by Denmark, as an expression of the radical strain of the alterglobalization movement, inspired by the Italian Tute Bianche. After the summit, activists from Globale Rødder were involved in actions concerned with Danish participation in the war in Iraq. The network was dissolved around 2003, but activists from Globale Rødder were subsequently involved in establishing the Danish Social Forum and Piratgruppen (the Pirate Group), combating the intellectual property rights regime, as well as in the EuroMayDay project, which focused on precarious relations of work. Much later, in 2007 and 2008, similar modes of action were reconfigured in the context of the G13 action (a mass civil disobedience action after evictions from the social centre, Ungdomshuset), which I describe in Chapter 2, and Shut Down the Camp (against a Danish detention centre for refugees), described in Chapter 5.

4. 'Do-it-yourself' (DIY) is used by activists to denote practices in daily life aimed at creating self-reliance and independence from market-based capitalism. The idea is that societal transformation can be brought about through concrete actions here and now (cf. McKay 1998).

5. Christiania is an area of former military barracks in the centre of Copenhagen, which was squatted in 1971 and transformed into a self-governed space. Christiania has approximately 1,000 inhabitants, and is an autonomous space that has most consistently developed its own economy, system of democratic decision making and activist infrastructure. For more information, see the Christiana website: www.christiania.org. Last accessed 26 December 2014.

6. The solution suggested by the squatters involved a local foundation (Himmelblå Fonden) purchasing the building from the owner, Ungbo (a society renting out cheap youth residences), in order to donate it to the municipality, under the condition that the municipality would turn the right of use (usufruct) over to the squatters (Heinemann 1995: 129–30). This model was later reiterated in the case of Ungdomshuset, where a private foundation offered to buy the building from Faderhuset (lit. Father House, a Christian sect) on the condition that its usufruct rights would be handed over to the young activists for one Danish krone (US$ 0.20).

7. The Free Gymnasium is an alternative secondary school founded in 1970 that focuses on the development of direct, consensus democracy among students and teachers.

8. The agreement was signed by 'forhandlingsgruppen for BZ-brigaden' (the squatting brigade's team of negotiators), but in the contract they were referred to as 'the users' (*brugerne*). Under the agreement, the users were responsible for the management, while the municipality paid 90 per cent of the running costs. The agreement could be cancelled by the municipality if the house was not kept 'open', had too few activities, the buildings were not maintained, the house was used for accommodation or if

drugs were found on the premises. As I describe in Chapter 2, these requirements were cited later in the public debate to argue for the cancellation of the contract (see US and FBZB 1982). In 1997, the contract was cancelled and replaced with another agreement, which could be cancelled at only three months' notice (KUC 1997).
9. In 2004, the Danish state made an offer to Christiania for 'normalizing' voluntarily. This entailed turning part of the historic ramparts of Copenhagen, presently part of Christiania, into a recreational area, as well as the development of the remainder of Christiania into a mixed residence and commercial area. The relationship between Christiania and the authorities has been marked by conflict-ridden negotiations and a lawsuit by Christiania against the state where they claim usufruct rights over the area. In 2011 an agreement was reached, by which Christiania will now buy the land from the state, and manage it collectively through a foundation. The conflict also concerned the open and undisguised selling of marijuana in so-called Pusher Street, but this was stopped, in part by the inhabitants themselves and through police action in March 2004.
10. Curiously enough, this part of Nørrebro is also considered more safe according to an annual *tryghedsindeks* (safety index) issued by the municipality of Copenhagen, whereas the area on the other side of Nørrebrogade (the former black rectangle) is considered less safe. For the safety index, see http://tryghedsindekset.kk.dk/sites/tryghedsindekset.kk.dk/files/uploaded-files/Resultater%20p%C3%A5%20distrikter%20og%20bydele%202010.pdf. Last accessed 26 December 2014. The visitation zones are, according to the Police Act § 6, a 'security generating measure' (see 'Krim: Københavnske visitationszoner er ulovlige', *Politiken*, 15 December 2007; and 'Ministerium blåstempler politivisitationer', *Ritzau*, 22 March 2010).
11. My inspiration to make this point derives from Annelise Riles (1998), who compares the aesthetics of UN documents with Fijian mats. She argues that the meaning of a UN document is not in the document, but resides in the relationship between documents and between bracketed and non-bracketed text in the documents. One important element in producing a beautiful document, she argues, is the repetition of language, that is, the intertextual references between documents. This implies that the UN documents are 'layered' like Fijian mats, which are piled on top of each other in particular ritual circumstances.
12. I was involved in a mass arrest in connection with recurrent protests against the building of Øresundsbroen in 1995 and 1996. Yet, the Danish High Court found us, the accused, not guilty, because the public prosecutor was unable to establish individual guilt, or in other words, to prove that each of the arrested had violated the law. This concrete experience has a bearing on my interest in how activists decouple individuals and intentions during planning meetings, while the police base their investigations on the assumption of individual motives and intentions (see Chapters 3 and 4).
13. On this issue, see the EuroMayDay website: www.euromayday.org/about.php. Last accessed 18 March 2014.
14. Decisions can be about where the next ESF will take place, or issues of principle about the ESF programme, fees for participation and so on. The EPA also engages in ongoing discussion about how to develop and enhance the ESF. See the ESF website: http://esf2008.org/about/who-organizes-esf/european-preparatory-assembly. Last accessed 7 August 2012.
15. See 'Undercover Police: Officer B Identified as Mark Jacobs', *Guardian*, 19 January 2011.

16. My Ph.D. dissertation was, without my knowing, used both by the prosecution and by the counsel for the defendant in a case about the legality of arresting just under 1,000 participants in a demonstration during the Climate Summit. Moreover, my observations of the activities of a British undercover police officer on Danish soil have been debated in the media, and led to so-called Paragraph 20 questions in the Danish Parliament (which are written questions from a member of parliament to a minister on an issue of public concern) about the activities of foreign police officers in Denmark, to which the Ministry of Justice never managed to provide answers.
17. Etymologies from the Etymonline website: www.etymonline.com. Last accessed 15 April 2012.
18. On this, see also Maeckelbergh (2011). For a critique, see Razsa and Kurnik (2012).
19. Durkheim focused explicitly on forms of religious life. According to Durkheim, however, the true function of the rites performed by Australian clans is not what they (the clan members) understand it to be – to increase their totem species – but to produce socially useful effects. During the rite, the Aborigines experience intense enthusiasm, and as a consequence they are 'transported to another level of reality', which makes them feel they are outside and above normal moral life (Durkheim 1954: 216, 226).
20. In Strathern's later work, this is more consistently developed into a theory of the fractal person, where the relations that we usually consider as external are thought of as internal to the person (Strathern 2004; see also Wagner 1991).
21. Underlying this is the idea that some relations are 'eclipsed', a concept that refers to how relations of a more subordinate order are nested, occluded and latent within relations of a more encompassing order, the consequence being that the subordinate relation is only accessible through the encompassing order (Gell 1999: 41–43).
22. Povinelli (2006: 27–94) describes a sore on her body acquired during her fieldwork among aboriginal Australians. The sore was both discursively produced as 'contact with Dreaming', and as staphylococcus because of the filthiness of indigenous communities. But sores still sicken the body, she argues, and for aboriginal Australians the sores often have the effect that they die much earlier than the non-indigenous population. Povinelli draws a distinction between corporeality, which refers to how forms of power shape materiality, and carnality, which is the material matter, such as a sore.

1

'Other Worlds Are Possible'

A Political Cosmology of Capitalism

Weeks ahead of the 2009 Climate Summit in Copenhagen, Never Trust a Cop, a network formed to mobilize anarchists and other Left radical activists to participate in the protests, uploaded a 1 minute, 20 second trailer on YouTube titled *COP 15: War on Capitalism*.[1] The trailer caused an uproar in the Danish media, and journalists, backed by an army of experts, foretold that black-clad activists would come to town to stage street riots similar to the ones seen in the video. The video comprised printed text over still pictures accompanied by the lyrics to Franz Ferdinand's 'This Fire', and it opened with the question: 'You thought the COP 15 in December was about climate? Well ... think again!' Against a background of clouds floating across the sky, the video continues, 'What we usually talk about as a crisis for the climate is only the ultimate symptom of a capitalism in crisis'. The trailer then cuts to a power plant, with the text: 'Capitalism is stumbling all over the world. In order to save its profits capitalism is prepared to let us all drown'. The statement is followed by several pictures of natural disasters and their human impact. The text continues, 'They talk about "green capitalism", but it is still the *same* capitalism'. Against the backdrop of the inner city of Copenhagen and the tower of Copenhagen's municipal building, the text reads, 'In Copenhagen 7th to 18th December at COP 15 they will try to get capitalism back on track'. At this point the film changes pace with a picture of a masked black-clad girl stating: 'We don't! We will go to Copenhagen, to teach a dead system how to die', which is succeeded by a long sequence of photos of street riots, barricades and burning cars accompanied by Franz Ferdinand's lyrics: 'Now / There is a fire in me / This fire is out of control / We're gonna burn this city / Burn this city / This fire is out of control / We're gonna burn this city / Burn this city'.

The broadcasting of this kind of video is a recurring phenomenon before summits, and also an integral part of summit mobilizations (Razsa 2013). Yet, in spite of the grandiose language and expression of apparently clear intentions, they tell us little about how actual protests develop. Instead, the videos have a lot to say about how activists see capitalism and the world around them.

In this chapter I describe how activists talk, and do not talk, about capitalism and the possibility of radical change. I show that there is a significant difference between Left radical activists and the traditional Marxist Left, based on different perceptions of time and, particularly, the future. I will make this argument based on an ethnographic description of the European Social Forum (ESF) in Malmö, Sweden, in 2008. Social forums can be thought of as an integral part of the global justice movement; they are spaces shared by various tendencies on the Left, aimed at developing alternatives to the prevailing economic model. Drawing on newer works on discontinuous time (Hodges 2008; Robbins 2001, 2007b), and in particular a debate in *American Ethnologist* concerning the 'evacuation' of the near future (e.g. Guyer 2007; Robbins 2007a), which entails a reorientation of people's attention and political projects to immediate situations and distant horizons, thereby abandoning midterm reasoning and organization, I will discuss how activists perceive time as discontinuous, and how the future becomes paved with dates around which they must mobilize.

I will use political cosmology as a heuristic term to explain the logic of activists' perceptions of the world around them, the order of things in the world and the possibilities of radical change.[2] The basic question I address concerns what the world, and capitalism in particular, looks like through the eyes of activists. Phrased this way, the question allows us to discover that the logic of the cosmos is not order and integration, as often assumed in classical studies of cosmology (Handelman 2008: 182; Schrempp 1992), but disorder and discontinuity. Cosmology is obviously a tainted concept – associated with relatively stable models of cosmos and continuity in cultural anthropology – but maybe it is time to dust it off and imbue it with new meaning (see Chapter 5). Understanding cosmology as an emergent effect of actions rather than their holistic backdrop.

I deliberately use the term political cosmology rather than ideology, because activists' views of capitalism cannot be seen as an ideology in any strict sense of the term. In conventional political science, every political tendency is associated with and informed by an ideology, which is usually defined as a more or less systematic set of ideas about society and how it should be organized. This definition of ideology implies mid-term reasoning about necessary reforms, or steps to attain political goals. As already stated in the Introduction, Left radical activists generally refrain from providing images of the ideal or utopian society towards which they are striving, which challenges our implicit understanding of politics as a goal-oriented practice.

Many activists can be considered 'small-a anarchists' (Graeber 2002: 72) because they do not explicitly associate themselves with a specific anarchist ideological tendency, but do give priority to self-organization, direct democracy and action over theory (Graeber 2009: 219; Epstein 2001). Particular views and utterances can obviously be traced to 'big-a' Anarchists such as Proudhon, Kropotkin or Bakunin, and their writings on self-organization and mutual aid, their scepticism towards the state and rejection of private property rights. In practice, inspiration also stems from modes of organization and experiments with participatory democracy in the student and feminist movements, the direct action groups of the anti-nuclear movement, as well as experiments with new lifestyles in the 1960s and 1970s. In a European context, the influence of autonomism is still significant and traceable to the Italian organizations Potere Operaio (Worker's Power) and Autonomia Operaia (Worker's Autonomy) in the 1960s and 1970s, as well as the theoretical works of Mario Tronti, Paulo Virno and Antonio Negri (Katsiaficas 2006: 6–8). It is important to note, however, that many young activists do not themselves associate their practices with particular historical predecessors. In a Scandinavian context, most activists do not even identify themselves as anarchists, and people have seldom read the works of anarchist thinkers, nor do they consider it important to tie themselves to a defined ideological standpoint.

This chapter proceeds with a description and analysis of the European Social Forum, which will be supplemented by discussion of YouTube videos and a more in-depth presentation of Danish activist Aske's experience of going through 'dead time'. This first approximation will neither provide a description of how capitalism is experienced in all situations, nor fully account for all internal variations; nevertheless, the inquiry will point to some key issues and concerns, these being that activists seldom talk about capitalism explicitly, that action in the world is favoured over theoretical analysis of the world and that capitalism is simultaneously seen as all-encompassing and pervasive yet unstable and transformative, filled with interstices and potential ruptures.

Another World Is Possible

The first World Social Forum (WSF) was held in Porto Alegre, Brazil, in 2001, as an alternative to its 'evil twin', the World Economic Forum in Davos, Switzerland, where selected politicians, CEOs and celebrities meet at a ski-resort to debate the world's economic problems. From Porto Alegre, the name and form of social forums spread around the world, resulting in an infinite number of local, regional and thematic variants. At the same time, the WSF continued to grow, with 150,000 participants at the 2005 event (Juris 2008; Osterweil 2004).

Porto Alegre was said to be 'the place where the so-called anti-globalization movements in their various guises come together and demonstrate how global they really are' (Hardt and Negri, in Ponniah and Fisher 2003). The social forums are sometimes referred to as the visionary arm of the global justice movement for developing concrete alternatives to capitalism (or to neoliberalism, for the less radical participants) under the slogan 'Another World Is Possible'. The social forums are visited and organized largely by the same people as those participating in summit protests, but they are seen as opportunities to 'assess the strength' of the movement and to analyse general social, political and economic trends, discussing strategies and alternatives, forming networks and planning actions. The social forums usually consist of a mix of self-organized workshops, more formal or academic panel debates, cultural events and at least one large demonstration where the sheer number of demonstrators, according to one participant, is supposed to display the strength of the social forum network in the streets. Outside the workshop areas there are vendors and stalls selling magazines, t-shirts and fair-trade products, as well as disseminating information on specific organizations or future mobilizations and events.

Academics and journalists associated with the social forums often focus on the lively sound and colourful visuals when describing the events (Osterweil 2004: 495). They are depicted as part Woodstock, part political rally (Juris 2008: 236), or even as a political jam session (Wainwright 2004). These descriptions support the values expressed in the WSF's Charter of Principles, namely that a social forum is an 'open meeting place' that gives room to a diversity of activities and ways of engaging (art. 1, art. 9).[3] The number of people in attendance is an important criterion of success when participants and organizers evaluate a forum; other key outcomes are the number of people backing proposals for action, the diversity of the individuals and organizations present and entering into new networked relations, and the success of self-management in practice.

According to the International Council of the WSF and the Brazilian organizing committee, the aim is to have the social forum become 'a permanent process of seeking and building alternatives, which cannot be reduced to the events supporting it' (Charter of Principles, art. 2). However, the relationship between process and event, and how process should be interpreted, is a major point of conflict. Most Left radical activists stress that the forum should be self-organized and that the planning and running of the forum must embody the aim of creating a better world (Maeckelbergh 2009: 72). In this light, the means are seen as more important than the outcome of the event, and apparently apolitical questions about how the forum is financed and how decisions are made when organizing the event come to the forefront as politically significant matters.

This perception of the social forum is distinct from both that of the Marxist Left and the ideas held by many trade unions and NGOs. The Marxist Left, on the one hand, places more emphasis on where the process is going, that is, on the goal of creating alternatives to capitalism in the long run. From this perspective, it becomes crucial to build smooth-running and disciplined organizational structures that allow for efficient decision making and a well-organized event. The radical change envisioned here can best be understood as a process of linear accumulation: forces must be gathered and more and more people brought into the process in order to reach the revolutionary moment that will overthrow capitalism in its totality (Nunes, cited in Maeckelbergh 2009: 97). Whereas the Marxists' view of the future is one of linear accumulation that reaches a tipping point in time, trade unions and most NGOs are, on the contrary, oriented towards the near future, and use the social forum to discuss and launch more moderate advocacy campaigns or proposals for policy reform.

Other discrepancies around social forums are connected to this fundamental conflict concerning how social forum actors orient themselves in time. For instance, the WSF Charter states that the social forum cannot be considered representative of participants: 'No one, therefore, can be authorised, on behalf of any of the editions of the Forum, to express positions claiming to be those of all its participants' (art. 6). By emphasizing 'open space' and abjuring collective representation, the forum process brings together different ideological tendencies on the Left in spite of their various political inclinations. However, there are several meanings attached to the word 'open'; for some, the emphasis is on bringing more people into the process, while for others the key point is internal diversity. Moreover, there is disagreement about the future of the forum. Some have argued for years that the social forum should transform itself into a movement with shared political goals and agendas; others believe that this will inevitably lead to the formation of new hierarchies, and that many actors will refrain from participating. This is the view held by many Left radical activists, as well as moderate NGOs. Nevertheless, at every forum an array of organizations get together to convene an Assembly of Social Movements that issues a final declaration. The declaration is one or two pages long and presents some general views on current issues (the financial crisis, migration policies, war) and a long list of dates of events around which activists must collectively mobilize. However, the so-called 'horizontal tendency' (anarchists or activists of a Left radical inclination) argues that in spite of the formal exclusion of political parties, there is a reproduction of traditional party discourse or political culture within the forum (De Angelis 2006; Ponniah and Fisher 2003; Sen 2004a: 214; 2004b).

Following the success of the WSF, the first European Social Forum (ESF) was held in Florence in 2002, and it claimed to have 60,000 participants (Juris 2008: 50). Despite conflicts and dilemmas, the ESF was marked by enthusiasm and optimism, particularly in its early years. This enthusiasm was also noticeable during the official opening of the forum in Malmö in 2008, where the compère, Veronica, excitedly announced (while speaking to the issues of capitalism, expansion and open space):

> I love the social forums. I love you. ESF is a space where you can meet fellow activists, where it is normal to hate capitalism because it doesn't work, where it is normal to fight neoliberalism because it doesn't work, and where it is normal to work for a better world. I am proud to be part of a growing movement. That's why I love the ESF.

The rare experience of being the majority and the rewards from being able to engage in exchange with fellow activists are reiterated whenever people talk about their participation in a social forum. The compère also addresses another important issue, which I shall return to at length in Chapter 2, namely the positive experience of being part of something larger than oneself, which is described as a particularly exhilarating experience given the individualism of capitalist society.

After the first ESF meeting in Florence, followed by Paris, London and Athens, the ESF moved to Malmö in 2008. This is, at first glance, something of an odd choice, made by the European Preparatory Assembly (EPA) – the highest authority in the organizational process – because the alterglobalization movement is considered to be not as 'strong' in Scandinavia. However, in the selection process, several groups from Sweden, including ATTAC,[4] Friends of the Earth and several large unions, declared themselves ready to take on the enormous task of organizing the event. Moreover, they were able to commit to raising the necessary financial resources. At the EPA meetings that I attended during my fieldwork, organizational capacity and financial resources were underlined as important in choosing the location of an ESF meeting, but not the only considerations. Participants tended to support bids to host the event from their own political tendency (cf. Juris 2008), but the desire 'to expand the process' was a factor in choosing Malmö as the location of the ESF event. Various EPAs had discussed the need to expand towards Scandinavia and Eastern Europe, and in deciding on Malmö there was a hope that both could be reached at the same time. More than 20,000 people were expected to attend the five-day meeting in Malmö, and among these the organizers expected many who had not previously participated in a social forum. A committee was established to mobilize financial support specifically for encouraging participation from Eastern European countries. To reach out to social movements in Eastern Europe, an EPA meeting was furthermore held in Kiev, Ukraine, three months ahead of the social forum in Malmö. I present here a brief account of this meeting in order to describe the dynamics of expansion and the resulting dilemmas.

Kiev, June 2008

It is the first time that an EPA is being held in a former Soviet republic. The conference hall where the meeting is held is located inside a grandiose union building in the centre of Kiev, half the size of a football pitch. The light green colour on the walls matches the green fabric on the rows of seats, a checked pattern on the carpet and heavy dusty brocade on each side of the stage. Nonetheless, it has an unmistakable air of the past. Approximately a hundred participants sit scattered around the room; they are, for the most part, representatives from unions and movements in Western Europe as well as local organizers from the ESF secretariat set up in Malmö. Peter, from the Danish Social Forum, is the moderator of the morning session; he summarizes a key rule of the game: in not being a representative forum, and because decisions are made by consensus, he explains, there will be a limitation on how many times people are allowed to intervene during the debates, with new speakers and women being given priority on the speakers' list.

The first day of the meeting consists of detailed reports from the different organizing committees responsible for preparing the Malmö forum: translation, demonstration, accommodation, scheduling and logistics, budgets, cultural events and mobilization. Alma, one of the activists working full time at the secretariat, explains the logistics. She places great emphasis on the plan to spread the event throughout Malmö, specifically to the immigrant neighbourhood of Rosengård, in order to reach out to local inhabitants. Smaller details, such as the proposal to provide free drinking water instead of selling bottled water, are also discussed at length. Budgets and mobilization receive special attention, as well as prices and rates for different groups such as the unemployed and participants from Eastern Europe. The Swedish organizers express their concern over how to raise funds to pay at least part of the travel expenses of Eastern European participants, but no conclusion is reached. While debating these issues, a woman sitting next to me whispers, 'I find it quite strange that we don't discuss politics'. I simply shrug my shoulders and smile, as it was not until months later that I fully came to register this absence.

In the evening, the meeting is interrupted by the Ukrainian union which owns the building because they need to use the room for other purposes. The Norwegian moderator protests, as he had also previously criticized the local organizers for not taking responsibility for providing a co-facilitator. This creates a very tense atmosphere and sparks a conflict that seems to have been suppressed all day. The Ukrainian participants criticize 'the West' for not giving 'space for the participation of the East', concluding that it had been a mistake to hold the EPA in Ukraine, arguing that the Southern Europeans 'see themselves as the core of the ESF' and are not ready to reach out and include others. The meeting breaks off, but further into the night most of the Western Europeans meet again at the Association for Friendship Between Cuba and the Ukraine to hold an Assembly of Social Movements. In a cramped coffin-like room without windows, carpeting on all the walls and too little air, participants share their views on capitalism's impending crisis, and what they interpret as the interconnected crises of social movements. Most seem to agree that the movements are not able 'to respond to and gain from the crisis'. The meeting ends with an exchange of preliminary dates for mobilization over the next two years.

The next day continues like the first, though the agenda is now focused on the ESF programme. The deadline for submitting proposals for seminars, workshops and cultural events has already passed. Eight hundred proposals were submitted, which must be reduced via a merging of the proposals to 250 workshops and panels, due to time and space constraints. The programme committee is criticized for 'hiding' and not making their decisions in public. Principles for merging the proposals are debated, and a lengthy process is initiated whereby all proposers have to be contacted again. The meeting ends with debates over the content of the opening and closing events. The Swedish organizers propose a cultural programme, but the Southern Europeans argue that the opening and closing must reflect 'the multiplicity of the movement' through many short interventions. On my way back to Copenhagen, I wonder how this attention to minute details, such as not selling bottled water, can be understood as a critique of capitalism, and if it will in fact mobilize more people to participate in the social forums.

At the EPA in Kiev, I agree to meet up in Malmö with Alma in order to learn more about these issues. Alma is a member of ATTAC and had moved to Malmö to work for the ESF secretariat. During our conversation, she explains that she considers the issue of self-organization to be crucial, and that this is why she is preoccupied with logistics. In her view, self-organization means that the proposers of seminars and workshops should be deeply involved in the organization of them, and that the form of organization should reflect 'what we are aiming to do'. Moreover, in her view the forum has to be a generator of alternatives:

> It is not about changing society in one go, but about the forum generating alternatives that slowly become mainstream, you know what I mean? At the same time, the forum process has to continue and create new alternatives, alternatives that can be offered to others: 'Here you go, it costs you nothing, but it is the solution to the problems that the world is facing'. Several intellectuals talk about the crisis of capitalism: the climate crisis, the food security crisis, the energy crisis and the financial crisis. They say that we are at a turning point. But actually, these are some of the issues that the social forums have been working on, and that we can offer solutions to.

In other words, she rejects the view that the ESF is about generating a revolutionary situation in the classic sense of the term. In her view, the strength of the social forum is based on both self-organization and the continual development of alternatives that can be taken up by others. She recognizes that if governments do not take up the alternatives, and given that capitalism is not likely to break down by itself in the near future, the only other available tactic is to involve more and more people in thinking and acting differently. The unintended effect of such efforts at expansion is, however, that the events also become increasingly costly (in fact, most ESF events end up with a huge budget deficit) and there are conflicts over the politics of fundraising.

This leaves the ESF with something of a dilemma between the goal of continuous expansion and the conviction of Alma and others that means are ends in themselves. According to the WSF Charter of Principles, the process of organizing the forum is actually more important than the event itself but, on the other hand, the social forum must continuously expand; more people should attend and be inspired by the propositions and become engaged in the process for this to be a plausible 'theory' of change. If the growing movement – which Veronica, the compère at the opening in Malmö, talked so warmly of – fails, there is little hope of this theory succeeding. This was exactly the realization by the end of the ESF meeting in Malmö, which I now turn to in order to describe the participation and views of Left radical activists.

Dates and Fringes of the ESF

At the outset, Left radical groups participated in the overall coordination of the social forum in Malmö, but then withdrew because they felt that the municipality of Malmö and the trade unions, which were also the main financial contributors, were controlling the process too rigidly. Instead, groups of Left radical activists decided to organize their own parallel space at Utkanten (the 'outskirt' or 'fringe'), a new self-managed social centre in Malmö.

A month before the forum, I meet up with Mariann, who is part of the newly formed Action Network coordinating the alternative programme. Mariann is in her early 20s and is a student of law and human rights. We meet up at the train station in Malmö, and then walk to somewhere 'secure' to talk. We sit down at a café, but she is concerned about other people listening in on our conversation, and I leave with the feeling that I have asked the wrong questions. Our second meeting is in her home, a small house that she shares with a handful of activist friends in Lund, a small but vibrant university town in southern Sweden. Whereas several of her room-mates have formed a local clown army,[5] Mariann is mostly active in Anti-Fascist Action (AFA), a network that 'keeps an eye out for skinheads' and mobilizes against the annual Nazi marches in Lund and the rest of Sweden. At the kitchen table she serves coffee with soya milk and rye bread with hummus, while explaining her view of the official ESF:

> We have also held a local social forum here in Lund, and that was more a grassroots thing. You can always criticize that kind of event – too many organizations, too much discussion and too little action. But it is a huge step forward from the ESF, where you have to pay to talk, and then there is the top-down style of management. That's why we formed our own Action

Network. We don't want to waste time talking ... It is the Social Democrats doing the opening speech, because the ESF is completely dependent upon the municipality's financial support. It is obvious that if you have 15,000 [Swedish kroner] to offer, then you get 15,000 worth of space. We want to be political and don't think one should pay 2,500 [the price of a stall] for being political in a political context ... It is not a fair attempt at creating something free from capital management. We find that way of thinking pretty exhausting.

According to Mariann, Action Network places greater emphasis on organizing actions than on talking about change. In her view, the official ESF is too focused on inviting clever people to panel debates, which will then analyse the situation for you. Action Network, in contrast, intends to focus on actions against the immigration services' office, a climate-related action to block traffic in the streets, an anti-war action targeting one of Sweden's arms manufacturers, and it wants to hold a vibrant Reclaim the Street party. She insistently repeats that we have talked enough; now it is time to take action.

While the official inauguration of the ESF meeting a month later is held in Malmö's historic People's Park,[6] with bands and a long list of speakers addressing a range of political themes, Action Network holds their inaugural Reclaim the Street party outside the town hall. And while the official ESF celebrates the get-together with speeches, Left radical activists dance and spray-paint the street, a party that later develops into a clash with the local riot police. Apart from direct actions, left-wing radicals are also organizing so-called radical assemblies at Utkanten for participants to exchange experiences on issues such as squatting and free spaces, precariousness and workplace struggles, and the EU's security policy for major events; they also plan for future mobilizations.

In Mariann's view, the contradictory relationship to the official ESF – both being a part of it and yet not – has much to do with the rift created at the EU summit in Göteborg (Sweden) in 2001. The police repression and street riots that followed the event were extraordinarily violent and fierce, she explains, as the police stormed the schools where people slept even before the protests had started. She was 16 years old at the time, and it taught her a lesson:

> To have many people gathered at one place makes us extremely vulnerable. Since Göteborg we have tried to move away from that way of acting. We have become more invisible and more a part of the crowd ... But we also experienced other things in Göteborg, which created a lot of commotion and hurt the movement a lot, namely the betrayal of the established political parties

on the left. The Socialist Party and the Trotskyites deceived us, because they publicly denounced our actions. That created divisions, and we do not trust the official organizers of the ESF.

In other words, the conflict between the established Left and the radical Left in the context of the ESF lingers on, and builds on previous experiences.[7] The protests in Göteborg occurred before attempts to build consensus around a 'diversity of tactics' (see Chapter 5 for more on this), and the established Left's public denunciations back then influenced the decision made among Left radical activists to create their own self-managed space during the ESF seven years later. But the break is not complete; for example, Mariann expressed the need to be 'part of the crowd', that is, to be inconspicuous so as to avoid becoming the target of police repression again. Moreover, she underlined the fact that the official ESF offers a platform to make their own struggles visible. Left radical activists would, therefore, still participate in the large demonstration by forming their own anti-capitalist bloc, and individual participants would still ramble back and forth between the official and alternative forums during the five-day event in Malmö.

When I arrived at Utkanten for the assembly on squatting and free spaces during the social forum in Malmö, some fifty people were hanging around the vegan soup kitchen set up in the yard of this abandoned factory building on the outskirts of the city. People were sitting in small groups on the ground, talking and eating lunch. Both the inside and outside walls had long ago been covered with graffiti. The assemblies were held in the only main hall, a high-ceilinged room without windows, with a bar and a kitchen at one end and groups of chairs and tables scattered throughout the rest of the room. On the wall, among a number of tags and slogans, an over-sized baby with a hoodie looked down at us: 'There will always be a new generation' was the accompanying text.

During the radical assembly on squatting and social centres, different activists gave short briefings on the situation in their city or country. The room was crammed with people, and I found a seat on the armrest of an old sofa next to Mikkel, who had been actively involved in planning some of the large demonstrations and actions in Copenhagen for a new social centre after the evictions from Ungdomshuset (see Chapter 2 for a detailed analysis). Some people related their experiences about the hardship of repeated squatting and evictions, while others focused more on the challenges of running squats and trying to put the beautiful words about 'free spaces' into practice. Faces were grave, and the sombre atmosphere was broken by cheers and laughs only when somebody told a spellbinding story about successfully squatting in a house in a Swedish town. Two girls from the new Ungdomshus in Copenhagen were received as heroes due to the success of their struggle, in which many activists from southern Sweden had also participated. They addressed the challenge of moving into a new house, and particularly 'how to keep the good energy from the streets' when the everyday routine settled in, and about trying to maintain a balance between the many different groups that laid claim to the new space.

After the presentations, we broke into smaller groups and spent an hour or more discussing solutions to concrete problems raised by someone in the group. My circle included activists from London, Sweden, Ukraine and Spain, and we talked about what the Ukrainian social centre could do to get themselves supplied with electricity and water. It is sometimes difficult to bridge different contexts and organizational histories when trying to come up with solutions, Mariann later commented.

After the workshop, I headed for a panel discussion on the criminalization of social movements, which was part of the official ESF programme. ESF organizers had, as previously mentioned, decided to spread the workshops across the city. This particular event was held in Rosengård, a so-called immigrant ghetto some 5 kilometres from the centre of Malmö. As my companion and I arrived at the neighbourhood's local square, which mainly contains a police station, a welfare office and a city-run social centre, we bumped into a middle-aged man from the Socialist Workers Party (SWP), which claimed at this time to be the largest far Left party in Britain. He had set up a small bookstall on the square, and quickly started a conversation with us by asking, 'You know about the crisis?' We replied that we did, because in September 2008 the economic crisis was on everybody's lips. 'This crisis will soon be generalized', he continued. 'Capitalism is using military power, because it is in crisis'. I glanced at the books on the table; there were books on Trotskyism and Marxist theory, and works on anti-war and anti-capitalism by SWP's international secretary, Alex Callinicos. 'This time it is serious', he continued, 'we face the Third World War unless the working class gets organized and rises up to fight capitalism'. In the end he sold us a subscription for their quarterly magazine *International Socialism*, and let us off the hook.

Towards the end of the forum, I attended the Assembly of Social Movements, which was held in a large hall in People's Park. The hall, which two days earlier was bursting with people in expectation of a talk by Antonio Negri, was now half empty. While most of the participants at the Assembly of Social Movements meeting were in uproar due to news of an extraordinarily low number of registered participants at the forum in Malmö, the huge financial deficit and the lack of remuneration for Babels, an international network of voluntary translators that was key to the success of any social forum, the facilitators managed to finalize a one-page final declaration, the gist of which is given below, listing the following:

1. On the social issue: We are immediately launching a COMMON EUROPEAN CAMPAIGN against EU social and labour policies ... [T]his campaign will have different steps (ex. December 6 in Paris).
2. Against NATO and War: We call for a large demonstration on April 4th in Strasbourg Kehl ... We propose that the WSF in Belém [Brazil] declare April 4th to be a day of international mobilisation against NATO.
3. Against the climate crisis: We call for a global day of action on December 6th during the Poznan summit ... We are calling for a massive international mobilisation next year to make [sic] the critical Copenhagen talks in December 2009.
4. In July 2009, the Sardinian and Italian social movement will invite all movements to come to Sardinia where the G8 summit will be held.[8]

Agreement on the dates for mobilization is considered to be of paramount importance to leaders of the traditional Marxist Left, trade union members and Left radical activists alike. After much discussion, everybody agreed to the concrete list of events, which carefully reflected the calendars of the heads of state. Since the EPA meeting in Kiev there had also been a plan to issue a statement on the financial crisis, but the participants were not able to complete the statement before the next EPA meeting in Istanbul three months later. Interestingly, the statement launched 'We won't pay for their crisis!' as a shared slogan, which would come to resound in European protests against government austerity measures and bank bailouts as the economic crisis escalated over the following years. The slogan epitomizes the importance of these spaces of coordination, which send new ideas into broader circulation. However, what surprised me most was the list of dated events. What can be made of these dates?

In a provocative contribution to a debate in *American Ethnologist*, Jane Guyer explores what she sees as a strange evacuation of the temporal frame of the 'near future' in the Western world. She argues that the near future has been substituted with a combination of 'enforced presentism' and 'fantasy futurism' (Guyer 2007: 409–10). According to Guyer, this tendency is most evident in monetary (that is, neoliberal) economic theory and in evangelical ideas about time. Both work with an infinite horizon: monetarism through abstract mathematical models for analysing long-term market developments, and evangelical notions within an apocalyptic horizon (see also Robbins 2001). The evacuation entails that the near future has no interim stages, no organization work or mid-term reasoning (Guyer 2007: 416). Instead, the mid-term is perceived as morally dangerous and filled with punctuated time; that is, with dates and ruptures. She writes, 'I perceive a similar rising awareness of a time that is punctuated rather than enduring: of fateful moments and turning points, the date as event rather than as a position in a sequence or a cycle' (ibid.: 416).

If we look at the list of dates put forward by the Assembly of Social Movements in the light of Jane Guyer's thoughts on the near future, we can appreciate how the near future is punctuated and turned into a list of important events around which movements must gather to protest. But even if there is agreement about the importance of dates, and about mobilization for these dated events, different logics can be identified among the participants of the ESF. The traditional Marxist Left perceives the dates not only as stepping stones towards the final revolution but also, as the SWP leader in the square explained, as opportunities to get organized and draw more people into the movement. From this perspective, mid-term strategizing and organization building, as well as ongoing analysis, are important in reaching the moment of revolution (Graeber 2009; Maeckelbergh 2009: 88–89). To Left radical activists, the dates offer a chance to get together to practise a kind of figurative politics where the distinction between means and ends ceases. The dates in the near future seem to represent moments where the evil forces of capitalism materialize, which presents activists with a chance to rebel, or put differently, to stage a moment of rupture.

Even though Left radical activists and the traditional Marxist Left organize around the same dates, there is a qualitative difference in their orientation to the future, which is important to keep in mind when trying to grasp the logic of their forms of action. Left radical activists are not simply 'bad Marxists' unable to state their objectives in a clear way; their lack of linear foreclosure regarding the future is deliberate, but entails both frenzied activity, despair and inaction, which I will delve into by returning to Aske and the COP 15 in Copenhagen.

Aske's Dead Time

The Left radical activists I have encountered throughout Northern Europe seldom talk explicitly about capitalism. In their meetings, they do not spend much time talking about or analysing capitalism in its various guises, contrary to the practice of previous generations of the extra-parliamentarian Left who seemed to place greater value on long oratories and in-depth critiques of the political economy of capitalism. During a warm-up rally and party held in Christiania two days before the Reclaim Power action during the Copenhagen Climate Summit (COP 15), a spokesperson for Climate Justice Action briefly talked about the issue of capitalism and how it can be overcome in the following way:

> What has fifty years of COP [Conference of the Parties] ever done for us? Excuse me for sounding like the *Life of Brian*. The COP is not about solving the climate crisis, but about solving the multiple crises of capitalism. That's their dirty little secret. The aim is to legitimate the fucked-up business as usual and create a new green market to invest in. The COP is a shield around capitalism ... We need to think about how to destroy capitalism, but we do not know exactly how to do it yet.

In this description of the forces of capitalism, certain actors pull the strings and shield the system from attack. From the spokesperson's point of view, these are the corporate lobbyists and the politicians, who are the custodians of representative democracy, but who nevertheless require cohesive force to make others submit themselves to decisions (see Graeber 2009). Moreover, there are the police officers that defend the system for money, and other individuals who constantly give in to their desire for consumer goods and a comfortable lifestyle.[9] To the spokesperson, the moment of crisis is seen as the territory for capitalist expansion. Such a view is not limited to activists on the street: Naomi Klein has formulated this view most consistently in *The Shock Doctrine* (Klein 2008), where she develops a neat analogy between Ewen Cameron's experiments with electroshock therapy at McGill University in the 1950s, aimed at 'depatterning' his patients, and Milton Friedman's economic 'shock treatment'. Klein argues that during the shock-and-awe campaigns of wars (for example in Chile or during the War on Terror), during natural disasters (such as tsunamis and Hurricane Katrina in New Orleans) or economic crises, neoliberal actors get the opportunity to expand and fortify the existing system. Wars, disasters and crises are moments for turning common goods into private property (ibid.: 6).

The quote from the speech at the Reclaim Power rally also speaks to another issue, namely the experience of not knowing how to break down capitalism, if it is at all possible, and what should replace it. It reiterates the view held by my activist friend from the study circle, who I referred to in the Introduction, and who found that it was best to avoid painting pictures of a future paradise or ideal society. Interestingly enough, not knowing how to undermine capitalism or exactly what the final aim of activism is plays out both as a frenzied activity, for example around certain dated events, and as a sense of despair, leading to apathy and inaction.

In my first interview with Aske he spoke about this issue. Aske is a graduate student of history and temporarily lives in co-op housing on the outskirts of Copenhagen, rented by a group of his activist friends a few years ago. Even though he has only been politically active on the Left radical scene in Copenhagen for a few years, he has become a key figure, that is, someone you call up when direct actions are to be planned. He is pleasant and outgoing with a rare mixture of macho recklessness and theoretical self-reflection, and he almost always seems prepared to engage himself in a variety of tasks. Aske is from a middle-class background and his parents are left-wing. Before starting university Aske had been a student at the Free Gymnasium, an alternative secondary school in Copenhagen that stresses direct consensus democracy among students and faculty, and which is often talked of in public as a stepping stone to the radical Left milieu. Aske did not 'get engaged' (*blev engageret*, which in Danish carries the meaning of getting involved and becoming absorbed) in activism right away, he explained, but used to turn up at the local self-managed social centre Ungdomshuset (the Youth House) for parties and to hang out with friends.

On a sunny afternoon, I interviewed him in the garden of the house he lived in, while the neighbour's lawn mower threatened to drown out our conversation:

> My political interest started through reading texts, even classical Marxism and critiques of political economy. I was very negative and quite apathetic at the time. I was not engaged in anything specific. When I began university I teamed up with some people from the Front of Socialist Youth – but that was too much organization ... Direct action is more my kind of thing. [He lights up a cigarette and continues.] Sometimes problems just become too big, too structural: it is like hitting a cushion. Climate issues, for example. That is probably why I started with Ungdomshuset.

Aske spoke of a quite widespread experience among activists, namely that it seems impossible to change or even influence capitalism: its cushion-like quality implies that one's actions do not really matter or change the way things are, which often leads to the conclusion that it does not seem worthwhile even trying. Aske described this experience as 'a time of apathy'. And apathy is also the word he used two years later to describe his state of mind after his involvement in another lengthy political controversy resulting in the eviction of a group of Iraqi refugees from a church in Nørrebro and their subsequent forced repatriation. He was not the only one who, after this experience, kept to himself, was said to have 'burned out' or become depressed, claiming not to have the energy to participate in the ongoing preparations for the Climate Summit in Copenhagen.

Aske described this sense of not being able to influence the way things are in a bodily idiom, as being 'apathetic', which was not healed by reading political theory or by becoming a member of a formal youth organization of a leftist party, but only when engaged in 'direct actions' with others. I believe that Aske's experience of apathy and 'not being engaged in anything specific' is intimately tied to an experience of capitalism's pervasiveness and persistence. According to the people I spoke to, capitalism is in what you eat, how you travel, if you drink bottled water during the ESF, in the goals you might set for your life, the way you relate to other people and how you fall in love. When capitalism is intrinsic to all relations, changing it can seem a huge task. Just as when you hit a cushion you can make a dent in it, but it quickly regains its shape, capitalism is likewise perceived to recover from its recurrent crises.

Again, this view can also be identified among other observers of the movement. De Angelis, an intellectual involved in the conflict-ridden planning of the European Social Forum in London in 2004, has argued that since the fall of the Berlin Wall the European Left has been suffering from a 'TINA syndrome', that is, the idea that 'there is no alternative' to capitalism (De Angelis 2006). This view might have changed slightly in light of the financial and economic crisis that took root in Europe in 2008: the expectation of actually being able to supplant capitalism seems to be on the rise again, even though it is still accompanied by the concern that capitalism will simply become reconfigured as a new 'green' version of its old self.

In Aske's reasoning, his political engagement, therefore, started with something that did not seem as 'big' or 'structural', namely the fight against the eviction of Ungdomshuset that hitherto had mostly been a social base for him. Like many other Left radical activists, he has had a short-lived attachment to more traditional leftist organizations, in this case the Front of Socialist Youth,[10] but that was experienced as 'too much organization' – which is, as previously mentioned, a common critique of the more hierarchically organized political parties, NGOs and labour unions. Instead, he took an intense interest in the effects and tactics of direct action. In addition to interpreting this as an expression of an anarchist aversion to leaders and formal organization, I believe it can also be understood as a particular temporal template: while many organizations found on the European left aim to mobilize people to act at a later stage, direct action makes it possible to take action in the present without the finality of revolution. In this context, direct action can be conceptualized as an attempt at creating differentiation or internal distance, which has to be opened from within the system (Critchley 2007: 113).[11] In this view there is, so to speak, no Archimedean point from where capitalism can be perceived and attacked in its totality; rather, it demands constant work to keep the encroachment of capitalism at bay.

During my talk with Aske in the garden of his co-op, he told me about his experience of participating in the protests against the G8 summit in Heiligendamm (Germany) in 2007. In Heiligendamm, protesters managed to block the summit venue by inventing 'a new form of action', which entailed an elaborate choreography of different colour-coded blocs converging on the same target. Aske showed me a video on YouTube with the rather dull name of *G8 2007 Promotion Trailer*.[12] While watching it, I was struck by how it reiterated key perceptions of capitalism and the future that are held by many activists: that capitalism is an all encompassing system with no point of transcendence, with no 'outside' from where it can be attacked; instead, any contestation has to take place from interstices arising from other social relations that can be opened up within the system.

Before major direct actions and other protests, activists post 'promotional' videos on the internet to get fellow activists to join them. The trailers usually follow a similar script – which Razsa (2013) has referred to as 'riot porn' – and I have found that these video are one of the few media through which activists engage in a kind of public exegesis concerned with the reality of capitalism. They begin by displaying the evils and injustices of capitalism: war and starvation, exploitation and global inequality, as well as the devastation of the planet. This is depicted as an effect of the insatiable appetite of corporate business for gain as well as political leaders' desire for power, both of which result in the use of cohesive power to keep the world under their control. Whether promoting protests against the summits of NATO, the G8 or the UN climate conference, the trailers convey the message that capitalism is the underlying force and shaper of affairs, as also alluded to by the spokesperson during the Reclaim Power rally in Christiania quoted earlier. The second part of the videos usually shows photos from riots and burning barricades, and then other photos where activists successfully defeat or trick police officers during confrontations in the streets.

This particular video for the G8 protests in Heiligendamm in 2007 is saturated with imagery of the apocalypse. In the opening it states that 'one demonstration will change the course of Earth's history', and lets us know that something new and better might be about to emerge. It continues with the statement that 'the world of our dreams lies beneath the ruins of the old', over the background of a city in ruins. Throughout the trailer a short sequence in black and white is repeated, namely that of a man and a woman slowly approaching each other, followed by their embrace and deep kiss. What the scene signifies is obviously hard to establish with certainty, but it definitely hints that a better world can be associated with the return of intimacy, the freedom of association and an experience of love between humans. Aside from this, what actually characterizes 'the world of our dreams' is left open and undetermined. In this particular video, a future otherworld is minimally depicted as glimmering sunlight in the shields held by a line of riot police while the written text tells us that we 'probably experience powerlessness and apathy in the present world', and have 'a sense of dead time'. It then goes on to state that taking action will 'reveal something' about a world to come or, in other words, that by participating in the protests one is likely to gain a bodily experience of the freedom, strength and undirected social relations associated with an anti-capitalist world order.

What struck me as particularly interesting about the G8 video, as well as the one promoting the protests against the Climate Summit in Copenhagen that I referred to in the opening of this chapter, is their talk of a dead system, dead time and apathy, and the particular way this seems to mirror Aske's bodily experience of powerlessness and apathy. The trailer's talk about dead time and Aske's experience of apathy, lurking indifference and inaction, have their own distinct temporal quality. I believe they say something essential about activism and activists' modes of being in and engendering time with their bodies, which I shall return to in Chapter 5.

A Cosmology of Capitalism

As previously mentioned, explicit references to capitalism are rare and usually confined to the frequent videos and written calls for action circulating on web listservs and homepages. What more can be said about the characteristics of capitalism transmitted by the videos, and what can they tell us about the models of the world that we as anthropologists employ?

In the promotional video for the Climate Summit protests in Copenhagen in December 2009, capitalism is imbued with the qualities of a sick and unbalanced human body: it is stumbling; it suffers from crisis, but may recover; it can be healed or left to die. It is depicted as simultaneously fragile and dangerous in its capacity to recover, and inherently unstable in its power to transform. So while in some instances – during certain critical periods or at particular dated events – it materializes and temporarily bears a resemblance to the human body (incarnated by the police officer), it is normally both far more pervasive and elusive.

Besides, from the corporeal metaphors used, capitalism is thought to hold crucial systemic qualities. For one, there are not several capitalisms. Green capitalism is still the same *one*, as the text in the YouTube trailer for the summit protests in Copenhagen implies. During the week of protests at the Climate Summit, apart from the approximately 1,000 preventive arrests, around a dozen activists were taken into custody for further criminal investigation. Two weeks later, they sent an open letter to fellow activists, which addressed the system of capitalism. They wrote: 'Even mild examples of civil disobedience have been considered as a serious threat to the social order. In response we ask – what order do we threaten and who ordered it?' In the letter, the prisoners continue describing an 'order' in which people are imprisoned without evidence of having committed a crime, where people do not own their own bodies, where power is beyond control and decisions shielded from debate (Tornatore et al. 2010). So, apart from being one system, capitalism is, in view of these activists, characterized by the irregular and disorderly imposition of order.

The experience that capitalism is everywhere and nowhere at the same time and yet penetrates every aspect of human life is widespread among activists. Many are concerned not only about police surveillance of their activities, but also about how to disentangle themselves from the influence of the state, at least in some parts of their lives, which results in attempts at doing politics at an (internal) distance from the state.[13]

This view of capitalism as pervasive is developed most consistently in Michael Hardt and Antonio Negri's first book, *Empire* (Hardt and Negri 2000), which is concerned with unpacking a new global logic or structure of rule called Empire. The book has been read by many of my activist interlocutors, and there seems to be great continuity between the thinking about world order in *Empire* and the sense of cosmological disorder encountered among Left radical activists.[14] According to Hardt and Negri, 'Empire presents its rule not as a transitory period in the movement of history, but as a regime with no temporal boundaries and in this sense outside of history or at the end of history' (ibid.: xv). In other words, Empire presents its order as permanent and ahistorical. In the book, everybody is described as absorbed within webs of capitalist exploitation and consumption, and subjects have interiorized the mechanisms of command (ibid.: 23; cf. Foucault 1982). Yet the fact that capitalism is all-pervasive also makes it accessible from everywhere.

At particular dated events in the near future, however, capitalism, or Empire as the global system of rule, materializes, and it is possible to act upon it in its totality. Among activists, the story goes that since the Paris Commune of 1871, anarchist and Left radical groups have been travelling from one rebellion to the next. But while the rule of nineteenth-and twentieth-century revolutionary and anti-imperialist tactics was to 'break the weakest link', particularly by fighting imperialism and capitalism in the Third World, among Left radical activists the tactic is to leap vertically, directly to the virtual centre of the Empire (such as summits of heads of state). Hardt and Negri have addressed the relationship between capitalism and rupture, chronological time and discontinuous moments, in *Multitude* (Hardt and Negri 2004):

> When does the moment of rupture come? ... Here we have to recognize decision also as an event. Not the linear accumulation of Chronos and the monotonous ticking of its clocks, but the sudden expression of Kairós. Kairós is the moment when the arrow is shot by the bowstring, the moment when a decision of action is made. Revolutionary politics must grasp, in the movement of the multitude and through the accumulation of common and cooperative decisions, the moment of rupture or *clinamen* that can create a new world. (ibid.: 357)

The meaning of all this is rather vague. As Guyer notes, it is as mysterious as evangelical prophecies and monetarism's ideas of growth through 'an infinite ripple effect', projecting a model of the future with no intermediary stages to reach for (Guyer 2007: 416). In physics, the term *clinamen* is used to describe how flow turns into turbulence, and as such it can work as a metaphor for rebellion.[15] Nevertheless, in the context at hand it would be wrong to think of capitalism as a system in equilibrium that is impelled into chaos. If we accept the activist view that capitalism is a disordered order – rife with crises, interstices and ruptures – *clinamen* would simply mean a creation of productive difference that is simultaneously inherent in a system, which is not necessarily ordered at the outset.

The idea of society as an ordered system is, to put it mildly, not strange to anthropology, which for most of its history has been concerned with describing the invisible order or forces of cohesion of 'primitive societies'. Marshall Sahlins argues that the sense of society as a systemic or self-regulating order is itself informed by a Judaeo-Christian cosmology (Sahlins 1996: 406). The tradition of seeing societies as an order has, as Sahlins says, been transposed to anthropological descriptions of the political systems of other people. Following the activists' lead, the challenge here is to think of a cosmos that is fundamentally disordered, in which evil forces and personal greed uphold the imbalance, but which also ruptures with crisis and is full of interstices and glimpses of other possible worlds. At the same time, however, even if the system appears disordered to activists, it is still seen as preserving the properties of a common life, and a common future, found within the more holistic models of society in classical anthropology.

If we return to the concept of political cosmology, a preliminary conclusion can be reached at this point: as argued, the anti-capitalist stance of activists does not appear to be very well or comprehensively elaborated, and it seldom manifests itself in speech. Many of my interviews are ripe with silence and beating around the bush on the topic, and activists have expressed their extreme boredom, or even outright fury, with the waste of time when, in meetings with representatives from the Marxist Left, the latter engage in long narratives on the state of capitalism. It is, in other words, not fully possible to describe Left radical activists' various perceptions of capitalism by relying only on an analysis of language, and this is in itself an important insight for coming closer to understanding the form politics takes in this context. In Chapter 5, I shall return to the concept of cosmology. I will employ a strategy similar to activists' approach to capitalism, that is, to hollow the concept out from the inside in order to imbue it with new meaning in light of the experience of 'the one big body acting together', which means that the cosmology of capitalism can be conceptualized as an effect of confrontations with the police that, so to speak, make the world fall into place.

For now it is sufficient to conclude that thinking and talking about the future poses a problem for the Left. This problem is rooted in an experience of radical discontinuity between a present of pervasive capitalism and another possible world. The future is not connected to the present in any straightforward manner: planning and setting goals for the near future are downplayed, while time becomes intensified around certain dated events (such as summit protests). This should have consequences for the choice of the anthropological concepts we use to think about time. Left radical activists seldom talk about revolution, and if they do, the meaning of the word is different from that of the Marxist Left, being more about rebellion, direct action and the creation of internal distance or temporary interstices (see Bey 1991). The slogan, aptly, is to build a new world here-and-now within the shell of the old rather than to wait for the revolution (see Gibson-Graham 2006; Graeber 2002, 2009). Activists want to overthrow capitalism (and rid themselves of the state), but 'don't know exactly how to do it yet', as the spokesperson for Climate Justice Action phrased it at the Reclaim Power rally.

Not knowing about and leaving the future indeterminate often creates impasses in the political projects of activists, such as when the ESF is caught between a desire for continual expansion and a strict adherence to a principle of self-organization. In hindsight, looking at the ESF in Malmö, the various dilemmas described in this chapter have without a doubt influenced the decline of the social forum process in Europe, and the reinvention of new forms of action such as permanent squatting in public squares (as performed, for example, by the Occupy movement to protest against austerity measures, leading to the performance of alternative forms of participatory democracy). To individual activists like Aske, not knowing can generate a bodily sense of apathy and inaction. Direct action is the road out of this, and much of the remainder of this book is concerned with how that happens.

Acknowledgements

Some of the ethnographic material included in this chapter first appeared in articles published in *Social Analysis* 54, 3 (2010) and in Anne Line Dalsgård, Martin Demant Frederiksen, Lotte Meinert and Susanne Højlund (eds), *Ethnographies of Youth and Temporality* (Temple University Press, 2014).

Notes

1. Retrieved 21 March 2011 from: www.youtube.com/watch?v=DWEzLoUgXw0.
2. Bruce Kapferer (1988) has previously used the term 'political cosmology' in a study of political culture in Australia and Sri Lanka that demonstrates how political values such as egalitarian individualism define nationalism in these countries.
3. For the Charter of Principles, see http://www.forumsocialmundial.org.br/main.php?id_menu=4&cd_language=2
4. Association for the Taxation of Financial Transactions for the Aid of Citizens (ATTAC) is an international network that is part of the alterglobalization movement. It was founded in France in 1998 around the demand for a tax to regulate speculative transactions in the financial market (the Tobin Tax).
5. The Clandestine Insurgent Rebel Clown Army emerged in 2003 in Great Britain. The Clown Army, which used clowning and non-violent tactics when engaging the police, represented a new form of action in the context of summit protests, and spread to a number of other European countries, including Sweden. It is described in further detail in Chapter 5.
6. Malmö's People's Park is the oldest of its kind in Sweden. The park was bought by the Social Democrats in 1891, and slowly developed into an amusement and recreational park for local working class families (see http://malmofolketspark.se). The Social Democratic Movement established similar parks in most other Swedish towns.

7. For a similar observation regarding the conflict between the traditional Marxist Left and Left radical activists in the context of the ESF in London, see Maeckelbergh (2009, 2011).
8. The text is taken from the declaration produced by the Assembly of Social Movements, ESF meeting, Malmö 2008.
9. In an article on the Judaeo-Christian cosmology that underpins contemporary anthropology, Marshall Sahlins has pointed to a generalized concern in the Western world with the constitutive power of human will. This concern, he argues, is particularly salient in anxiety about humans having wants beyond their means (Sahlins 1996: 397–98). Hence, whereas earlier in European history it was God who was considered to be 'the invisible hand' steering human action, now human desires have taken God's place as the ultimate providence.
10. The Front of Socialist Youth is affiliated to the left-wing party the Red–Green Alliance (Enhedslisten). The Red–Green Alliance is a socialist party with seats in the Danish Parliament and was formed by three small left-wing parties in 1989.
11. Other intellectuals close to the global justice movement have referred to this as the immanent labour of transformation (Gibson-Graham 2006; Hardt and Negri 2000: 396) taking place from interstices and moments of deviance within capitalism.
12. Retrieved 21 March 2011 from: www.youtube.com/watch?v=Uk-MBWp4vh8.
13. In a Scandinavian context, this experience of entanglement cannot be fully appreciated without also considering the role of the state. The Scandinavian welfare states were constructed in the wake of the Second World War. Today, the Danish state is present in many aspects of daily life, from birth registration, when every Dane receives a civil registration number and in setting the rules for the legal names that a child can be given, to the provision of publicly subsidized child care, free schooling until university, provision of subsidized community centres and support for voluntary associations, public libraries, health care and care for the elderly, among others (Jenkins 2011: 159–67). Denmark, together with other Scandinavian countries, has the lowest Gini coefficient (which measures income disparity) in the world (UNDP, cited in Olwig and Paerregaard 2011: 7). The Danish welfare state has few real foes: most people expect the state to provide for them, and pay their taxes reasonably willingly (Jenkins 2011; Jöhncke 2011: 31). If capitalism and/or the state is experienced as all-encompassing and perpetual, activists who wish to produce radical change need to produce interstices where other forms of living and doing politics can develop at an 'internal' distance.
14. At a talk in Denmark, Michael Hardt argued that *Empire* (Hardt and Negri 2000) and its follow up *Multitude* (Hardt and Negri 2004), which is concerned with the constitution of new revolutionary subjectivities, are the result of the influence of the movement on the authors' thinking, not the other way around.
15. The term *clinamen* means spontaneous or unpredicted deviation. According to Deleuze, whose thinking has inspired Hardt and Negri, it does not mean deviation from a present path (that is, a negation), nor a transcendence of the path, but the existence of productive difference in itself (Deleuze 1994: 232).

A Dumpster Dive

I meet with a group of seven people a little after 9 PM, nobody I know well except for Naya, who I had met during the preparations for the Climate Summit protests in Copenhagen. She is 27 years old, a dedicated shoplifter, dumpster-diver and vegan, and has lived almost all her life in the Freetown Christiania. It is freezing cold and I am full of presentiments.

I have been allowed to participate in a trip to forage for food in supermarket containers – food that is to be served as a free meal at a preparatory meeting for the Climate Summit. The practice of dumpster diving seems to have accelerated over the past ten years. Every night, Danish supermarkets full their rubbish containers with food past its sell-by date, and every night an increasing number of activists and young people turn up to collect the discarded unspoiled food. Naya has said it will be okay for me to come along as long as I do not mention names or our exact whereabouts. I have been told to bring a torch, preferably a headlamp, and gloves if I do not feel like touching the rubbish.

The plan is to split up into groups so as not to attract too much attention, and go to different supermarkets to 'recover' food to serve at the meeting the following day. I cycle with Naya and another young woman to a supermarket on Frederiksberg, a wealthier and conservative municipality within Copenhagen. The supermarket is located along a road with several lanes coming from the city centre, but at this time of night only few cars speed by. My head is full of questions, but I wonder if we can speak. 'They tend to throw out nice stuff', Naya says, 'and the container cannot be locked'. I ask if it is illegal to dumpster dive. 'Not really', she replies, 'when it is thrown away, it is not their property any more unless the container is locked, of course'. 'Can we talk or is it best not to be detected?' I ask. 'It is probably best to whisper', says a young woman with a crew cut, who I learn is called Anja and is a 'radical feminist'.

We arrive. We park our bikes around the corner from the supermarket, which has now closed, and walk into a small alley. After some 20 metres the alley runs into a back yard, and I realize that the light is still on in many apartments overlooking the back entrance to the supermarket. Luckily, it seems to be too cold for people to be outside at this time of night. I can see that Anja and Naya have been here earlier from the way they walk directly towards a large blue container located near the supermarket's entrance. Anja slips her gloves on, lifts herself to the edge of the container and jumps in. 'You are welcome to stay here', Naya whispers. My face must have revealed that I am not too comfortable about the whole thing; I keep imagining how my feet would sink into day-old mince meat. I feel acutely that this is against all I have learned, but nevertheless I follow her into the container.

As an anthropologist I know that dirt stands for moral disorder. In Scandinavia, ideas about purity and dirt were formed by the end of the nineteenth century, together with the emergence of the bourgeoisie. As Swedish ethnologist Jonas Frykman has phrased it, the bourgeoisie was seen as 'fit to lead because of its many virtues: its high moral standards, its self-discipline and moderation, its thrift and rationality' (Frykman 2008: 266). Even today, the smell of putrefaction is thought of as a symptom of illness and moral decline (Schmidt 1986: 43–44). Activists are aware that they break middle-class norms of cleanliness and respectability when jumping into a container, but they reject the thought that it should be morally wrong.

I am on firm ground. The sweet smell of decay hits my face and I try to block my sense of smell. A small heap of vegetables is visible at the farther side of the container, but besides this I can mostly see grey plastic. 'How do you know what to take?' I ask. 'It is not too difficult really. Look at the bread and vegetables: if it is not visibly rotten or mouldy, you can eat it. We don't touch the meat or the milk products, but that's because we are vegans, you know. I wouldn't recommend taking home meat, but it is not hard to detect if the milk products are too old. It is just like in the refrigerator at home', Naya explains. Anja abruptly adds, 'The best way to know what to eat is to take a sniff of it'. After fumbling about for a while we find a common rhythm. They dig and I hold a green box to carry home the vegetables in while I carefully avoid touching the sludge on the sides of the container. For a while they sink into their own little world and the only sound is that of plastic being ripped.

There is something odd going on here, which later makes me think of Lévi-Strauss. In an analysis of a group of young punks' dietary habits in the US, Dylan Clark (2004) argues that Lévi-Strauss's culinary triangle is a good concept to think with in order to understand the group's relationship to food and rubbish. To cook food is, according to Lévi-Strauss, what distinguishes humans from animals, and distinctions between the raw, the cooked and the rotten are universal (Lévi-Strauss 2008). Many activists prefer the 'raw', which in the present context would refer to organic and home-grown foodstuffs, while they disavow foods that are or appear extraordinarily processed or 'cooked' (see also Skrædderdal 2006). One could say that the ills of capitalism are absorbed through the processed food. But dumpster diving is an important exception to the avoidance of 'the cooked'. By passing through the container the foodstuffs are ritually cleansed and transformed into lawless and 'rotten' food (Clark 2004: 27), and thereby something desirable and edible. While in the dumpster, Naya and Anja do not refrain from collecting highly non-organic, highly processed and unwholesome food such as sweets and potato chips.

Naya and Anja are quite systematic and consumed by their endeavour: every single plastic bag and packet is ransacked, and the small heaps of thrown-out food are gone over with a trained motion of the hand. I try to participate, but continue to pause in order to listen for sounds from the outside. Nobody disturbs us. Naya digs out several packets of pasta from a plastic bag at the bottom of the container, and Anja laughs and presents them to me. 'I am amazed at how much is thrown away', I say. 'Yes', Anja replies in a much friendlier voice now, 'we have been lucky today. There is often an abundance of nice food on Saturdays. There is nothing wrong with it. It is kind of gross actually, they prefer to trash it than to give it to somebody in need', she pauses, 'but it is funny to know that you can live from the stuff that other people throw way'. I start digging too and am soon carried away by a feeling that it actually makes a difference.

I have lost my sense of time, but after what seems like 15 or 20 minutes we leave. We quickly load the green boxes onto Naya's platform bike – a bicycle with a platform or large box attached to the front, in which one can carry goods or children – and throw some empty rubbish bags back in the container. Naya's bike is loaded with tomatoes, peppers, squash, onions, apples and a few other fruits and vegetables. We also have pasta, tea, potato chips and biscuits. 'We were lucky with the tea. You seldom find that', Naya says. 'It must be beginner's luck',

I reply with a smile, relieved that nobody detected us halfway through the job.

Our little foraging trip makes me think of the issue of abundance and foraging practices among indigenous peoples in the Ecuadorian Amazon, where I have previously worked. Laura Rival has described how the Huaorani understand the abundance of the forest as resulting from the ritual activities of previous generations. The game hunted or food carried home from the forest is shared within the long house, and the food is generously given away rather than exchanged or sold. Everybody has access to the forest, which – at least in principle – puts everyone on an equal footing when it comes to sharing. According to Rival, the concrete acts of sharing tie individual freedom to social equality and to an egalitarian way of community life in Amazon societies (Rival 1999; Overing 1988). Among the Huaorani and other indigenous groups, the idea of an abundant forest is translated into public institutions and private oil companies. These should – like the forest – be 'harvested to the extent possible' (Rival 1999: 75; Krøijer 2003). Among activists, dumpster diving and food sharing in soup kitchens produce a similar sense of equality due to the fact that everybody can tap into the resources and can participate in the meal without reference to economic capability. Many activists, but not all, find it legitimate to make use of the excesses of capitalist society, and many look upon public institutions in much the same way. So even though Scandinavian activists seek to avoid governmental interference in their activities, this does not necessarily contradict the acceptance of unemployment benefit, free health care and public study grants.

'What do you do if somebody turns up?' I ask while we cycle back. 'A lot of people don't mind; we leave the place tidy. Sometimes I just leave if people get angry, and come back later. It is bad style [dårlig stil] to make a mess. But once I got into a discussion with a man who shouted that we should get ourselves jobs. I tried to explain to him how stupid it is to throw out a box of apples just because one has a brown spot'.

Silence falls on us again. It is freezing cold, and Naya and Anja take turns with one pair of gloves as we bike back to the kitchen with our booty. The other two groups have not arrived yet. 'We need to buy soya milk and oil tomorrow unless the others have found some. If they turn up at all, that is', Anja says in a sulky voice. 'Anyway, we can make a pickle of the peppers'. We are all exhausted, but carefully wash and wipe dry all the vegetables while we drink tea in the large industrial kitchen filled with large pots, pans and piles of very diverse plates. They are not really inclined to talk about the experience, though I try to understand why it is worthwhile to go dumpster diving instead of putting the same energy into organizing the protest. I am offered various explanations: Naya tells me that dumpster diving is 'as important as the protest', and that it gives her a sense of 'being able to do something' and 'the strength to continue'. Anja lets me know that this is how it is done at international meetings where money is seldom available to pay for food.

In Copenhagen, I have found that it is particularly activists involved in environmental and climate issues who tend to swing by a container on a regular basis, for example on their way home from an evening out; or they may drop by a bakery dumpster on their way to a meeting to surprise fellow activists with freshly snatched pastries. One would assume that people with a revolutionary outlook would find it difficult or even futile to invest time and energy in dumpster diving and alternative eating practices; or, to put it differently, that activists who invest so much in staging ruptures and orchestrating confrontations would care little about the humdrum of daily life. Instead, mundane actions are ascribed enormous importance and political value and come to provide a sense of autarky and autonomy in the fleeting performance of the act. The practices are in different ways concerned with reconfiguring the body, and in performing these acts activists come to materialize radical change in their bodies.

The next day our bounty from the dumpster is served as delicious vegan dishes. Large portions of pickled peppers, pasta and a lentil dish with vegetables are handed out to a long queue of people from behind a serving table. Next to the pile of plates is a little plastic cup for donations, but collections are meagre and the organizers end up paying a part of the expenses for the meeting out of their own pockets.

2

Becoming Absorbed

Youth and the Interstices of Active Time in Ungdomshuset

In March 2007, dramatic clashes between young activists and police took place in the district of Nørrebro in Copenhagen. The riots followed conflicts over the ownership of a house known as Ungdomshuset (the Youth House), which had been a self-managed social centre for autonomous or Left radical activists for twenty-five years. The Christian sect Faderhuset (the Father House) owned the place at the time of the eviction.

The present chapter relates the story of Ungdomshuset from its sale in 1999, over the struggle after the eviction of its users in 2007, to the inauguration of a new social centre a little more than a year later. The story will be accompanied by an analysis of intersecting public discourses with special attention to the question of autonomy. I argue that in the public debate the 'Ungdomshus problem' is understood in a generational perspective, namely as associated with young people's problematic process of 'finding themselves' in order to 'find their place' in adult society (cf. Gullestad 2006: 82–84). However, I also show that there is significant variation in how the resolution to this problem is envisaged. Some politicians argued that young troublemakers should be corrected so that they know their place (*kende deres plads*), while others argued that the youngsters had a right to a space of their own, and that Danish society should be sufficiently 'spacious' (*rummeligt*), a spatial metaphor used to express tolerance, inclusion and a willingness to accommodate difference. Either way, I argue, the process of finding oneself is perceived as the progressive acquisition of individual autonomy. To elucidate the latter point, I draw on Sally Anderson's book on youth and cultural policy in Denmark (Anderson 2008), as well as other works concerned with generation and youth in Scandinavia (Gullestad 1992, 2002, 2006; Korsgaard 1998, 2001; Olwig and Gulløv 2003; Whyte et al. 2008).

Whereas activists' forms of organizing and protesting are represented in public debate as concerned with the difficult transition to social adulthood, I argue that within the Ungdomshuset case lies another interpretation: an eclipsed sense of autonomy. In the second half of the chapter, I therefore turn to activists of Ungdomshuset and their practices within the house. To explore these ideas and practices, I draw on Elizabeth Povinelli's work on modes of governance in late liberalism, in which she distinguishes between two normative discourses of social belonging: the autological subject, which represents the individual as a self-authoring individual; and the genealogical society, which implies an imagination of the human as constrained by social and historical forces. Social difference and forms of life that do not correspond to this communicative rationality, she argues, come to exist in bracketed zones (Povinelli 2006; 2011: 77). I argue that the Ungdomshuset became such a bracketed zone, simultaneously understood as an interstice of autonomy, where activists experimented with other modes of organizing and being together (see Lacey 2005a: 403). The overall aim of the present chapter is therefore to draw attention to an alternative and qualitatively different understanding of autonomy within Ungdomshuset. This sense of autonomy rests, I argue, less on a distinction between the individual and society than on people implicated in common activity.

A Pile of Rotten Stones or a Space of Their Own?

On a summer's day in 2000, Ruth Evensen, of the small Free Church called Faderhuset, received a sign from God. Ruth is a charismatic, eloquent woman, and priest of the 150 souls who are members of the Church, which follows the Pentecostal creed. On this day, she was driving along Jagtvej in Copenhagen, and as she passed the black, graffiti-covered façade of the self-managed social centre, Ungdomshuset, on Jagtvej 69, she looked up at a large red banner declaring: 'For sale! Including 500 stone-throwing, violent psychopaths from Hell'. In *Deadline*, a news programme on Danish national public television, she later explained that while looking up she heard the voice of God requesting her to remove this abomination from sight. She instantly decided to pick up the gauntlet and use all means possible to exorcise evil from the streets of Nørrebro (Karker 2007: 114).

Ruth Evensen and Faderhuset were not alone in this quest. Politicians from the municipality of Copenhagen had decided the previous year to put the building on Jagtvej 69 up for sale. The municipality owned the building, but had delegated the running of the house to an undefined group of users since 1982. Right-wing politicians and respectable citizens had for years depicted the users of the house as 'spoiled middle-class kids' who had not been properly educated by their parents. In addition, the kids were renowned 'troublemakers', said to be displaying undemocratic behaviour in their recurrent violent clashes with the police. Ungdomshuset was described as a filthy, inhospitable and somewhat glowering and notorious place without contact with the surrounding world. In the debates of the municipal council over the sale, several politicians said that it had been their desire to erase this black spot from the map of Copenhagen all along. But in the end it was a fire in the building in 1996 and the cost of total renovation, partially undertaken by the activists themselves, which encouraged a majority of councillors to sell the house at a meeting of the city council in May 1999 (ibid.: 111–12).

As one former member of the council bluntly put it: 'I agree with Enhedslistens'[1] statement that young people are the gold nuggets of our society. We need to protect them and give them the best conditions possible. But not that pile of rotten stones at Jagtvej 69. Tear the shit down. Period! Let's get all the blather over and done with' (Copenhagen Municipality 1999, my translation).[2] On the most immediate level, statements like this reflected the need to characterize Ungdomshuset as dilapidated and poorly maintained in order to legitimize the termination of the contract.[3] But the view of the young users of Ungdomshuset as 'unruly children' and 'spoiled kids' who should be taught to stop making a nuisance of themselves in public also points in another direction: the young people were thought of as politically immature and hence in need of protection while going through a process of learning in order for them to be able to take full part in public politics, as mature adults.

Sally Anderson has made an excellent analysis of how recreational sport is considered an acceptable and widely accepted path for teaching children and young people to become active citizens. By 'going to something' (*gå til noget*), as it is called in vernacular Danish, children move into public space (a sports association) for short periods of time without their parents, being coached there by other, professional adults. While the children have little say in a sports association, the mere movement of going away and coming home is thought of as formative, and the fundamental figure of democracy (Anderson 2008: 3, 7). Besides addressing how young people are still thought of as incomplete citizens, these insights also point to how notions of space, physical movement and age are tied together in a moral condemnation of activists' particular mode of occupying public space.

By extension, it is also possible to discern how the quote addresses another widespread concern, namely the suitability of Ungdomshuset as a space for young people and under-age children to embark upon the journey of becoming fully fledged members of Danish society. In Denmark, and in Scandinavia in general, it is not unusual for children to be placed in special institutions, such as kindergartens, schools, clubs and sports associations, during most of the day. These are considered proper places for children as opposed to 'hanging around' and being subject to bad influences or 'roaming around public space', as the activists were thought to be doing. Not being able to recognize what is considered a proper place for children has moral consequences (Olwig and Gulløv 2003: 2–3), as we shall see.

Apart from these public concerns about the suitability of Ungdomshuset for young people, other more favourable voices were also heard in the debate that emphasized the cultural aspects of the activities in the house. Another member of the city council described the sale as 'an attack on creativity'. In his view, Ungdomshuset 'gave room' to many extraordinarily committed youngsters and should be considered 'a growth layer (*vækstlag*) of talented people' within the area of culture, organizational politics and small businesses (Copenhagen Municipality 1999).

According to this view, which was also broadly articulated in public debates, the young activists were still considered incomplete or unfinished, but should be 'given room' to 'find themselves'. Whereas children in Scandinavia only a few generations back had to learn to be obedient in relation to their parents and figures of public authority, today the goal is to 'find oneself' (*finde sig selv*), become aware of one's individual identity (Gullestad 2002: 255–57; 2006: 87–88) and potential. This implies both inner personal growth as well as learning how to manage on one's own (*klare sig selv*) on a more practical plane. However, in order to find oneself, one must be 'given room', and this became the leverage point in the public debate in favour of Ungdomshuset. The argument rested on a metaphorical association between a house as a limited physical space and society. According to this view, Danish society as a whole should be sufficiently egalitarian and 'spacious' (*rummeligt*) to encompass different forms of social living, and conversely, people should learn to 'make room for all' (*gøre plads til alle*) (cf. Anderson 2008). This expectation also holds for public space, I believe: people are expected to be able to limit themselves physically in public space in order to make room for others, and this became the activists' Achilles' heel.

Regardless of these public arguments, the municipality pushed through the decision to sell Ungdomshuset to the company Human A/S Under Foundation[4] in the winter of 1999, with only little more than half of the votes in the municipal council. A lawyer formerly employed by the municipality and a number of unknown investors formed the company, and in the contract with the municipality, the company committed itself to continue the activities of the house. In discussions within the city council, the conservative councillor of culture expressed his view of the intended sale: 'Sometimes you must dare to take a chance offered to you … We have to decide on the sale of a building, which we are selling very cheaply, but we are also selling a problem' (Copenhagen Municipality 1999).

After the contract was signed, a sense of relief was noticeable among the politicians, who felt that they had rid themselves of a tiresome problem. But the 'problem' came back to haunt the municipality when the Christian sect Faderhuset took over Human A/S in 2001 and immediately terminated the contract with the users. The majority of the population, along with politicians and commentators in the press, agreed that the property rights of Faderhuset should be respected. Other voices argued with equal force that the adolescents in Ungdomshuset had the right to a space of their own, and that society was sufficiently 'spacious' to encompass different values and forms of life.

The Limits to 'Spaciousness'

The activists from Ungdomshuset refused to leave without a fight when their contract was ended. They felt that the municipality had committed a major injustice by selling a house that had been given to them back in 1982. At the weekly 'Monday meeting', where decisions were reached by consensus, the activists decided, after long internal debate, to use a variety of means to defend the house. First, it was decided to 'open up', which implied explaining to people about the history and activities of the house. The activists invited school children and journalists to visit the house in order to mobilize support and counter prejudice about the place. Second, it was decided to employ 'a variety of tactics', involving black bloc demonstrations, humorous actions and 'soft squattings' of public places, to raise public opinion in defence of the place. Third, activists decided to take the fight to the juridical system. As we shall see below, they quite consciously framed their campaign in terms of both 'spaciousness' (*rummelighed*) and a 'right to difference' (*ret til forskellighed*), and saw themselves as adhering to these norms within the house.

Rune, a 28-year-old activist who became active in Ungdomshuset right after the house had been partly destroyed by fire in 1996, explained the reasoning behind the black bloc demonstration. After the sale, they had organized a black bloc demonstration in the inner city of Copenhagen, and this was needed, he argued, 'to show our strength and our willingness to go all the way in defense of the house'. They had sought advice among people who had been part of the squatter scene in the 1980s on how to do 'militant stuff'. As a consequence, the first rows of demonstrators wore crash helmets and balaclavas, and were armed with iron bars in anticipation of physical confrontation, Rune explained. As the demonstration returned towards Nørrebro, riot police at Queen Louise's Bridge (connecting Nørrebro and the inner city) blocked the demonstration. 'But we did not stop', Rune said. 'We continued towards them with unaltered speed. The first rows had prepared themselves and were willing to take a 119 [the paragraph in the penal code on violence against public servants]. But the police withdrew. It felt like a great victory and imbued us with a sense of actually being able to defend the house'.

In this sense, black bloc demonstrations were considered important as they gave people the 'strength' to continue, but according to Rune and other activists it was equally valid to engage in more humorous actions because, as the expression in Danish goes, they simply make you 'a happy head' and 'communicate to the public that we are not violent psychopaths, but just normal people with hopes and dreams'. Among the more humorous actions was a pirate take-over of a large restaurant-ship in the Tivoli amusement park, the occupation of a bus terminus opposite the municipal building in the centre of Copenhagen, and the squatting of an old fortress in the harbour. In addition, activists who called themselves the Movement for More Opera Houses (launched at a time when Denmark's richest man, Mærsk McKinney Møller, donated an opera house to the Danish people under the condition that the Danish state defrayed the running costs) humorously argued for public support for more opera houses instead of youth houses. Inside the municipality, a 'ghost buster' action was staged, which attempted to exorcise the evil spirits that had possessed the politicians, and a 'naked brunch' on Sankt Hans Torv on Nørrebro was a comment on the fancy cafés cropping up in the neighbourhood, and meant to communicate the point that 'we were being stripped of everything we had', as a participating activist explained.

Apart from public protests, the fight was also carried on within the juridical system between the users' claim to usufruct based on the 1982 agreement and Faderhuset's claim to private property. In August 2006, the activists finally lost the court case, and all political and judicial solutions seemed out of their reach. Thousands took to the streets several times in the autumn of 2006, after years of smaller demonstrations and other happenings. Whereas the house had only been used regularly by a couple of hundred activists during the late 1990s, an increasing number showed up at demonstrations under slogans such as, 'Against Regimentation and Normalization!' 'Free Spaces – Now!' or simply, 'Hands Off! It's Our House'. These were often accompanied by the song 'Our House', by the British pop and ska band Madness.

Many users of Ungdomshuset and the majority of supporters who joined the defence saw the actions of the state, represented by the police, as a violation of the egalitarian 'room for all' (*plads til alle*) dictum (cf. Anderson 2008). The explicit reference to a broadly shared value mobilized many supporters who had hitherto not even been guests at the house, while former activists also joined in with their experience of defending squatted houses. There was concern in many quarters that Danish society was becoming less spacious.

In the Nordic countries, popular education is seen as one of the key means for creating democratic citizens. In accordance to *Folkeoplysningsloven* (the law on popular enlightenment), municipalities are expected to provide financial support for community centres and the work of local associations. This is thought of as a way to link the individual to society (Anderson 2008; Korsgaard 1998), and to further this goal the state has traditionally also financed such associations and political initiatives that are not perfectly aligned with mainstream public opinion or the policy of the government. Ending the activities in Ungdomshuset therefore also raised fears of alienating or excluding the autonomous activists and their supporters from democratic society, and in this sense the demand for autonomy turned into a problem about social 'spaciousness' (*rummelighed*).

Even activists from Ungdomshuset experienced no contradiction in both demanding autonomy and simultaneously expecting the municipality to provide the building. They expected the municipality to finance the facilities, but apart from that they wished to manage it on their own. In the face of the sale, activists believed that taking back the streets, even with the means described by Rune, was a legitimate attempt to create a space of action, and hence to carve out a space for themselves in a society that was becoming less spacious. In a sense, fighting back and claiming rights was perceived as a superior realization of the values that the state was neglecting when it disregarded the demand for a self-managed social centre. The recurrent attempts to control the streets during demonstrations and actions could be perceived of as one way of actualizing the claim to autonomy, at least for the moment.

International activists and squatters from social centres around Europe were mobilized to participate in the Final Battle on the date of the announced eviction, 14 December 2006. Even though the police authorities postponed the date indefinitely, thousands of black-clad activists in crash helmets, armed with cobblestones, iron bars and ladders, took to the street two days later. The activists refused to cooperate with the police regarding the route of the demonstration or comply with the prohibition of masking during demonstrations.[5] When the police tried to block the street, they were taken aback by the rage of the assembled activists (Karpantschof and Mikkelsen 2009: 62). An activist later explained this as a 'necessary show of force' to demonstrate to the police and the politicians what would be in store for them if and when the house was cleared and the youth evicted.

In the early morning of 1 March 2007, two military helicopters launched police units from the anti-terrorist unit onto the roof of Ungdomshuset. An excavator was used to allow the police to break through the wall, and officers swarmed into the building, which was pumped full of tear gas and foam. Even though the police announced to the media that the eviction had gone swiftly and quietly, it was later admitted that battles had broken out (ibid.: 69). Over the next three days, Copenhagen became the scene of a riot in which activists engaged in physical confrontations with the police, armed with stones, paint bombs and Molotov cocktails; they also controlled several streets on Nørrebro by building barricades and setting cars, and any other available material, on fire.[6] Many activists, who would otherwise find it unacceptable to participate in a riot, felt that 'now the time had come' for a forceful response. Aske explained:

> How you define your style depends somewhat on the police. If they do not get out of their cars, then it makes sense to run around the cars and operate in smaller groups. You cannot be all alone because then you will get a beating. You have to be three or four, knowing where each other is at all times, but not more than that. That was how it worked. It was like being in a bubble of time – get up at noon and prepare yourself, and then be in the streets until late at night. It was something like: move ahead, make a fire, pour something on the street and then move away. Then the police would arrive, [someone would] throw stones at their car and then run away again.

With house searches and arrests in the early hours of 1 March 2007, the police tried to counter the kind of guerrilla tactics described by Aske, but in the streets the authorities only managed to disperse the crowds, not to control the streets. After about 800 arrests and the detention of some 200 people (Københavns Politi 2007: 53), the riots abated. The eviction of Ungdomshuset had led to the largest riots in Denmark after the Second World War (Karpantschof and Mikkelsen 2009).

National public television followed the eviction and the riots in a 'breaking news' show every hour. In an analysis of the press coverage, Asta Nielsen (2009) shows how the police were virtually the only source of input for the analysis. The activists did not appear to be providing their versions of the story, but the analysis was spiced up with statements from local citizens concerned about 'the lack of police control of the streets'. The day after the eviction, the Minister of Justice, Lene Espersen, also appeared on screen. Following a feature in which parents expressed frustration with their inability to contact their children in police custody, the Minister was asked if they look like 'bad parents'. She replied:

> No, but I would say it is a bit late to start worrying about what your child is doing. I am deeply offended by the number of parents who have no control over their children. It is not until the social services call them up and explains that they [the children] have been arrested, because they have been throwing stones and setting the entire city on fire, that the parents wake up. And I maintain that it is first and foremost the parents who have disregarded their obligations.

The interviewer continued by asking the Minister what impression it makes on a child of 14 or 15 to be handcuffed and dragged to jail. She replied:

> I am sure it's a very unpleasant experience. Maybe it's the first time they experience that their criminal acts have consequences. And of course it is a hard way to learn that we live in a state governed by the law (*retssamfund*), but at some point they have to learn. (quoted from Nielsen 2009: 173, my translation)

On television, the Minister uses ambiguous language, categorizing the arrested activists first as children, and subsequently as criminals who have to face the consequences of their own actions. This side of the debate (symbolically represented by Faderhuset, we could say) shows a concern for the apparent lack of values and proper upbringing of some of the younger generation. In this view, it was believed that the inability of young activists to perform in a proper way in public space was the fault of the parents and should be corrected by them or, if need be, by the institutions of law and order. The trouble was explained as being a consequence of psychosocial problems, both within the age group and in young people's relations with their parents. From this side of the debate, agency was ascribed to the police, the elected politicians and the parents of the 'unruly' youngsters. The fact that most activists were more than 18 years old was ignored.

In interviews, most parents supported the activities of their children, and hence their right to organize public demonstrations for what they believed in. Some parents and former activists even organized themselves as a 'grey bloc' (a reference to their hair colour), who participated in demonstrations and actions. Other parents established the network Parents against Police Brutality in order to document and file complaints concerning police violence. When interviewed, parents argued in support of their children, and reasoned that by making public demands and organizing themselves their offspring were manifesting themselves as proper citizens of democratic society. Moreover, they warned against the alienating effect of police violence. Yet, most parents stated that they 'drew the line' (satte grænsen) at the use of violence, which few described as acceptable under any circumstances.

Again, ideas of societal spaciousness seemed to be at stake. As described above, 'making room for all' was as much an abstract ideal as it was a tactile bodily competence that you were expected to learn from an early age. Young people are not expected to be able to conduct themselves appropriately in public space, and therefore they are a group of special concern. During demonstrations, and particularly in the context of the riots following the eviction at Ungdomshuset, bystanders came to the conclusion that, given that the activists were not accommodating towards others, their own demand for 'spaciousness' should no longer be considered as being valid. This shift in public opinion, triggered by the alleged violence, went hand in hand with a shift in the categorization of the group from 'youth' to 'criminals', as reflected in the statement of the Minister of Justice quoted above.[7] This implied that recognition was no longer relevant to the task at hand, and less caution was necessary when it came to the employment of repressive measures (cf. Povinelli 2011).

A few days later, Ungdomshuset at Jagtvej 69 was torn down under police protection. Young punks, former users of the house crying in despair, and curious bystanders gathered to place flowers, candles, teddy bears and an occasional beer bottle at 'Ground 69'. Faderhuset (the religious sect) called a press conference to explain their view of the events and to address the users of Ungdomshuset. Ruth Evensen began in a motherly tone:

> I can understand that the youngsters are sad, but when they have finished crying, they should dry their eyes. The house on Jagtvej has been damaged

by years of neglect and vandalism. It is a huge firebomb and the unhealthiest place in Copenhagen ... It is the intention of Faderhuset to create a popular place with music and doors open to the public. And of course the youngsters are welcome, if they can behave themselves. (quoted from Karker 2007: 136, my translation)

It is a remarkable irony that Faderhuset also refers to the same values about 'open space' and 'room for everybody'. This underlines the wide dissemination of ideas about spaciousness, but simultaneously draws attention to the many ways in which it can be practised. The irony is underlined by the fact that Faderhuset, whose property was protected by the state, was a party whose treatment of children and young people within the Church congregation was far from the social and cultural ideals that are generally considered praiseworthy in Denmark – as equal, independent and autonomous individuals.[8] While a majority of the Danish population seemed to agree with the reaction of the authorities, only a few people actively supported Faderhuset. Much of the criticism of and many reservations about the young people were centred on the 'violence' of those who burned cars and threw stones at shop windows or tried to roll over and damage police cars. The attitude seemed rather to be one of a certain discomfort with the whole situation and the dilemmas about spaciousness that it entailed, though people also thought that law, order and private property had to be respected and defended.

The 'Madhouse' in the Streets

But the story did not end here, and 'the problem' was not solved by the sale, eviction from and demolition of the house on Jagtvej. A movement rose from the rubble of the house and protests continued. Activists and supporters of Ungdomshuset saw the eviction as evidence of the state's forced 'normalization' of society, and of an unjust targeting of difference. Among activists, stories flourished about police brutality and random arrests (see also Christensen 2009), and these highlighted both the experience of being under constant threat and the urgent need to fight back.

It is not possible to mention all the different activities, which were launched to demand a new house, and impossible to unravel all the factors that went into building a successful movement, but I will, nevertheless, mention a few highlights. After the eviction, the 'Monday meetings' (the weekly decision-making space within Ungdomshuset) continued in other locations to enable collective decision making, and a weekly Thursday demonstration was organized to draw continuous attention to the problem. These demonstrations were organized by shifting networks and groups, under the auspices of the 'Monday meeting', and they became a new social space and fixed point for activists in the street. The Thursday demos continued for seventy weeks and drew heavily on police resources; one such demonstration lasted twenty-four hours.

The many actions were partially financed by the production of Optøj, a brand of clothes produced by activists playing on the double meaning in Danish of 'clothes' and 'riot'. During the summer of 2007, t-shirts with slogans in favour of Ungdomshuset and Christiania, and a group of activists calling themselves Fighters and Lovers (who had been convicted according to Danish anti-terror laws for sending money to FARC in Colombia and PFLP in the Palestinian occupied territories),[9] were very visible in the streets. The t-shirts were only the visible surface of the way these three struggles were discursively tied together, bound by their demands – for spaciousness, and against the 'normalization'[10] and conviction of people of a different political opinion. Moreover, activists and artists' groups reconstructed the Ungdomshuset at Roskilde Festival, a large international music festival, while situationist-inspired artists reproduced an exact copy of Copenhagen's street signs, all saying 'Jagtvej', which were hung throughout the city (Rasmussen 2008).

Before the eviction, a network of activists calling themselves the Movement for More Youth Houses had occupied various buildings in Copenhagen and in other major cities of Denmark. This multiplicity of actions, including the Thursday demonstrations, was able to reach out to and absorb many new activists into the concrete activities of the movement. In addition, the struggle for a new youth house was able to heal a division among Left radical activists in Denmark that had existed at least since preparations for the EU summit in 2002. Now, activists who had formerly been of a civil-disobedience persuasion (for example, Globale Rødder) and those with more anarchist leanings (organized during the EU summit as the Anarchist Federation) participated in and supported each other's actions. The occurrences on 1 September and 6 October 2007 exemplify this.

Six months after the eviction of Ungdomshuset, an activist demonstration and party at Ground 69 (after the address of the house on Jagtvej 69) on 1 September was followed by vandalism and the plundering of nearby shops. According to some activists, the police 'attacked' the approximately 1,000 activists, who were dispersed with tear gas (Karpantschof and Mikkelsen 2009: 87), while others held that the whole incident was staged by activists. The situation evolved into rioting, including the spectacular burning of a police car. The following day, shocked politicians affirmed that they were unwilling to negotiate with the activists, and that the municipality could not offer houses 'to people prepared to employ violence against the police'. Not all activists were happy about this well-orchestrated incident, but they did not publicly distance themselves from it, and they argued that it was what could and should be expected in the current situation. The action and the public statements played into already existing speculations in the press about radicalization and activists turning to urban terrorism.[11] In retrospect, several activists have described it as an act caused by a sense of powerlessness and despair after the first, immediate rage had subsided.

At the same time, however, preparations were ongoing for a large confrontational civil disobedience action named G13. This was inspired by the mass action near Heiligendamm in Germany, where thousands of activists had successfully blocked a meeting of the G8. As in Heiligendamm, the participants in the G13 action were divided into four blocs with different colour codes, and each bloc prepared their own tactics to reach and occupy what they described as 'their new Ungdomshus (youth house)'. The action was named after the address of the house, 13 Grøndalsvænge Allé, in the wealthier neighbourhood of Frederiksberg in Copenhagen, and the plan as well as the date were announced in the media several weeks ahead. According to Mikkel, who was one of the organizers who had worked for months on planning the action, the idea was 'to take for ourselves' instead of waiting for the politicians. The hope was, as he phrased it, 'to do politics at a distance from the municipality', and to move the conflict out of Nørrebro and into the wealthier Frederiksberg to demonstrate that Ungdomshuset 'concerned everybody'. The action was coordinated between various Left radical groups in Copenhagen, and the colour-coded blocs reflected different tactical inclinations.

The green bloc was the first bloc of the demonstration. According to the plan it was to stick to the route, and the participants were to use home-made shields to push against police lines along the way; the turquoise bloc was formed of black-clad activists with turquoise scarves who had planned an unpredictable and flexible 'swarming' tactic in smaller affinity groups; the red bloc stood for party, chaos and trickery, while the yellow bloc, a queer-feminist grouping, consisted of a tight bloc of 400 mainly female activists in canary yellow hoods, ingenious padding and goggles to endure tear gas and police batons. The first line of protesters in the yellow bloc carried a large banner saying 'Normalize This!', a reference to their grotesque outfits and a phrase ridiculing the increasing regimentation of public space.

The G13 action followed different routes after meeting the first police blockade and managed to include activists of different tactical inclinations.[12] At Grøndalsvænge, the action ended with a group of youngsters planting a black pirate flag on a rooftop, even though the police had besieged the area the previous day. The participants consider the day a great success, even though they were soon arrested. The success was described as a bodily sense of strength, but there was also contentment with the fact that all the participants had respected the confrontational, yet non-violent, style of the action.

The next day, the public media criticized the police for using excessive force and quantities of tear gas against 'the young activists'. The chief director of the police responded by calling the Ungdomshus affair a 'mad house', and requested a political solution to the problem.[13] Soon after this, negotiations about a new house were opened, and in July 2008 a new, self-managed social centre was inaugurated in Copenhagen.

Autonomy as 'Finding Oneself'?

The public debate about Ungdomshuset was embedded in a discourse about the activists' transition into social adulthood, which implies a particular understanding of both generation and time. In the anthropological literature, generation has been understood in three ways: as the genealogical relation of kinship; as a principle for structuring society and categorizing its members, for example in age groups; and as historical generation, that is, as groups sharing a common historical experience (Whyte et al. 2008: 3–5). The former two are clearly present in the public debate in the many statements made about parents' responsibility for educating their children, and in the phrasing of the entire conflict as a problem of the immaturity of an age group. The third understanding, a historical generation, was absent in the public debate, even though, as I argued in Chapter 1, activists seem to have a similar outlook to the future or, put differently, share the historically contingent experience that there is no real alternative to capitalism and that this ties into how politics is performed.

If we go into the representation of the activists as young, it is relevant to consider how the transition to social adulthood is envisioned. As previously mentioned, youth is thought of as a process of 'finding oneself', and a certain degree of independence and autonomy is considered central to this process (Gullestad 2006: 82–84). 'Finding oneself' is thus a process of gaining individual autonomy, which must be orchestrated by parents and public institutions with equal amounts of freedom and the setting of limits to behaviour (*grænsesætning*). References among sympathetic politicians to the creative activities inside Ungdomshuset were a reflection of the idea that young people can find themselves through expressive activities: the young activists needed a space of their own, and under the right circumstances, autonomy would emerge from inside the person.

This understanding of the activists can be further conceptualized with reference to the distinction Elizabeth Povinelli makes between two normative discourses on social belonging in late liberalism, which she defines as the discourses and practices of the autological subject and genealogical society. She writes:

> By the autological subject, I am referring to discourses, practices and fantasies about self-making, self-sovereignty and the value of individual freedom associated with the Enlightenment project of contractual constitutional democracy and capitalism. By genealogical society, I am referring to discourses, practices and fantasies about societal constraints placed on the autological subject by various kinds of inheritances. (Povinelli 2006: 4)

The young activists in Denmark are largely represented as being in the process of becoming self-authoring individuals. In short, autonomy is tied to the individual and is something one acquires in the process of growing up.

Yet, I believe there is a modification to this discourse on individual freedom and self-sovereignty in a Danish or maybe even Scandinavian context. If the post-Enlightenment idea of individual autonomy is foreground, the social whole and strong egalitarian ideals are the tenacious background, which should not be ignored (Gullestad 1992: 183). Several authors have argued that individuality takes a particular form in Scandinavia, in being historically associated with the independent and flexible life of freeholding peasants. The positive value of managing on one's own (*at klare sig selv*) is a widespread ideal, but in collective memory this goes hand in hand with the togetherness, closeness and commonality usually associated with local communities (Ekman 1991: 58–59; Gullestad 1991: 482; 2006: 113–14). What still binds society together, it is widely argued, is an active life in communality (Korsgaard 2001: 64–70; 2004: 449–52). This has a bearing on the issue we are discussing here, in as much as the young activists are perceived as having to be individualized, but in such a way that they simultaneously grow into adulthood and into society.

The use of the word 'growth' to describe the process of generational succession suggests that in order for the process of finding oneself to be a successful one, young people must refashion the values transmitted by the family, which imply that a certain level of resistance is acceptable and even desirable (Gullestad 1991, 2006; Olwig 2000). They are, however, not expected to completely 'uproot' themselves, because at some point they must also 'find their place' (*finde deres plads*) in adult society. Both parents and the Danish state are considered to have a legitimate role to play in the process: on the one hand, the family is expected to support, coach and give the child 'freedom within limits' by successively letting go, but on the other hand the state is expected to orchestrate the process by financing activities for young people away from home where they can acquire the skills necessary for becoming active citizens. Young adults are expected to increasingly venture into public space but, according to the Danish thinker Hal Koch, only grown-ups are fully fledged citizens, and young people must wait and learn before participating in public political matters (Korsgaard 2001: 73–76).

With this amendment to Povinelli's distinction between the autological subject and genealogical society, which points to a particular and permanent tension between the individual and the societal whole in public discourse in Denmark, we can start considering what happens to activists – the incomplete political subjects – who are placed in the position of waiting. Povinelli's thoughts are useful here, I find, because she considers what happens to people who do not fit, or defy fitting, into the communicative rationality. She argues that forms of radical alterity are simply ignored, or bracketed, whereby people are abandoned in a state of 'bracketed time' (Povinelli 2011: 76–77), which involves a temporal suspension of the relationship of justice and recognition by which people are left to wait and endure in a 'disquieting limbo' (ibid.: 78). Defining the activists around Ungdomshuset as young was one way to abandon them since only time – that is, their coming of age – would be able to resolve their undesirable behaviour. Moreover, the sale of Ungdomshuset and the later recategorization of the activists from youths to criminals in light of their so-called 'untimely' protests only added new layers to this abandonment, because it thereby became legitimate not only to ignore them but also to suppress their actions (ibid.: 92–93).[14]

As Povinelli has convincingly argued, people tend not to be waiting in the 'imaginary waiting rooms of history' that they have been confined to. Instead, they often begin experimenting with what we think of within a Western scholarly tradition as self and society (ibid.: 100). In this light, we now turn to the social life that developed within Ungdomshuset, and how activists describe their experiments with forms of organizing and being together. This entails a different form of autonomy that does not pertain to the individual 'autological' subject, but to being enmeshed in active time together.

Active Time and Dead Time in Ungdomshuset

Ungdomshuset was considered the backbone of the squatters' movement in the 1980s, and over the years, the house served as an alternative scene for punk music, street theatre and circus performance. It had a weekly vegan soup kitchen, a café, a bookshop and a printing workshop, a weekly film show and the yearly K-town Festival.[15] The building also housed meetings, seminars and action-planning sessions, and served as a general hangout for young people between the ages of 13 and 30. Among the Danish public, Left radical activists are associated explicitly with Ungdomshuset; although several other activist spaces were located in the same area, Ungdomshuset was the most explicitly anarchist-inspired place, and was frequented by activists with a strong interest in music and a preoccupation with alternative lifestyles.

In my interviews with activists from Ungdomshuset, consensus decision making and self-organization were stressed as particular to the place. These practices were thought to hold out the promise of true democracy, more so than the representative democracy praised in parliamentary politics. Moreover, self-organization was described as qualitatively better than the pacifying rule of so-called 'dead-boring grown-ups' and educators in conventional Danish community centres. At Ungdomshuset, collective decision making and basic rules of social interaction were defined at the weekly 'Monday meeting' (*mandagsmøde*), where core activists would meet up in order to discuss concrete activities and take decisions on various issues. These ranged from who was in line to organize the next party, to how to defend the house in case of eviction. Most concrete activities, such as vegan cooking for the soup kitchen and concert planning, were organized in smaller groups without much interference from the 'Monday meeting'.

The insistence on a 'good meeting style' (*god møde stil*) meant that everybody had the right to voice their opinions and that nobody should try to dominate, for instance by laughing at others or by taking a leading role in the process of decision making.[16] Katrine, who lives in a once-squatted house named BumZen (meaning 'pimple', but which also refers to BZ, from the word *besæt*, that is, 'occupy' or 'squat') and who had been an activist in Ungdomshuset for about ten years at the time of the eviction, recalled that it was sometimes hard to live up to these ideals:

> After the house was put up for sale, we had discussions all night: Should we go to court? Do we want a press group? Do we want to be part of the system by doing so, or should we fight right away? We had long, long

discussions, and four or five people, representing the two wings, sat far into the night discussing these issues ... I don't think people are proud of how it was done; that it was the most stubborn and persistent who got to decide. It was a contest of perseverance, which I don't think people would accept today.

All attempts, conscious or not, to rule others became, at some point, the subject of heated debate about 'hierarchies' and domination. Though many found these long discussions tiresome at times, Katrine nonetheless considered them to be formative, insofar as they enabled people to rid themselves of the subtle forms of domination associated with the rest of Danish society. Whereas, in the mid 1990s, derogatory or sexist comments were not uncommon, and alleged 'faggots' could get a beating in Ungdomshuset, Katrine and many others tried to change this way of relating to one another:

> Before I became active, it was all about food and ecology. When I came into the house, discussions about homophobia and sexism emerged. It was hard core in the beginning because somebody, namely the white heterosexual men who don't believe that these issues concern them, always believed that these matters should be saved until after the revo' [revolution] ... There was a couple – when they were drinking they would get into a fight, and she would sometimes get a beating. To many it was hard to overcome the fact that he was a friend: 'Why doesn't she just go back home to France', or 'She is just so annoying'. Some feminists left the house because of this, but I stayed to take the fight [further]. Now, it [anti-sexism] is part of the house, so something has happened.

Notwithstanding the existence of other forms of domination within Ungdomshuset – particularly expressed in the fact that people with many friends, long experience and the most active would have more influence – activists described it as a 'free space' characterized by the slow but steady work needed to create voluntary and undirected social relations. Many activists therefore stressed the importance of relatively permanent activist spaces such as Ungdomshuset because they were a place to come together; they facilitated this kind of work on social relations, and also permitted the imposition of sanctions for undesirable behaviour.

The goal was that the meeting, and the house in general, should 'make room for everybody' (*gøre plads til alle*). This expression has the same connotations as the Danish idea of 'spaciousness' (*rummelighed*), in that it stresses how social relations must be worked on in order for differences to be encompassed within a defined and finite space. Activists felt that their modes of being together implied a superior realization of 'spaciousness' and democracy, but simultaneously they nevertheless implied a rupture with what was experienced as the hypocrisy of the parental generation, the state and representative democracy. Careful practices of consensus decision making were developed, and by mid 2000, no utterances reflecting sexism, homophobia or racism were tolerated in Ungdomshuset, and wrongdoers would be corrected at the weekly meeting. They could be asked to voluntarily submit to 'social service' as punishment, the worst of which was cleaning the stinking toilets by the back staircase. If individuals were unwilling to improve, they were ultimately expelled from the house.

In Ungdomshuset, all aspects of social life and organization were thought of as political. Rune, who had started frequenting Ungdomshuset after the fire in 1996, recalled the political meaningfulness of the practical work:

> It was a period when the house was kind of dead – only three or four activists and a kitchen crew. I had been a member of Rebel,[17] but I was tired of that kind of politics because the only concern was how many beers you can drink, and how many girls you can score. In Ungdomshuset, you do politics by repairing a house that could eventually become the framework for a lot of people and a lot of activities. I found that much more political than theoretical discussions while drinking beer. That is what made me [get] involved.

Many activists in Ungdomshuset were, like Rune, recruited from other political organizations on the left, or started coming to Ungdomshuset with friends from the Free Gymnasium (the alternative upper-secondary school also located in Nørrebro). Like Rune, these activists describe how they slowly became absorbed by different concrete working groups, such as the building team and kitchen crew, and the concert-organizing, band-booking or theatre groups.

Rune, who like Katrine became a vegan at Ungdomshuset, is also an activist with the Animal Liberation Front (ALF). Today, many activists are vegan, which entails that in their diet and other aspects of life they avoid eating animal products – meat, dairy and eggs – and reject the use of fur and leather, and cosmetics tested on animals. The basic endeavour is thus to avoid inflicting harm on animals as a concrete reaction to how animals have been reduced to just another means of production in industrial capitalism. I once talked to Rune about the relationship between humans and animals that being an ALF activist entailed:

> RUNE: Animal Liberation Front (ALF) fights for animal rights and liberation through direct action. ALF do not inflict physical harm on people, but economic harm on the industry. To me there is a difference between animal

rights and animal welfare: with animal rights, you work at extending rights to animals; they have a right to life and freedom, not to be bred for slaughter and killed in the most barbaric ways, et cetera. ALF works in a very loose way [it is not formally organized]; there are some guidelines, which must be fundamental for any action: you must be vegan or vegetarian; you must not inflict physical harm on people, et cetera. If you act based on these points then you are part of ALF in the moment of action.[18] ... A meat-eater will never understand why you do what you do because then they would become vegan or vegetarian. The gap between what is considered right and wrong is huge, and these people cannot understand why you would destroy a mink farm. I have lost friends because they did not understand why I would defend it, and because I publicly express that I found it perfectly legitimate because that farmer was a murderer, a torturer, and that it is a bloody and dirty business.

S.K.: I do not quite understand that 'rights' thing. To liberate animals – is that to equate animals with humans? Are they a kind of people?

RUNE: In a sense yes, but then it is a different kind of people ... We do not want to abolish the distinction between humans and animals altogether. We do not think that animals should have the right to vote, for example, but we do think they have the right to a life of freedom. It is not up to us to govern them. My motivation is anti-capitalist; it is a reaction to the exploitation of animals, but others [ALF activists] feel that animals are like humans.

During the interview, Rune established a relationship between the way human and animal bodies are exploited for economic advantage, and affirmed that moral legitimacy cannot be equated with the legality of actions.

Most studies of veganism and animal-rights activists draw on symbolic analysis, and focus on the symbolic aspects of eating as well as the ritual process of identity formation. The respect that activists show for animals has been interpreted, in this context, as 'standing for' the respect you have for other people and for the planet (Fiddles 1997: 256–58). Particularly in works inspired by studies of sub-cultures (Clark 2004; Fiddles 1997; Krogstad 1986), the eating habits of activists are understood as symbolic practices, that is, actions aimed at constructing a common identity or a symbolic way of challenging the dominant order. Anna Krogstad (1986), for example, analyses the relationship between external provocation and internal morality in the context of the squatter movement in Oslo, Norway. Krogstad makes a distinction between declarative and regulative punk symbols. Declarative symbols are associated with hair and clothes, music and graffiti; that is, the black, ugly and trashed style that sneers at conformity, and is said to create a counter-image of its surroundings. Regulative symbols, on the other hand, are ingrained in food, sexual and organizational practices, and are thought of as indicative of the morally correct way of action. In the case of young squatters in Oslo, it was particularly 'becoming vegan' which had the effect of regulating internal practices.

Krogstad's distinction between two types of symbolic action draws, in my view, on the outdated idea of sub-cultures (see Clarke 2006), particularly because it rests on an idea of a homogeneous culture supported by shared symbols. Nevertheless, the analysis is insightful as it points out how food becomes what Krogstad calls an important 'autonomous field of action' (Krogstad 1986: 519). She argues that these particular fields are rendered important by activists themselves because they facilitate the construction of community without resting upon hierarchical relations (ibid.: 519–20). While I agree that changing one's food practices does not rely on an endorsement of the surroundings, it is nevertheless important, I believe, to take into account the fact that the food practices of activists are not completely egalitarian either. Some people such as Rune get the knack of it better than others, or are in a position to teach others the right way, and this introduces a hierarchy of values (Dumont 1970: 20).[19]

But what is also interesting is how Rune considers humans and animals to be basically 'of the same kind'. From an anarchist perspective, humans should not rule over other humans, and this is extended to also include human rule over animals, who share human emotions and craving for freedom. Rune expressed doubt whether it is correct to equate animals with humans in all respects, but argued that to some of his fellow activists animals are considered a kind of person. In other words, there is a strong anti-anthropocentric current within the milieu according to which the ambit of sociality and norms should be extended to include other kinds of humans – that is, animals. So, what animal-rights activists like Rune seem to be doing, though with some hesitation, is to extend human categories and ethical considerations (that is, culture) to the animal world (cf. Descola 1992).[20] What concerns me here, however, is how such a view is a political one, and how it speaks to autonomy and activism in Ungdomshuset.

Rune had, over the years, been engaged in the kitchen crew and in tending the bar during concerts; furthermore, he was the official spokesperson of Ungdomshuset for a couple of years, while also participating actively in organizing black bloc demonstrations to protest against the sale of the house. Besides being a vegan and animal-rights activist, Rune describes himself as 'straight edge', which to him also entails periods of abstinence from alcohol and sex. This 'straight edge' trend coexisted with heavy drinking in Ungdomshuset in the 1990s, but became increasingly dominant. According to Rune, if you want to do politics you need to 'think straight', and in his view this group was, with few exceptions, 'the most active' in the everyday running of the house.

Besides being skilful at playing punk music, to 'be active' (*være aktiv*) and 'become engaged' (*blive engageret*) was considered something positive, and was the personal and political quality most widely appreciated in Ungdomshuset. To be engaged in doing something practical and to show a disposition to act on a problem were signs of a willingness to take one's life and future into one's own hands, Rune explained. In my view, becoming a vegan connects to a (bohemian) tradition of writing off the comfortable lifestyle of mainstream society, but it also implies an experience of becoming absorbed in common activity; in this way, eating and eating practices mirror an array of other modes of generating politics in the body. This is epitomized in the fact that, according to Rune, one is only considered an ALF activist in the moment of action. The practices revolve around bodily reformation and the transformation of social relations, which in the fleeting act segregates the body from capitalist norms and values. Being engaged and becoming active is hence also a temporal phenomenon, which could be described as a bodily experience of active time.

This appreciation of activity, of organizing and being physically active together, has a long historical tradition in Northern Europe that ties together the ideals of the civil (civilized and civic minded) and the physically fit and educated person (Anderson 2008; Frykman 1993: 170–73).[21] In Ungdomshuset, the emphasis was on the activities – a concert, a meal in the soup kitchen, a debate or a demonstration – which an engaged action enabled, more than on the individual person. This implied, I believe, an understanding of politics as immanent in practical action, but also as something that must continuously be enacted to restore its vitality. 'To be engaged' referred to the relationship between what is usually thought of as the individual and the collective. If anyone incarnated this, it was Sara.

Sara, a 26-year-old artist, who lives in a small one-room apartment only a few blocks from Ungdomshuset, has been engaged in a whole series of different activities, both inside and outside the house. She started out by playing music in a punk band and 'hanging around' the house with friends. Later, she became involved in the running of the soup kitchen, but soon came to see the house as a point of departure for activities in public space, such as the Folkets Park Initiativet (People's Park Initiative), which was aimed at restoring, running and defending a local park and playground between Stengade and Griffenfeldsgade for the benefit of the local inhabitants. To be an autonomous activist was, in Sara's view, a constant labour: 'Obviously, walking through the door to Ungdomshuset was not like taking a shower that would wash away all the norms, values and hierarchies of the surrounding society, but we did work hard to *do* things differently', she explained on one occasion.

Sara used her involvement in setting up a printing workshop to exemplify the activities of the house. At one point, she got the idea for a portable printing machine in order to print flyers, posters and artworks. In her own words, she just carried the idea through together with a couple of fellow activists and with materials they could pick up for free without needing to ask for permission. To Sara, Ungdomshuset was a place where you were allowed to 'take initiative on your own and create something concrete'. Sara recalled the feeling that 'everything fitted together, from the cleaning and bar jobs in Ungeren [Ungdomshuset], the vegan cooking and dumpster diving, to the meetings and the demos'. She characterized this as a positive experience of 'becoming part of something larger than you', something she also later pursued as an artist.

Most activists – such as Katrine, Sara and Aske – describe how they started frequenting Ungdomshuset as 'users', which mostly implied they were hanging around the place with friends, drinking and going to concerts. At some point they became absorbed by different concrete activities, and thereby 'became activists', which in practice also implied going to and participating in the weekly 'Monday meeting'. Activism is, in other words, not associated with frequenting certain places, but depends on being involved in common activities: it was talked of in the passive voice as something you are either 'absorbed by' (*bliver optaget af*) or 'become engaged in' (*bliver engageret i*). This very widespread way in which activists talked about how they became involved implies that the person is seen as the recipient of the action rather than its initiator. In this understanding, activism is less a reflection of the existence of an intentional agent pursuing political goals than something defined by the common activities which persons are absorbed by.

Activism in Ungdomshuset hence implied vital common action, which – although it plays out in different ways – work as a kind of antithesis to the apathy and dead time described in the previous chapter. The two existed alongside one another in Ungdomshuset, which in practice meant that those working on creating meaningful decision-making processes had to put up with people just wanting to 'drink and destroy' (and vice versa). Katrine explained:

> There has always been a chaos-punk or drunk-punk [*druk punk*] wing of Ungdomshuset. They did not go to meetings and simply insisted on the right

to be chaotic and drunk. They are very political, but in a very hands-on way, which concerns how many beers you have in your bag [laughs], and [they] definitely do not want to participate in meetings or let anyone tell them what to do. They can be incredibly annoying and completely irresponsible ... To them, participating in a meeting is a drag (*dødens pølse*) – then you have to sit and listen to each other and to all kinds of people that you do not want to listen to ... and follow the rules on how to behave ... Now [after the eviction], the physical and social framework is gone; it takes place at the Thursday demo. We have made a flyer about good demo style: about not getting pissed when you are at a demo, because if something happens you are unreliable and unable to take care of your friends ... After the eviction, the milieu has lost its ways of acting on destructive and self-destructive behaviour. In Ungdomshuset, if people had been pissed and smashed up the bar or the toilets, then we could say – if people agreed – that for the next months you are not allowed to get drunk, but have to form a crew to repair the toilets. We had sanctions, a way to react collectively, which we are lacking now. People could become aware that we are responsible for each other here, and some people have become good activists through these demands.

It was hard to overlook the fact that some of the so-called booze-punks had social or psychological problems, but Ungdomshuset offered itself as a place to hang around outside their case officers' and psychologists' field of vision. Fellow activists, like Katrine, found them annoying at times, but they were also good for a laugh, were a pool of crazy ideas and, not least, someone to hang out and drink with. Sometimes activists tried to care for them by giving them a couch to sleep on, a meal or a place to shower.

A young homeless punk boy nicknamed Tossien ('the foolish one') was one of those who frequently 'hung around' Ungdomshuset, who got a laugh out of the others due to his constant drunkenness and many crazy ideas; he was widely known for having driven a car into the façade of a police station in his home town of Aarhus, for stealing beer from the local social security office or simply flashing his enlarged testicles in Ungdomshuset at a time when he was suffering from a hernia. In 2005, he committed suicide by hanging himself with his shoelace in Hersted Vester Prison after the prison personnel had tried, nine times, to transfer him to a psychiatric hospital. While still at Ungdomshuset, he would stop drinking at times, say that he felt better, and would engage in concert planning and some of the other common activities. Everybody knew that he was not well, but also felt that not much could be done to help him.

Activists like Tossien did not have much expectation that the representatives of the Danish welfare state would help them out, and fellow activists generally accepted their presence and behaviour. I believe this acceptance originates in part from their sheer embodiment of the 'no future', punk ethos of the place; their stories also reinforced a widespread experience of systematic injustice and abandonment. This acceptance, however, also rested on the fact that most other activists had experiences of going through difficult times of apathy and despair, or would get caught up by periodic depression, prolonged periods of drinking and other self-destructive behaviour. Fellow activists would often express their understanding, but little is jointly done to cope with the individual experiences of 'burn out', as it is often associated with a shameful weakness.

After the evictions at Ungdomshuset, however, Parents against Police Brutality, which had been formed to observe the behaviour of the police during riots and demonstrations tied to the conflict over Ungdomshuset, formed Gadeterapeuterne (Street Therapists), consisting of several psychologists whose aim it is to curb traumatizing experiences and offer help when activists run into the kind of existential crisis that Aske was talking about (see Chapter 1). The therapists understand anger, depression and 'burn out' as an individual, politically motivated rebellion against the prevalent ideas of normality.[22] According to the therapists, depression was seen to emerge when activists placed the political cause ahead of individual well-being.

Among activists on the other hand, dead time is associated with bodily weakness, apathy and with being physically pressed down, as the word also etymologically implies, which results in the inability to engage in common activities. Instead of understanding 'burn out' as the rebellion of an individual subject, Left radical activism is, in my view, a way to challenge the particular way that young people in Scandinavia are turned into self-authoring individuals. As one interlocutor phrased it, in the face of difficulties such as depression, 'it generally helped us to be in Ungdomshuset and do things together'. Though active time and dead time coexisted in Ungdomshuset, the place was generally associated with the former, and framed against the resignation, apathy, loneliness and greed of surrounding society.

Interstices of Autonomy

Ungdomshuset was a composite of a variety of people, where activists strove not only to 'make room for all', but also to mould and reconfigure social relations. In public debate, however, the activists were, as mentioned earlier, depicted as young troublemakers who were expected to acquire autonomy and status as adult members of society by going through a process of 'finding themselves'. I have argued that the representation of the conflict over Ungdomshuset as a generational conflict was a way to render the alterity of the activists tolerable and understandable to the surrounding society. Looked at from this perspective, individual autonomy was depicted as a slow and continuous process, something that the young activists would acquire in the course of time.

In the 1990s, many Left radical activists defined themselves as 'autonomous' (*autonome*). The term is derived from the Greek *auto-nomos*, referring to those who live by their own rules. Danish activists adopted the name from German Left radicals, but this particular notion of autonomy can be traced to the Marxist theorists Mario Tronti and Antonio Negri, and the Italian movements Potere Operaio (Workers' Power) and Autonomia Operaia (Workers' Autonomy) of the 1960s and 1970s. From this perspective, political parties and trade unions were no longer considered the vanguard of political struggle; rather, liberation was seen as something to be fought for in all aspects of social life, the goal being a life in communality, under collectively defined rules (Castoriadis 1991; Katsiaficas 2006: 6–8).

Among activists, autonomy is usually spoken of in overtly spatial terms – that is, as a conflict over space, for example in opposition to the gentrification of an urban neighbourhood, or as the establishment of safe and permanent autonomous spaces that allows for the development of other norms and values. The eviction of Ungdomshuset actualized the feeling of being under constant threat and the sensation among those that frequented the house that their space was being invaded; it affirmed the experience that autonomous places need to be fought for, won and defended in a sea of hostility.

This spatial understanding of autonomy is also recognizable in the more or less politically engaged academic literature on the subject in which autonomy is linked to the occupation and control of the (urban) terrain, and to the problem of how free spaces can be opened up at 'an internal distance from the state' (Critchley 2007: 113–114; see also Graeber 2009; Hodkinson and Chatterton 2006; Lacey 2005a, 2005b). While this focus on space is pertinent, spaces such as Ungdomshuset also have a temporal dimension, which is tied to the common activities that activists are absorbed by. The creation of a distinct form of daily life at the same time implies 'a work on time'.

The interstices of active time are riven with contradictions and seldom take the form of glorious resistance (cf. Povinelli 2011: 78–79). When sustained over time, however, dumpster diving, asceticism and making a life from what other people throw away are difficult endeavours that require significant endurance. This can be exemplified with reference to another situation, when international activists were setting up the protest camp prior to the summit marking NATO's sixtieth anniversary in Strasbourg: food and money were scarce, and the task of building infrastructure for the 4,000 to 6,000 activists expected was not easy. It was freezing cold on the open field assigned for the camp in the early spring, the food retrieved by dumpster diving was of poor quality and our plates were dirty. After having eaten a grey, oily soup, one of my interlocutors, Natalie, who we will meet again in the next chapter, cried out, 'I can't believe that we are eating trash'. When I later asked her about it, she explained that she was fed up and disappointed about people not taking responsibility for building the camp and procuring food for those who did. She said that the camp was not turning out as she had hoped, and that she was considering giving up the 'militant' life. The lack of common dedication and involvement in procuring and preparing a good meal implied that the food remained in its state of 'trash'.

The forms of sociality found in Ungdomshuset departed from the individualist notion of autonomy, but involved a radicalization of Scandinavian notions of spaciousness and equality. In this context, individual freedom and creativity can only be conceptualized as the offspring of the common activities that people engage in. Rather than understanding autonomy within this context as an individual experience of the sacrifice of egoism (Graeber 2009: 130), or as the transcendence of the self in the social (Korsgaard 1998: 14), I have found that it is social relations that are primary: people become activists by becoming engaged or absorbed in common activity. The careful work on reconfiguring social relations – for example, through experimenting with decision-making procedures, in cooking a vegan meal or in organizing an action together – are world-making procedures. They imply that a new world comes into view – of the sort Sara referred to in talking of her sense of everything 'fitting together'.

Acknowledgements

An earlier version of this chapter, co-written with Inger Sjørslev, appeared in *Social Analysis* 55, 2 (2011).

Notes

1. The Red-Green Party (Enhedslisten) is a socialist party with seats in the Danish Parliament. Three small left-wing parties formed the alliance in 1989.
2. The quote is from the minutes of a meeting of Copenhagen's municipal council in May 1999.
3. The failure of 'the users' to maintain the house was one of the few circumstances that, under the original contract, would give the municipality the right to close Ungdomshuset. For more on the contract, see US and FBZB (1982).
4. The name of the company, Human, is said to be the short form of Hjælp til Unge Mennesker til at tage Ansvar for sig selv på en Nænsom måde' (Help for Young People to take Responsibility for Themselves in a Gentle Way), which underlines a broad focus on teaching young people to care for themselves in a proper manner. Nevertheless, the meaning of the name cannot be confirmed as the company no longer exists.
5. According to an amendment to the Danish penal code § 134, ratified in May 2000, it is illegal to cover your face or possess items that can be used in order to hinder one's identification during public meetings or demonstrations.
6. Karpantschof and Mikkelsen define an urban riot as the takeover of (a significant part of) urban public space (streets and squares) making everyday life and the working of the city come to a standstill (Karpantschof and Mikkelsen 2009: 74).
7. A similar debate about spaciousness can be found in discussions about Danish state-run schools, which are also expected to be spacious (that is, inclusive, particularly in relation to children of immigrant descent). However, in this context too, it is generally agreed that the limit on spaciousness is set at violence and other serious disturbances of peace in the classroom.
8. Admittedly, Faderhuset never received as much regular and extensive attention in the public press as did Ungdomshuset, but a few scandals and front-page articles, mainly in the tabloid *Ekstra Bladet*, concerning excessive authoritarianism and alleged child abuse found within the Church's congregation, are nevertheless revealing. In 2008, Faderhuset again hit the front page, this time with a headline about the abuse of children as part of an excessively authoritarian style of upbringing. Later scandals have focused on the leader Ruth Evensen's relationship with her own daughter, who publicly stated that she has no contact with her mother or the Church due the extremely authoritarian treatment of children within the sect.
9. FARC (Fuerzas Armadas Revolucionarias de Colombia) and PFLP (Popular Front for the Liberation of Palestine) are two irregular military organizations that activists wished to display their solidarity with.
10. 'Normalization' is the term Foucault uses to describe the discursive construction of norms for proper conduct (Foucault 1977). In the present context, the word normalization (*normalisering*) was used both by politicians and government officials to account for the bringing of law and order to a specific area, and by people living in that area and opposing the process (in the latter case, the word implied regimentation and the unnecessary attempt to assimilate difference).
11. See 'Ungdomshus-talsmænd afviser terrorplaner', *Politiken*, 10 June 2007.
12. For a more complete description of the action, see Krøijer (2008).
13. 'Politichef om Ungdomshus-balladen: "Et galehus"', *Jyllandsposten*, 14 October 2007.
14. It can be contested whether all activists involved in the conflict can be categorized as young, but the obstinate insistence in public debate about the activists being *young*

troublemakers also pointed to certain solutions: either parental disciplining, setting limits to children's behaviour, or lenience and tolerance in the face of youthful rebelliousness. The stubborn focus on activists as young, particularly at the beginning of the conflict, suggests that a certain degree of rebelliousness could be allowed for, as it opened up the expectation of their smooth reintegration into adult society.

15. The K-town Festival (K for København, the Danish for Copenhagen) was a yearly punk festival at Ungdomshuset.
16. As argued elsewhere, this aversion to hierarchies is mixed with a stubborn insistence that consensus decision making is not and should not be free of conflict. Ideally, the aim is not to reach agreement through a sameness of ideas, but to find a workable solution respecting difference of opinion (Graeber 2009: 327–28; Maeckelbergh 2009: 17).
17. Rebel was a revolutionary youth organization in Denmark. It was formed in 1992, but in 2001 it joined the Socialistisk Ungdomsfront (Front of Socialist Youth) affiliated to the left-wing party Enhedslisten (the Red-Green Alliance).
18. That ALF is defined only by these guidelines and not as a formal organization or network simultaneously reflects openness and secretiveness. The choice has been made for security reasons; ALF activists have several times been legally charged according to Danish terror laws, but being defined only by guidelines reveals a consideration for openness and equality as everybody, in principle, can become an ALF activist. ALF in Denmark is mostly known for direct actions against mink farms, but the concern for animal liberation in activist circles can be traced at least to 1975, when Australian philosopher Peter Singer published his book *Animal Liberation* (Singer 1975).
19. Dumont puts it this way: 'To adopt values is to introduce hierarchy, and a certain consensus of values, a certain hierarchy of ideas, things and people, is indispensable to social life' (Dumont 1970: 20). In Scandinavia, hierarchy is associated with economic difference and unequal political power, and hierarchical differences are handled with a certain discomfort and uneasiness as it is considered socially unacceptable to articulate them. Yet, the appreciation of equality does not imply that notions of what is good and right do not exist, and the ability to master what is considered good and right introduces hierarchies (Bruun et al. 2011).
20. There is nothing that indicates that this extension of human qualities to animals is limited to animal-rights activists; one has only to think of the way many people in the Western world ascribe human attributes and dispositions to their pets. As also suggested by Matai Candea in a paper on scientists studying animal behaviour, a multiplicity of worlds may lie within Euro-American (mono) naturalism (Candea 2010).
21. Since the beginning of the twentieth century, physical training has been tied to the process of civilization, the reinterpretation of 'popular character' (*folkelighed*) and nationality. According to Frykman, physical exercise was seen as both a way to discipline people to become active and individual citizens, as well as having emancipatory potential insofar as it allowed otherwise invisible groups to make their bodies visible in public space (Frykman 1993: 163,167).
22. See 'Gadeterapeuterne', *Weekendavisen*, 9 December 2011.

Naming and Raising a Child

I first met Jürgen, who is in his mid 30s, when I tried to get involved in the preparations for the actions scheduled for NATO's sixtieth-anniversary summit in Strasbourg in April 2009. After the local organizers of the Revolt Network initially refused to allow me into the international preparation meeting, I was – through the intervention of an activist friend – allowed to attend, but asked to go to Berlin to meet Jürgen (and get his approval) before continuing on to the first planning meeting in Strasbourg. On my way to Berlin, I had no way of knowing that the encounter would not only bring me into the frenzy of summit mobilization, but also open my eyes to activist ways of coming of age.

We meet at 10 AM at Café Taqueria Florian in Kreutzberg. Located south of Mitte in Berlin, Kreutzberg is one of the poorest neighbourhoods, and it has the highest population density and proportion of migrant inhabitants in the former West Berlin. In the 1960s and 1970s, many small businesses closed down in this former industrial area in the centre of town, resulting in several buildings being left vacant, which were subsequently squatted. Before the fall of the Berlin Wall the neighbourhood, which was enclosed on three sides by the Wall, contained more than 200 squats, and was the home of a vibrant punk scene and other expressions of alternative culture.

When I arrive at Taqueria Florian, Jürgen is sitting by the window drinking coffee, in a worn black hoodie and Naver workpants. After ordering coffee for me, he questions me about my project, and this leads to a two-hour conversation about the renewal of forms of action in the face of police repression and surveillance, the EU's security architecture around major events and the cooperation between the French and German police in keeping the Revolt Network under surveillance. Jürgen has worked with these issues for years, since the so-called 'summer of resistance' in 2001 and the G8 protests in Genoa, where protests and repression were particularly intense. He has also been involved in organizing and doing press-release work during the protests at the G8 meeting in Heiligendamm in 2007, but explains that now he mostly works on his own on police repression and public security policies.

Jürgen is an 'atypical' activist as he continues activism well into his 30s, and not least because he is still engaged in summit mobilizations. Most activists seem to become involved in Left radical activism between the age of 16 and 19, and continue only till about their late 20s. While people in their 30s and 40s are not a rare sight in social centres, or during demonstrations, their rhythm of engagement in activism changes. Younger people consider full-time activism to be the ideal, but this is something most activists are only able to do for short periods during their 'activist career'. Jürgen no longer has an affinity group in Berlin, but while many in his situation drop out of activism entirely, because they are unable to spend the large amount of time demanded on planning meetings or they drop out of the social contexts where ideas for actions are generated, others learn to limit their involvement to one project, or to particular realms of life. Not being able to live up to the high level of activity that activists expect from each other and from themselves often leads to a feeling of inadequacy and loneliness.

Jürgen says that he does not expect the protests in Strasbourg to be as large as a G8 protest because it will be too easy for the police to prevent people from crossing the French–German border and moving around the city. He wishes to take advantage of the preparation meeting to create a group that can follow the developments of the European security architecture. In our e-mail conversation, I have been asked to 'involve myself', and before we leave the café he asks if I will be able to help moderate the meeting in French or do some translation. I decline, as my French is poor, but offer to help out with cooking or other practical matters, and assist in facilitating the meeting if it is held in English.

After having talked for a couple of hours, we walk to his home, a caravan in an activist-run children's zoo in the neighbourhood. While we walk, he explains that the zoo and activity playground was founded twenty-seven years ago while squatting in the area was still at its peak. Self-built and self-managed playgrounds were very popular in the 1980s, and the caravan village was set up to look out for the animals at night. Jürgen has lived in the village, which amounts to approximately twenty caravans, for the past ten years. I learn that he has a daughter named Ayo, who is seven years old. The caravan village has been evicted several times, and the self-managed playground closed down, but every time people have returned and rebuilt the place, he explains.

Obviously, not all activists live in squats, trailers or caravans, not even while they are young, but making a choice about where and how to live one's life is considered important, and collective forms of dwelling are common among activists throughout Northern Europe. While squatted houses were quite common in the 1980s, fewer are left after the gentrification and housing boom since the mid 1990s. There are no illegal squats left in Denmark; several houses have been legalized and continue as collectives. In Germany and Sweden too, many squats have been neutralized by eviction, or been the subject of fierce battles.

Jürgen has been a full-time activist for many years, living on the dole, and due to a 'constant feeling of urgency' he has not had a rest or 'been on holiday' with his daughter for years, he says. Now he is in his mid 30s and he says that he needs to rethink his working life, as the social security office is pressuring him to find a job, saying that they will cut off his unemployment benefit if he does not find one. What was before a desirable option, that is, not being subject to the decisions of others during working hours and 'freeing up' time to pursue activism, is turning into an enduring circumstance of his life.[1] Being unemployed becomes tiring over time, he explains. Living mostly on espresso coffee and roll-up cigarettes, Jürgen's life in the caravan involves few expenses. He has already toured Germany, giving critical lectures on the EU's security architecture, and hopes to be able to do more touring in the future in order to earn a bit of money and lessen his dependence on unemployment benefit.

The area around the caravan park smells of wet soil; it is early spring, and we follow a muddy path to his wagon. Along the way we say hello to a couple of neighbours who have defied the cold to chop wood. We leave our shoes outside his caravan on a small wooden terrace and step inside. To the left of the door, he has built a double bed with open shelves above for his and his daughter's clothes. To the right, an old sofa and a writing desk with a laptop and book shelves take up most of the space. Further on, I catch a glimpse of a small kitchen with a wooden stove, which heats the caravan. I drop my sleeping bag on the floor and Jürgen shows me how the water and the stove work as well as the way to the outdoor compost toilet. Then he leaves to pick up his daughter from nursery.

An hour later he returns with his daughter, Ayo, and in the afternoon we hang out on the worn brown sofa watching a Pippi Longstocking movie, based on a book by the Swedish author Astrid Lindgren, while we eat pretzels. Having children of the same age myself, Jürgen and I talk for a long time about child rearing. This is clearly a subject that occupies his thoughts. He explains to me that in the summer Ayo tends to run off to play in the park and seldom comes home before dinner, but this winter she prefers to stay inside and watch a movie. 'But it is difficult to find films that don't preach traditional nuclear family values and gender roles', he comments. 'This Pippi movie is kind of cool ... though they use the term "negro king", so maybe it is not that nice after all'. I mention that Pippi is my daughter's dearest hero, and after some discussion we agree that her inventiveness and anti-authoritarianism are great, but that the films are also products of their time.

Jürgen explains that he does not live with Ayo's mother, in part because he never desired living as a nuclear family and in part because she got tired of the amount of time he spends on activism. She lives in a normal apartment in the neighbourhood, and during the week Ayo spends three and a half days at each place. While looking distractedly at the movie, he recounts that he and Ayo's mother spent a long time looking for a kindergarten for her that would be free of gender stereotyping. Then he turns towards me: 'Sometimes I ask her, are you a boy or a girl today? And I often get different answers', he says, with a satisfied smile. 'People have a hard time accepting this, though. The postman once asked her if she is a boy or a girl, and she answered that she is both. He got all confused and told her that it isn't possible'. We laugh, and continue talking about gender, while Jürgen works on his homepage on police repression, and Ayo and I take turns playing on her little pink piano. He says that he hopes that Ayo's mother will teach her Linux and coding – free software collaboration is thought of by internet activists as a sphere outside capitalist control – so that these subjects do not end up in her consciousness as male domains of interest.

Jürgen's naming of his daughter is a case in point of the form politics can take when one is not, or no longer, engaged in spectacular confrontations with the police in the street. Ayo is a unisex name and embodies Jürgen's hope for a world where little girls are not 'gendered', that is, brought up to believe that gender has to be performed in accordance with some predetermined societal norms. Her name is fused with a vibrant potentiality because she, as in the story Jürgen tells about her, has the option of giving different replies when the postman questions her about her gender. The political becomes a potentiality in every aspect of daily life – such as when giving a name to a child.

The naming of Ayo was an interesting way to pursue politics, which engenders intentions for the future. Not only does the name materialize

Jürgen's hope that Ayo might be able to live a different life from that of other girls, but the ritual practice of giving someone or something a particular name is also a magical way 'to get hold of it' (Malinowski, quoted in Jackson 2005: 84–85).[2] Anthropologists have long recognized that different ideas or rhythms of time may exist within the same culture or society, but we have tended to assign them to different domains of life: linear time has been associated with everyday life and cyclical time with rituals (Bloch 1977; Leach 1985; Robbins 2001: 530). In this case, ritual time and daily life are not easy to segregate, which means that the daily life of activists is not a passive backcloth against which we can understand visible and spectacular protests in the streets.

In Jürgen's case, the act of naming simultaneously implies or contains the solution to the problem addressed. Hence, the naming can be perceived to be what Judith Butler has called an illocutionary speech act, which furthermore 'ritually exceeds itself in past and future directions' (Butler 1997: 3). In Ayo's answer to the postman – and all other future postmen – language is a form of action that is tied to the materiality of her body, and not just an expressive tool that reflects Jürgen's hope for the future.

Before dinner they take off to her mother's home, as we have to leave early the next morning for Strasbourg. In the evening, before going to sleep, we sit in the kitchen; Jürgen rolls a joint and we talk about the G8 summit at the German resort town Heiligendamm and activists' press strategies, then we pack our rucksacks and two big boxes of solidarity CDs to be sold in Strasbourg in support of a group of imprisoned activists convicted for burning German military vehicles.

Notes

1. Framing activism simply as a matter of individual choice is a trivialization at best, which does not take into account how endurance and exhaustion are woven together (cf. Povinelli 2011), how past choices and occurrences condition present possibilities and, on a more abstract plane, how intentions are immanent to form, not prior to them.
2. The question of time and naming has been studied from an anthropological perspective on how mytho-historical pasts are concretized in places and in the topography of landscapes (see Basso 1988; Hill 1988), but few anthropologists have looked at how what we normally think of as future is concretized through naming practices.

3
'A Common Choreography of Action'
Preparations and Intentions

Kara was given two days in court for her trial. It is the first of a series of cases against people charged with orchestrating the protests during the Climate Summit in Copenhagen in 2009. She is accused of organizing vandalism and violence against the police as well as disruption of public order. The maximum penalty for these offences in Denmark is a twelve-year prison sentence. Kara is not a Danish citizen. Plain-clothes police picked her up while she was riding along the side of the road on her cycle three days before the Reclaim Power action. 'I asked them if they were just picking up anybody in black clothes. They said, "No we have been hunting you". It was really frightening', she later said. The arrest was made on suspicion of 'potential action'. According to the public prosecutor, Kara was an instigator and coordinator of a series of violent acts for which reason she and a handful of other activists (who were similarly charged) had been arrested and kept in preventive detention for three weeks in order to block the execution of their plans.

What caught my attention about the court case was neither the preventive nature of the arrests nor the fact that the accusations had little relation to what actually happened in the streets of Copenhagen during COP 15, but the peculiar way the prosecutors substantiated the intentions of the accused. During the first day in court, Kara was interrogated about her intentions and plans had she not been arrested. From the witness stand she replied repeatedly, 'I do not know; I was arrested after all'. In the face of this, the prosecutor used snatches of tapped phone conversations and produced some photocopies of Kara's notebook to substantiate the charges and provide evidence of her intentions.

Among the scribbled notes and drawings, the attention of the court was drawn to a drawing of a 'bolt cutter'. This, the public prosecutor argued, pointed to the fact that Kara and other activists intended to cut down the fence around the Bella Centre where the official summit was held. In court, Kara explained that the bolt cutter was a prop for a two-metre-tall papier mâché bolt cutter that had, in fact, been placed on the roof of the van accompanying several actions. To substantiate her explanation, two people in the audience went to pick up the papier mâché bolt cutter from a social centre on Nørrebro and brought it along to the court the next day. Its presentation in the courtroom was accompanied by bursts of laughter, not only from friends and family, but also from the journalists crammed into the small courtroom. The prosecutor's attempt at abducting[1] intention from the drawing fell flat.

The present chapter addresses the issue of intention in the context of action planning because, as the prosecutor rightly assumed, protests and direct actions are seldom completely spontaneous. They are often preceded by months or years of preparation, which again makes it relevant to consider how activists deal with the near future. How do activists handle the time span associated with immediate intentional action and the setting of specific goals? And why, as the prosecutor's attempt illustrates, is it so difficult to tie intentions to single persons?

Hence, the purpose of the present chapter is not only to venture into how actions are planned, but also into how activists deal with intentions. I will go into details of two international preparation meetings in the run-up to the protests over the summit of NATO's sixtieth-anniversary in April 2009 in Strasbourg in order to provide insights into how protests are planned. Though I have participated in a range of preparation processes, it was in Strasbourg, at a planning meeting organized by Revolt Network, that I first became aware of the peculiar way in which activists handle intentions during the events that precede an action. The second meeting I focus on was an 'action conference' hosted by the European peace movement in order to agree on an overall 'choreography of actions', as it is called in activist jargon. Drawing upon Alfred Gell's *Art and Agency: An Anthropological Theory* (Gell 1998), I will argue that during the preparations for an action intentions are distributed to non-human forms, such as puppets, and to other determinate forms, such as meetings. This implies that intentions are innate to material and ritual forms, which has the corollary that actions cannot be traced back to single persons.

My argument will proceed as follows: Based on an introduction to preparation processes and an ethnographic description of the meetings in Strasbourg, laying out a 'choreography of actions' for the summit protests, I introduce and discuss the nature of meetings among Left radical activists, drawing on he work of other anthropologists (Graeber 2009; Juris 2008; Maeckelbergh 2009). In particular, I will take issue with Maeckelbergh's description of meetings as 'intentionally prefigurative', a phrase which implies that individual or collective actors intentionally make meetings foreshadow the future (Maeckelbergh 2009: 69, 220). Instead of relying solely on persons as actors with conscious intent, I will bring objects and other determinate forms into the equation, such as oversize bolt cutters, giant penguins and 'blockading points', onto which intentions are distributed during meetings, and that take on the role of 'agentive entities' (Gell 1998: 17–18). Rather than prefiguration, I advance the idea of 'figuration of the future', which is defined as the act of giving determinate form to the indeterminate. This occurs when forms become ripe with intention. I argue that the form intentions assume involves a temporary abeyance of human agency. This will bring us back to the bolt cutter, and how activists and the police alike 'abduct' intention (ibid.) from material objects.

Following the analysis of planning meetings and puppets, I turn to the last element in planning, namely action training. I draw on ethnography from both Strasbourg and Copenhagen (firstly the Climate Summit, and second the action known as Shut Down the Camp, aimed at shutting down a refugee retention centre). The material presented here stems both from preparations for civil disobedience and black bloc actions, as well as large demonstrations, which have some common features when it comes to practices and intentions in connection with meetings. The question addressed is: How do relatively coordinated protests come about in a situation where individual intentions are concealed, innate to material forms, if not completely absent?

Action Planning in Strasbourg

In the analysis of the European Social Forum in Malmö in Chapter 1, I described how a series of events – the meetings of heads of state – punctuate the near future with specific dates. Significant amounts of preparation need to be made ahead of the protests and demonstrations tied to these dates. Usually, it is activists from the local town or host country who become aware of a summit approaching, and take on the task of local organizers. They call on international activists through 'calls for action' via the internet, and by undertaking 'info-tours' to different towns and neighbouring countries. The role of local organizer of a summit protest also includes organizing several international meetings of activists; sometimes the first one is up to two years ahead of a summit, at which the participants agree on action concepts, choreographies of action and media strategies, as well as a vast array of practical matters. The local organizers also need to take care of living arrangements, sometimes for several thousand persons, the provision of food (usually through large itinerant soup kitchens), information points, convergence spaces and media centres for the unknown number of visiting activists, as well as medical and legal support for the aftermath of the actions.

By the summer of 2008, ideas were developing about how to disturb the NATO summit, and three months ahead of the event the Revolt Network called for an international planning meeting. The meeting was advertised on international listservs and various homepages. As already mentioned, at first my participation as a researcher was rejected. Mariann from Action Network in Malmö intervened on my behalf, but getting a final clearance meant I had to travel to Berlin and meet Jürgen, with whom I ended up travelling from Berlin to Strasbourg.

The meeting was held in secrecy, and information on the exact location of the venue was distributed with care to avoid police interception. We were met by some of the local organizers at the square outside Strasbourg's central station, and after a quick hello our bags were loaded into an old Citroën. We later continued our journey by train, accompanied by Natalie from Revolt. I was still unaware of our exact destination, but after half an hour on the train we got off at a small deserted station. We followed a narrow dirt road on foot through the forest, until we arrived at a camp school where the meeting was to be held. Rolling hills surrounded the school; it was mid-winter and the forest was still dressed in white.

After a long wait, the Citroën with our bags arrived and we could start preparing for the meeting, which would start the following morning. We carried boxes of food into the large industrial kitchen, and in the adjoining dining hall tables were moved to allow the approximately seventy participants to sit in a large circle. Natalie and Alain, who told me they were from Paris, hung maps of the city of Strasbourg on the walls indicating 'places of interest', that is, possible targets of direct actions. Finally, the windows facing the forest were covered with black cardboard. Jürgen explained that at a previous meeting the participants had been filmed by the police, and that today they would do everything possible to avoid a repeat of that experience. All evening people continued arriving, but went to sleep early after a bowl of vegetable soup.

The meeting begins a little after 10 AM the following morning. The participants are seated in a large circle with their backs against the yellow-painted walls. Natalie and Alain introduce the agenda while several people are still trying to grab the last bite of their breakfast or running into the kitchen for more coffee. Fabienne, an activist from the social centre Molodoi, in Strasbourg, goes around with a plastic box to collect everybody's mobile phones. They are carefully switched off and stored in the kitchen pantry. 'We have thought of spending today in gaining an overview of international mobilizations and discussing proposals for different action days in connection with the NATO Summit', Natalie begins explaining. The idea, we are told, is to present a proposal for a 'common choreography of actions' to be discussed at an action conference organized by the European peace movement about a month later. Moreover, the French organizers propose that we spend some time discussing our relation to the media and the idea of turning Revolt into a permanent network in addition to a range of practical issues concerning the camp and kitchens, convergence centres and information points and, not least, the legal, medical and trauma support to be set up for the week of action.

There are no comments on or changes to the agenda, but before starting Alain gives a brief introduction on the hand signals that are often used to smoothen decision making: 'twinkling' is a shaking of the hands in the air that signals agreement; raising the hands while pointing your two index fingers means 'direct point' and is used to comment directly on what has been said by the previous speaker; making an L-sign with your fingers means 'language' and signals lack of translation or that someone is not able to follow the debate. Also, there is 'technical point', shown by making a T-shape with the hands which signals either comments on the procedure or simply an announcement; finally, there is the raised fist, which implies that the person wants to block a decision about to be taken. I have never experienced the block actually being used; usually the facilitators will attempt to change the proposal up for approval, or sometimes people 'stand aside', which allows the rest of the group to continue, while the people standing aside are free to follow a different course of action. Alain also organizes the translation between French, German, English and Spanish, and Natalie asks everybody to sign up for practical tasks during the meeting, such as cleaning and cooking. She requests that people respect the rule that smoking is not allowed inside the building, and adds that the caretakers of the school do not appreciate use of footwear in the dormitories.

We start off with a round of introductions and reports on the status of mobilization. Among the participants are activists from France,

Germany, the Netherlands, Belgium, Britain, Spain and Italy. I introduce myself as coming from Denmark, and after agreement with Natalie, tell the group a bit about the plans for the Climate Summit in Copenhagen. A couple of British activists speak about a direct action against a power plant, and say they will arrive with a couple of buses even though the NATO summit might coincide with the G20 summit in London. A young, articulate woman from Mannheim, with long dreadlocks, reports from an action against the headquarters of NATO's infantry, while a punk-looking girl describes the successful employment of a five-finger tactic in Cologne, which was adapted from the one used to block the G8 meeting in Heiligendamm in 2007. She says that several hundred activists from Interventionistiche Linke (IL) will come to Strasbourg for the summit. A bearded young man with a green cap explains that they plan on a week of action prior to the NATO summit; they are setting up a convergence centre for activists and an Indymedia homepage in Freiburg,[2] some 65 kilometres from Strasbourg, and they will organize shuttle buses to Strasbourg. A young blond girl, whom I later learn is called Laura, from Résistance des Deux Rives, describes the work her group is doing to set up a camp site in Kehl (on the German side of the French/German border), which the official delegates are expected to come through to make a 'diplomatic footstep', a walk by the heads of state on a bridge connecting the two countries in order to display the alliance between countries formerly separated by war.

Listening to the presentations, I am struck by how the interventions remain on a very practical plane – nobody presents their views on NATO or suggests common political positions – and this is an impression that stays with me all weekend. Jürgen explains to me that by calling it a Revolt Network meeting of 'the radical resistance movement', we are able to skip the part about common identity and positions and move right to coordination and action planning. Moreover, keeping discussions on a practical plane also enables people to work together in spite of belonging to different political tendencies on the Left, or having different tactical preferences during actions.

A bald, corpulent man from a German peace group interrupts my thoughts by adding that they plan to organize a peace march from Kehl to Strasbourg. There have been rumours that the Schengen agreement will be suspended during the summit,[3] thereby disenabling normal people's travel between France and Germany, but the peace groups want to march to and open the Europe Bridge connecting the two countries. 'It would not be right', he finishes, 'to leave the symbol to Merkel and Sarkozy', with reference to the diplomatic footstep meant to link the peaceful relation between France and Germany to NATO's operations around the world. Jürgen looks up from his computer and says in a loud voice, 'So, if they [the police] block the border will there be a peaceful riot?' People laugh at this attack on the peace movement and their alleged lack of ability to follow through when the police take their gloves off, and the peace activist writhes under the taunt.

Fabienne gives us a report from the local organizers in Strasbourg about the location of the camp, and of the red zones,[4] as well as about rumours that the police plan to seize and keep people out of the entire inner city of Strasbourg. He also introduces their problems in coordinating with the peace movement, but because his English is poor, Natalie takes over and provides a status report. The hope is to build a common choreography of action where a 'diversity of tactics' will be accepted, she explains, and continues:

> But there are some problems we need to address. The peace groups have already met in Stuttgart and approximately 300 of them signed a call for action: 'No to war, No to NATO'. The problem is that they have decided that no action should interfere with other initiatives. They [the peace movement] plan a large demonstration on Saturday, April 4, in the afternoon, but we would like to block the NATO summit about the same time as the demo. I know that it was possible to build a common choreography in Heiligendamm, but France has no history of broad mobilization and coordination. They say we are illegitimate. At any rate, all decisions are supposed to be taken at the action conference in mid February.

The explanation about the difficulties in building a common choreography is mostly addressed to the German participants, who have had a positive experience with a common choreography during the G8 summit in Heiligendamm. The floor is opened for comments. A German woman in her late thirties, wearing a black motorcycle jacket, notes dryly: 'Some people in Germany also found it [the common choreography] a waste of time, but in any case: the coordination should not be control, but coordination! We will coordinate with them, which means that we will tell them what we want to do'. Her friend adds: 'We should believe in our own strength and that they have a problem, not us. If we do a blockade, people will want to participate in that [instead of in the demonstration]'. Natalie complains that the peace groups have already produced flyers with dates, in response to which somebody proposes to make 'a call', stating that we do not accept this way of preparing. The peace activist argues that the police will use all the divisions between us, and that it is important to reach a consensus at the action conference. An anarchist from the UK replies that he has a problem with attempts at controlling forms of protesting: 'Is it not enough with the control of the state?' he asks rhetorically. 'They will distance themselves from us anyway', says Fabienne, and continues: 'We have wasted our time trying to coordinate with them. Even if there is agreement before an action, they always shoot at us afterwards. We have the strength to do our own thing, so let's go!'

The debate about coordination and the perspective of a 'common choreography' continues until lunch. There are different views on the appropriateness of coordinating closely, or at all, with the peace groups. The two facilitators do not have to do much, simply queuing the speakers when necessary and from time to time encouraging people to remember about 'twinkling' to show agreement. Noting the intensity of twinkling, the facilitators propose that we take a common position, namely that the blockade should be in the morning and that the peace groups will have to back down on the no-two-actions-at-the-same-time principle. Several people suggest that this will be widely accepted by the peace groups and other actors at the action conference a month away, as it is the radical groups doing all the practical organizing of the camp, the convergence spaces and music for the demonstration, which everybody is relying on for the realization of the joint NATO protests.

Before breaking for lunch, a chubby Frenchman with a short Mohawk shouts, 'So who is the spy?', a common joke at activist meetings where everybody expects police infiltration. It produces the anticipated laugh, while I am reminded of my own double role, and it makes me aware of how most people seem very reserved in sharing information about themselves. I am relieved from contemplating the ethical dilemmas of participant observation by Natalie, who asks me to take notes at the session on the action days after lunch, and she also asks me to help in facilitating the meeting the following morning. I accept as we step out onto a porch, where literally everybody is gathered for a smoke, knowing that getting involved in practical tasks is my ticket to acceptance.

After lunch the meeting continues. Large posters are placed on the floor in the centre of the dining room. We are presented with a plan of the official summit. On Thursday, 2 April, the official delegates will probably arrive at the airports of Lahr, Süringen and Strasbourg, but it will be impossible to hold a protest there due to the heavy presence of military police. On Friday, 3 April, the heads of state will be at a gala dinner in the resort town of Baden-Baden in Germany. That evening, or in the early hours of Saturday, they will be moved to Strasbourg to attend the diplomatic footstep and photo session on the footbridge connecting France and Germany, and from there they will go to the conference centre, Palace de la Musique, near the European Parliament. Then we turn to action planning. The activist from Freiburg again announces a day of action on Monday, 29 April. Natalie notes this down on a large sheet of paper. Jürgen suggests an action day in Strasbourg on Wednesday, linking issues of internal and external security. He says that it might make sense to link it to 'the border-crossing issue', namely the expectation that activists will be held back at the border and denied entry to France during the summit. He also argues that a mass action on Wednesday 'would be suicide' and that it is important to conduct an action that does not entail too many arrests. People nod and twinkle. A friend of Jürgen's from Berlin proposes a day of action on Thursday focused on the link between oil, war and the climate crisis. A tall man with a wild beard and hair, in his late 40s, says he would like to 'organize something' in Baden-Baden on Friday based on small groups making decentralized actions. 'There are many transport routes and narrow streets in town', he argues, 'so if we are a bit less black that day we can really move and smash'. He finishes by asking people to join his working group, because hands are needed if there should be actions in Baden-Baden. On Saturday, there are various possibilities for action – trying to interrupt the diplomatic footprint at 10 AM, organizing a blockade of the summit or organizing a black bloc for the large demonstration. The authorities will not let the large demonstration into the city centre or near the conference area; instead, it has been assigned a route south of the city, Natalie explains. For the moment the organizers from the peace movement are not in agreement with this route. Natalie says that she would like to help organize a solidarity action on Sunday to go to the prison where arrested activists will be held.

After the presentations we split into groups to discuss and elaborate on the different proposals. Around fifteen people join a working group on the blockade. As I wonder if it will be appropriate for me to join, a man called Nicola from Revolt Network and the Anarchist Federation pauses next to where I am seated, and while taking down a map of the city he asks if I would like to join them. I slowly follow the group, which gathers on a soccer field opposite the main building. For two hours we stand in the cold discussing everything from the starting time of the blockade to the tactics that can be employed in different streets to effectively block the summit. We decide that it should start at 7 AM and that it should continue even if the demonstration organized by the peace movement starts 'because they are never productive', as the green-capped man from Freiburg phrases it, again displaying some of the contradictions inherent in the NATO protests.

We carefully analyse the map of the streets around the summit venue and decide on possible blockading points. We agree on a so-called 'action concept', where different groups and organizations take responsibility for different blockading points in the street and decide on the form and tactics for themselves. Similar to blockades of other summits, there will be different colours indicating different 'tactical preferences', that is, modes of holding the street and entering into and handling a confrontation with the police. In spite of this agreement, we spend a long time discussing possible options at the different blockading points: along one street there could be a mass of people in a passive blockade (in the sense of being immobile, but also not resisting arrest); at another large intersection there could be a more 'confrontational' style, which could try to hold the street by use of smoke bombs, or by building barricades of cars and other available materials. Nicola seems to be interested in this. We also decide that there must be action training in the camp in the week preceding the action, and the young punk-looking woman called Alisha from IL promises to look into this. She also suggests a public meeting place on Saturday from where people can be directed to the blockade points (as these will not be revealed beforehand) in order to give everybody a chance to join in. We develop the action concept in some detail, but then we have to return to the afternoon plenary session.

Alisha and the green-capped man from Freiburg report back to the plenary on the discussions just held, but the details are only spoken of vaguely. They say that we have decided that the blockade should continue independent of the large demonstration, and that there will be different colour-coded blockade points and room for both pacifist and more active tactics. Another meeting is announced for 9 o'clock that night. Some people try to ask for more details, but they are simply told that the blockade will focus on the main streets in the area and that 'there is a concept'. Alisha says that she hopes that different groups will take responsibility for particular points, and that people should join the groups. She carefully avoids mentioning anything about people, places and times with regard to the blockade.

The discussion develops in various directions. Jürgen's friend from Berlin intervenes by saying that she would actually like to take part in the demonstration and that it would be 'cool' to organize a black bloc. A punk from Paris suggests that there should be information for affinity groups on the homepage, and this spurs a larger discussion. One of the British activists, whom I later learn is a vegan truck-driver called Harry, asks: 'You want to open [point out] targets, why? Then the police will be everywhere. People should find their own targets'. Someone else argues that we should make such a big list of targets such as financial institutions, big corporations and police stations that it will keep the police busy. 'If they are everywhere it will in itself be a victory', she states. The Mohawk-man says that the police always seek to turn non-violent actions into violent ones, and that we will help the police do that by publishing the list. Some argue that a list will be useful, while others say that finding a target in Strasbourg is hardly a problem, and that there is no need for a list.

I stop listening to the exact words of people and turn my attention to the facilitator. It is the articulate woman from Mannheim with long dreadlocks. She sits calmly, managing the speakers. When everybody has spoken she presents a proposal for consensus, then handles comments, concerns and amendments. Finally, a decision is reached, namely that the local organizers will spread information on 'the environment' without identifying 'targets', and that it preferably could also include locations of police stations, cameras and so on. There are no 'stand asides' (abstention from agreeing) or 'blocks' (veto of decision), so even though there was strong disagreement, the participants managed to reach a consensus that everybody could live with. People smile and seem overtly satisfied, not least with how the decision was reached. It is a good example of how a decision comes into being in a situation where nobody wants to take explicit and apparent leadership, but prefers instead to rely on a highly formalized decision-making procedure that slowly brings a decision into being.

We eat around eight. Large pots with potatoes, rice, mixed vegetable stew with peanut sauce and salads are placed on a table outside the kitchen. Small signs indicate the vegan and vegetarian dishes, and next to the pile of plates a box is placed for donations. Beer – the only thing sold at the meeting – is brought out from a store room behind the kitchen. Nicola, who is behind me in the queue, starts talking about the highway intersection and how it could be blocked using tyre spikes (caltrops), or by throwing burning tyres from a bridge. Alisha, who stands nearby, quickly cuts him off with, 'Don't talk about that kind of thing'. Again, I start wondering about the way that any expression of clear intention is avoided, which seems quite paradoxical in a context of trying to plan action.

Some people hang around drinking beer after dinner while the blockade group announces that they will meet again. We walk back to the soccer field. The evening plenary session to discuss relations with the media has been postponed to give more room to the planning of the actions. It is dark and piercingly cold, and we have brought the map along, again. Fabienne from Strasbourg points to a street north-east of the congress centre that it will be good to blockade because it is easy to get away from. The large highway intersection is discussed for a long time; it is important for hindering the access of the heads of state, but also difficult, because activists could easily be trapped by the police.

Nobody says explicitly who will take responsibility for which points, but Alisha mentions that IL could take care of the peaceful mass blockade of a southern access road in the city centre, and somebody says that Revolt might do a 'movable blockade' (of the highway). At least two other groups still need to be found. The group is amazingly focused and people stand in the cold for hours, while we sometimes slip into the dining hall for some warmth or to fetch beers and chocolate. We agree on exchanging PGP keys to enable email communication that is hard to intercept.[5] We also agree to meet again during the action conference three weeks later. It is quite intense, and after fourteen hours of discussions I finally fall into bed.

I see concentrated faces bent over the map, going over the action concept again when I enter the dining hall the next morning. People eat breakfast and several have a visible hangover. The meeting begins around 10 o'clock, after people finally succeed in waking up Alain and Natalie. We get our mobile phones back and a mailing list is passed around. I facilitate a short discussion about the press strategy. Jürgen proposes the formation of a press group like the one in Heiligendamm that could at least support the media work of different groups and organize daily press conferences. Most people do not agree to this, as they do not want 'someone to talk on behalf of others'. Instead, it is agreed that a list of press contacts will be made for everybody to use.

After this, there is supposed to be group work on all the practical organizing, particularly with regard to the camp, which Alain quickly changes to 'village' because, as he argues, 'only the authorities build camps, we build places, villages, for people to live in'. Many people are dashing about, going into the kitchen or outside to smoke, and are starting to pack their bags. We go through a mountain of details regarding the location, building and organization of the camp/village, and I lose my focus due to the level of practical details that must be agreed upon in common. Around mid afternoon, Fabienne drives me to the station. Before leaving, I fix up with Natalie to stay with her at a friend's place when I am back for the action conference.

Three weeks later: the night before the action conference, I arrive in Strasbourg again. I call Natalie, but nobody picks up the telephone. After several attempts, and a long walk to a possible meeting place, I check into a cheap hotel near the train station. I meet Natalie the next morning at the conference. She explains that her phone was hidden all evening and night in a cupboard at Aimée's place while they were discussing Revolt's involvement in the blockade. They have had second thoughts on the whole thing, she says, as 'it will be suicide to try to block the highway intersection'. The action conference is held at the university, which is a large, imposing concrete building. In itself, the building contrasts with the camp school where the Revolt meeting was held. Registration is inside a big hall, and everybody must put down their name and other personal information in exchange for a name tag. Nicola shows up, and I get a hug before we walk to a large auditorium. Approximately 300 people are seated in the auditorium listening to a panel discussing the role of NATO. We sneak in and I say hello to the two Danes from No to War who are organizing buses for people who plan on coming to the large demonstration. At the back are gathered several people who were at the radical meeting at the camp school, visibly bored. Harry sits bent forward with his forehead on the table, he looks up and hisses in my direction 'Where is the bloody pub?' We laugh and remain seated for a while. Around us the hall seems to be gradually emptying as the people who participated in the meeting at the camp school are gradually leaving.

Nicola, Alain, Natalie, Harry and at least ten other people are standing outside the university entrance, smoking. They find the analysis both boring and irrelevant. 'I just came down to find out where and when to fight the police', says Harry, gesticulating with an imaginary matchbox that he puts something on fire, and then runs away. Alain adds, 'Yeah, I do not want to listen to "the king" [referring to Reiner Braun from the German peace movement, who has taken on the role as host of the meeting and coordinator of the planning process]. They will turn against us anyway, so why bother. When the police asks who burned that car, I will reply that Stalin did'. People laugh. 'He thinks he can control everything', Alain finishes. Nicola says, 'And then they ask for our names and e-mail addresses. I do not want to give them my information. But when it comes to organizing all the important things such as the camp, they do not take any responsibility'. 'I suspect they do not care because they will be sleeping in a hotel', I say. 'To them the camp is not important, whereas the demonstration and the counter conference are'. There is no food at the conference and Nicola and I walk to a sandwich bar. He tells me that he is an architect and has worked abroad in both England and Dubai and, moreover, that he suffers from Asperger's syndrome and needs to write down anything he needs to remember. People are still standing outside as we return. Some are discussing the launching of an Indymedia homepage in Freiburg, and others are talking about the work of the anti-repression group. Harry and I decide to go for a workshop on the blockade.

The workshop is being held in a classroom. Alisha and Lucas, who is from a Belgium anti-war group, introduce and facilitate the meeting. Alisha presents the action concept. She says:

> We have been reworking the blockading concept from Heiligendamm and Cologne – where the five-finger tactic was adapted to an urban setting, and where we worked a lot with creating positive press before the action – to the context in Strasbourg. In Heiligendamm, the concept successfully shut down the G8 summit due to the high number of activist groups, the careful training and the ability to find different routes to get around and through the police lines. The idea was to 'focus on the gaps'.

By this she means the particular tactic where groups managed to approach the summit venue from different sides so the police were dispersed. Following this, activist groups could take advantage of the gaps between police officers to get to the fence without getting into direct confrontation.

Lucas takes over: 'The blockade in Strasbourg should also have a real impact on the summit. The idea is for different groups to take a spot and make an action'. There are two proposals: one emphasizes non-violence while the other argues that the blockade should resist but not attack the police. 'We have decided that it should be a bodily blockade, and that means no material barricades. The idea is to make an effective blockade of the summit, but do we have enough people?' he finishes. I am a bit surprised by the exclusion of the option of using 'materials', because from the earlier meeting I had understood that this was seen as the only way to effectively block the highway intersection. A man in his mid forties from IL interrupts my thoughts: 'There are no Revolt people here today, but they have said they are ready. The idea is that different groups take different points, and that we respect the tactical differences of each spot within the overall concept'. Alisha takes over again, 'We will have a common aim, but each blockade point will talk for itself. This is not just a demonstration; the idea is to take action'. To my mind, things are getting a bit blurred because on the one hand there is an overall concept, but on the other hand each point is supposed to 'speak for itself' and employ its own tactic. In light of Natalie's comment this morning, I am no longer sure that Revolt will actually take part; the concept of action for the blockade is getting narrower. But the blurriness is also at another plane, I realize, namely in the ascription of tactical differences and giving a voice to blockading points, not to persons.

The session develops as a question and answer session, and Harry's forehead is again on the table. A few groups actually say that they will consider taking responsibility for a point. Alisha ends the session by stating:

> It will be a civil-disobedience action, which means it is illegal, but legitimate. We will tell people what we plan to do and when. But we want more than a

symbolic action; hopefully we can effectively block the summit. Whether we are successful will depend a lot on our numbers, the tactics of the cops and the energy of the day. Strasbourg is difficult due to all the canals. There will be a public meeting point that can send people on, at each point there will be a moderation team, plenaries of affinity groups, a police contact, finger tips leading the way, et cetera. We also need to organize first aid, scouts to check on police positions, some press work beforehand and, most importantly, action training at the campsite.

This all reflects the tactics discussed at the radical meeting at the camp school. As far as I can gather, there is now IL and a coalition of anti-war groups taking up a blockade point each; possibly Revolt will coordinate a third point, and a German group of socialist youth might take responsibility for a fourth one.

I will sleep at Aimée's place along with Natalie, Nicola, Harry, Alain and three or four other people. We return from the meeting at around 7 o'clock and cook a large vegetable soup. Around eleven we go to Molodoi, the local social centre, for a concert. We hang out in a large black-painted room with a bar at one end and a stage at the other. It is impossible to talk, and Nicola suggests that we grab some beers and head upstairs. The little upstairs room is papered with posters from past concerts and actions, while four old sofas make up the only furniture of the room. We sit on one sofa opposite Natalie and Lucas, who are discussing Revolt's participation in the blockade. To judge from their gestures they are not coming to an agreement, but I am not able to listen in because Harry is telling me about his work as a truck-driver. 'I am probably the only vegan truck-driver in Britain', he says with a smile. 'When I drive to a lay-by everybody shouts, "Oh, there is the vegan"'. We laugh.

Harry, Nicola and I leave at around two in the morning with a dubious-looking friend of Nicola's. Outside Aimée's apartment, where she lives alone with her nine-year-old daughter, two police officers pull us over, and everybody in the car panics. The driver has had a couple of drinks too many, and one of the headlights is not working. 'Let me do the talking', Nicola says. 'Don't tell them where we are going. It would not be nice if they are directed to Aimée's place'. We step out, and have to show our identification papers. A female police officer points our attention to the fact that the headlight is not working and asks the driver to park the car. They search the car, but then we are let off the hook. 'Maybe it was nothing', Nicola says as we walk back to the apartment.

Nobody gets up until noon. Harry and I do a lot of 'anarchist hanging around', a term he uses to describe the fact that nobody is supposed to take the lead and get us out the door. Instead we have to wait until everybody signals that they are ready. Finally we walk to the university for the final plenary session. Alisha is giving a brief overview of the blockade to all those assembled as we walk in. Nobody objects to the blockade being the same morning as the large demonstration; instead, everybody is consumed by figuring out how to react to the fact that the police will not allow the demonstration into the city centre for security reasons. They are concerned about the lack of visibility that a trajectory south of the city implies. In the end, a 'choreography of action' that involves a demonstration, a blockade, a counter-conference and a camp with attendant action training is agreed upon. Natalie shows up just in time to report to the plenary on the plans of the camp together with Laura from Résistance des Deux Rives. They want support for the decision to do just one camp in Strasbourg, cancelling the one in Kehl for both political and technical reasons, they explain: opting for only one camp will underline their argument for open borders. They explain about the kitchens, the organization of the camp according to a barrio system, and the aim of the camp, which is that it should 'represent our political vision by building alternatives regarding environment and climate'. Finally, they ask for €20,000 to build the camp. They do not get much of a response, but Reiner promises to look into it. Shortly after this, Nicola accompanies Harry and me to the train station. I am returning home, but have agreed with Natalie and Laura that I will return at the end of March to follow the building of the camp. Natalie is talking about coming to Denmark and Sweden as part of the info-tour to mobilize participation, and we all might go to another blockade meeting in Germany two weeks later. Harry is not returning home just yet; first he will take a walk around the city to check out some targets, he says. Nicola asks if he needs company, but Harry explains that it is best to do these things alone.

Years later, when I learned that Harry was actually a British undercover police officer, I speculate about his role during those days.[6] Did we get along so well because we were both in a marginal position? Was he pumping me for information about the Climate Summit, during which his colleague, an exceptionally militant-looking undercover police officer, participated, or was it simply his unusual bodily appearance and life story, his secrecy and good humour, that attracted my attention?

On the Form of Meetings

What mainly concerns me here, however, is the form of the meetings and how intentions become immanent to form. Left radical activists consider the form of meetings to be especially important, but they are starkly different from the form celebrated by the traditional Marxist Left and most other organizations that I am familiar with.

Smaller meetings like the one in Strasbourg often start with a round of introductions, and everybody is encouraged to take part in the discussions. A meeting usually has one or two facilitators, who introduce a theme, put people on the speakers' list, and try to frame and put forward proposals for consensus. This model worked for the radical preparation meeting in the woods outside Strasbourg because the size of the group was manageable, but also because the sense of time pressure led people to favour plenary discussions. The hand signals were used to smoothen decision making, allowing people to express their point of view without talking. The participants particularly used 'direct point' and 'twinkling' in the discussions, but as meeting-fatigue kicked in twinkling became rarer, and the meeting went on longer because the facilitators had difficulty in decoding the viewpoints of the participants and their support for a proposal for consensus.

Meetings do not always comply with the ideal form, implying horizontal decision making and respect for diversity (Maeckelbergh 2009); some people, either by talking more than others or due to being more experienced, may come to dominate discussions.[7] During the preparations for the Climate Summit in Copenhagen, several meetings were held where international activists also participated. At one meeting, where the aim of the various planned actions had to be agreed upon and coordinated, one of the spokespersons of Climate Justice Action (who also spoke during the Reclaim Power rally in Christiania described in Chapter 1) pushed quite hard to make his idea for a mass action of civil disobedience prevail. This led to a division of the group, and the formation of a separate group that called itself Never Trust a Cop – a name playing on the double meaning of Cop as police officers and 'conference of the parties', as negotiations in the United Nations are called – which decided to plan street riots to coincide with, though at some distance away from, the peaceful demonstration. Among these more militant activists was Harry's colleague, who was arguing for the orchestration of riots. The meeting showed that strong opinions, the ability to argue the most or simply stand one's ground sometimes makes it difficult to reach consensus. In Copenhagen, the lack of agreement about the appropriate form of action led to the splitting of the group and the division of the city into spheres of action, in order to let both tactics prevail. However, returning to the meeting at the camp school in Strasbourg, the form there ensured that participants sometimes gained a genuine experience of respect for different viewpoints, and of equal participation in the construction of solutions and decisions. The discussion about publishing targets was an example of a successful experimentation with the form of consensus decision making, in which conflicting viewpoints were respected, and where people were obviously satisfied, not by the solution as such but by the way a consensus was reached.

Larger meetings often work with a so-called 'spoke' model: each affinity group chooses a 'spoke' (spokesperson), who works as a temporary representative. What distinguishes a 'spoke' from an elected politician in a representative democracy is that the person is not empowered to take decisions on behalf of others. After hearing what all 'spokes' have to say on a subject, the facilitators may try to develop a proposal for consensus, which is then discussed in smaller groups, or they may go to the smaller groups directly in order for the groups to develop proposals for consensus. Either way, the small-group-to-large-group process continues until consensus is reached.

Marianne Maeckelbergh (2009) has conceptualized meetings as 'prefigurations' of horizontality and diversity. Her study is an exploration of democratic decision-making practices, and mostly focused on the preparatory meetings for the European Social Forum in London in 2004 and the mobilizations for the anti-G8 protests at Gleneagles in Scotland in 2005. Her basic argument is that actors participating in movements are intentionally prefigurative of the other worlds they are aiming at (ibid.: 4). Meetings, she argues, are a way in which movement actors intentionally create an ideal world in 'mini' form (ibid.: 194). Maeckelbergh explains 'prefiguration' as follows:

> In my experience as an activist, practising prefiguration has meant always trying to make the processes we use to achieve our immediate goals an embodiment of our ultimate goals, so there is no distinction between how we fight and what we fight for, at least not where the ultimate goal of a radically different society is concerned. In this sense, practicing prefigurative politics means removing the temporal distinction between the struggle in the *present* towards a goal in the *future*; instead, the struggle and the goal, the real and the ideal, become one in the present. (ibid.: 66–67)

Seen from this perspective, in prefiguration means and ends are collapsed, which corresponds well with the many discussions described above and the careful attention to how 'our means must reflect our goals'. Moreover, prefiguration also entails a merging of the present and the future which, in Maeckelbergh's understanding, is oriented towards one ultimate goal (a global horizontal democracy). Even though Maeckelbergh still operates with an ultimate goal, she argues that this is nested within short and mid-term goals (ibid.: 94–95).

The idea of participatory democracy as a prefigurative practice, that the means used should reflect the ends desired, is historically ascribed to the New Left that popularized this form in the 1960s and 1970s (ibid.: 13; see also Epstein 1991; Franks 2003; Graeber 2009), whereas the particular form of consensus decision making described here has been traced to Quaker decision-making practices, from where it was adopted into the peace, anti-nuclear and women's movement (Graeber 2009: 43; Maeckelbergh 2009: 15). According to Maeckelbergh, the alterglobalization movement came to conflate the two forms in their decision-making practices, but it has simultaneously sought to overcome some of the weaknesses, namely the tendency of 'unity as sameness', inherent in the identity politics of new social movements, and the forging of conflict-free consensus (Maeckelbergh 2009: 17–18). The alterglobalization movement is, in other words, not united around a common identity, but around experimentation with non-hierarchical decision-making practices. As previously mentioned, this does not entail that everybody must submit to the consensus reached. Individuals and groups are free to 'step aside' (not agreeing, but accepting the decision) or pursue a different course of action.

Instead of the optic of identity, Maeckelbergh argues that the movement should be comprehended through the idea of process, which is understood as 'a practice, a fluid action, an ongoing activity' (ibid.: 21).[8] While I share her view that a focus on identity politics is not conducive to an understanding of the global justice movement, Left radical groups and the events related to them, I want to take issue with her argument exactly in her use of the word 'process' in combination with the idea of prefiguration.

Movement actors extensively employed the word 'process' during the European Social Forum in London (see ibid.: 73–76), as they also did during the Malmö social forum that I described in Chapter 1, but by employing it as an analytical concept to explain an activist's orientation towards the future, Maeckelbergh is representing time as flow,[9] thereby glossing over what I have described as the frequent experiences of discontinuous and non-linear time among activists. So even though I recognize that activists participating in the organization of social forums employ the term 'process', the word is, in my opinion, used to describe the form of decision making, not a series of actions aimed at reaching a predetermined goal. By looking at prefiguration from the perspective of process (and strategy), Maeckelbergh does not, I believe, collapse the distinction between the present and the future as claimed, but reproduces it. In this vein, continuous prefigurative practices become steps on a linear scale that bring the present closer to goals in the future (ibid.:

228). This means that prefiguration is understood as a progressive realization of future possibilities.

However, although I am not altogether averse to thinking of meetings as prefigurative of horizontal decentralized democracy, I propose rethinking it slightly, first and foremost in order to highlight the discontinuous and nonlinear characteristics of activist practices, but also by taking into account the lack of clear vision and the underdetermined character of goals for the future, which I have described in Chapter 1.

In this endeavour, the question of intentionality comes into the picture. Maeckelbergh argues that the actors involved in the movement intentionally turn meetings into prefigurative events. She never clarifies exactly what she means by intentionality, but towards the end of her study she draws on Bourdieu to underline the conscious intentions of human actors within the alterglobalization movement (ibid.: 214).[10] Maeckelbergh also draws on Inden and Strathern to develop a less homogeneous concept of the person in arguing that 'the agent in the alterglobalization movement is understood as actively constructed through the combination of parts of people into groups of people through communication' (ibid.: 216). On the other hand, Maeckelbergh distances herself from Strathern's key argument about people not being the authors of their own acts (ibid.: 220, n.16; see also Strathern 1988: 273; 2004: 35). Following her line of reasoning, we end up with an understanding of intentionality as being tied to either individual actors or groups of people. In this light, meetings – understood as processes – become series of intentional actions aimed at unfolding the ultimate goal of a radically different society.

I believe, though, that there is more to intentions and activist meetings. In the following, rather than talking of process and prefiguration, I will talk of form and figuration. A form is simply conceptualized as the (temporary) mode in which a thing or procedure exists, acts or manifests itself. During planning meetings, intentions are not the property of individuals or groups of individuals, but emerge in the particular relational space that the meeting offers. In other words, the intentions largely pertain to the form of meetings, and to a much lesser extent to the participants. As I shall discuss in the following, I see this as part of a particular way in which intentions are distributed to non-human forms such as puppets and meetings, whereby intentions are decoupled from single persons.

The primacy of form (Sjørslev 1999) that I am advocating might become more apparent if we turn to an example from a distant place, namely the *oho* chant of the Waiwai of the Amazon (Fock 1963).

According to Danish anthropologist Niels Fock, the *oho* chant is a ritualized form of speech characterized by strict formalism.

> The Waiwai term 'oho-karï' means 'yes saying'. It covers a special mode of expression in official announcements, requests, and claims. It is a characteristic of the oho that the speaker, or oho-opener, in short, fast and firm sentences chants what he wants to tell his opponent, who at the end of each sentence answers 'oho'. The oho is always carried out by two individuals, who sit on low stools opposite each other. The questioner will invite his opponent to take a seat, and then in a special chant-tone he will make his requests in short sentences rising in pitch in the end. After each sentence the opponent answers with a hardly audible 'oho', that is, 'yes'. (ibid.: 216)

Fock argues that the chant is used on several occasions, for example to prevent severe conflicts in the context of marriage and trade agreements (ibid.: 217–18). In the absence of formal political authority, it hence becomes a way to enforce agreements and social norms and act on the disobedient, that is, a kind of 'pre-political form' that brings legitimacy to a decision or agreement (Veber 1997: 276).

The meetings of Left radical activists are obviously starkly different from the *oho* chant, but the concern for appropriate form is a possible point of comparison. In both situations, it is the form and its appropriate performance that gives rise to intentions, without these being attributable to any individual participant. The 'twinkling' at proposals for consensus in activists' meetings is a case in point: a way to bypass the authorship of single persons. Instead, intentions pertain only to the fleeting hand gestures and to the social space of the meeting. The lack of authorship and of formal leaders makes it difficult for the police to single people out for prosecution, as in the case of Kara described in the introduction to this chapter.

Hence, meetings are not intentional in any straightforward way. As with the description of the meetings in Strasbourg, activists consider it particularly dangerous to talk of targets and any kind of purposive action in the context of direct actions. Thinking of Kara and the charge against her that could mean a twelve-year jail sentence explains why this is so; the police and the judiciary are, as we shall see to in the next chapter, eager to find intentional individuals behind acts. In the face of this, Left radical activists have developed various ways to protect the intentions of single persons in a context of the widespread surveillance of dissenting groups. These practices are often talked of as a 'security culture', referring to the norms regarding what may be discussed, where and with whom (Robinson 2008: 232).

The security measures of activists can be summarized as follows: targets and detailed action plans can only be spoken of with people you know and trust, such as those belonging to the same affinity groups, or those equally involved in the planning. In larger forums, only the most necessary information is shared and, as Graeber has also noted, a part of the picture is always left vague (Graeber 2009: 68). This implies that you never talk of your own involvement, knowledge or plans in public, and that you do not ask for personal details about fellow activists (something that, incidentally, renders an anthropologist conspicuously similar to a police agent). Action planning does not take place in familiar meeting places, such as homes or cars or via telephone or the internet. All these practices are considered dangerous, and by not complying with security measures one may endanger oneself and others, or give rise to the suspicion that one does not belong and cannot be trusted.

As noted in the description of the camp-school meeting, discussions are often held on a very practical plane, going into all sorts of details about actions and the logistics of camps. This can in itself be seen as a way to avoid the conflicts that are the inevitable by-product of ideological discussions. But as I mentioned earlier, one consequence of collective decision making and the construction of consensus is that the decisions and targets of mass actions do not belong to one person, nor to a group or a collective, but to the meeting or action as such. In this sense, an action may have the goal of blockading a summit, but no individual should start talking about sprinkling tyre spikes on the road.

In general, the importance of meetings cannot be underestimated. Meetings are a mechanism through which intentions are distributed to other forms – such as a blockading point (that is, a place where a blockade is to be set up), of which Alisha spoke during the action conference as having 'tactical preferences' and the ability 'to talk for itself'. To most activists, moreover, the meetings are as important as any action, but this does not mean that they foreshadow the future in any straightforward manner. So while meetings are obviously organized deliberately, the intentions they produce cannot be ascribed to single persons. Meetings are neither singular nor plural; it is not a group that can be dissolved into its parts (that is, individuals). And the way meetings are performed continues to produce indeterminacy about activists' intentions for what we conventionally think of as the future. Together with activists' general avoidance of outlining a plan for the future and the contours of the ideal society they are aiming at, there seems to be enough ground for rejecting the concept of prefiguration as the most adequate for understanding the meeting practices. A well-facilitated meeting is a 'figuration' rather than a prefiguration, which in my terminology means that meetings are the way in which the indeterminate (indefinite and uncertain) gain a determinate form. So, what I call figurations are determinate forms, which become ripe with intention due to the performative procedures of activists.[11] This should become clearer in turning to activists' relations to puppets.

Puppets and Thoughts on the Agency of Objects

Let us take a step back. I have argued that intentions take a form, yet it need not be a human form. The forms looked at here can also include a specific procedure or a thing that becomes political when understood as a mediated manifestation of intentionality. In the discussion that follows, I shall consider puppets and other effigies that are used during mass demonstrations and civil-disobedience actions. It is important to consider them here partly because they are another form, in this case material, that intentions are distributed to, and partly because agency is abducted from them, both by activists and the police.

Alfred Gell has developed one of the most persuasive arguments about the relationship between (art) objects and persons, in which people as agents are in certain contexts substituted by art objects (Gell 1998: 5). The whole idea of his theory is 'to explore a domain in which "objects" merge with "people" by virtue of the existence of social relationships between persons and things, and persons and persons via things' (ibid.: 12). In Gell's view, art objects are not signs with meanings, but visible, physical entities that acquire agency and intentionality by being embedded in social relationships, and that may be the cause of events in their vicinity.

This brings me back to the bolt cutter mentioned in the opening of this chapter, and to other giant puppets, which are found at almost any major action of the radical Left and the alterglobalization movement in general (see Graeber 2009). I suggest thinking of these giant puppets as objects that intentions are distributed to in the context of action planning. During the Climate Summit in Copenhagen in December 2009, besides the large red and black papier mâché bolt cutter placed on the roof of Climate Justice Action's truck that was involved in the actions, a multitude of extremely large models of endangered species, such as penguins and polar bears, as well as puppets resembling world leaders, accompanied the mass demonstration in which more than 100,000 people participated.

David Graeber has described puppets as the main sacred objects of the movement; they are 'a matter of taking the most ephemeral of materials – ideas, paper, wire mesh – and transforming them into something very like a monument, even if they are, at the same time, ridiculous effigies' (ibid.: 490).[12] He describes the puppets as ridiculous gods that try, in a spectacular way, to seize power and ridicule it at the same time; they are 'the point of transition; they represent the ability to start to make ideals real and take on a solid form' (ibid.: 491). This, in a sense, anticipates my own thinking about figurations as the moments where an indeterminate future gains determinate form.

In the streets of Copenhagen during the Climate Summit, it was possible to identify three kinds of puppets: marionettes or puppets worked by string, resembling world leaders; iconic figures of endangered species; and an-iconic figures like the bolt cutters. In line with Gell, these puppets can be thought of as extensions of persons, and are hence examples of what he calls 'distributed personhood' (Gell 1998: 21). It is worth noting that Gell distinguishes between primary and secondary agents: while social agency can be exercised both relative to things and by things, primary agents distribute agency through secondary agents. Hence, like the soldier described by Gell who distributes his agency through a landmine or a military tactic (ibid.: 20–21), activists distribute their agency through a puppet as well as through tactics and other determinate forms such as blockading points. But aside from the fact that they are enmeshed in social relationships, how do puppets gain agency?

In his book on art and agency, Gell examines the production of idols. Idols, he argues, are the visual forms of gods (ibid.: 26).[13] Idols, both figures and images, may physically resemble the gods – that is, be iconic – or they may be an-iconic (such as, for example, a holy stone), but what matters is that they are in fact the body of the god. Viewed from a similar angle, activists' puppets may also be considered materializations, but of various kinds: the marionettes mimicking world leaders are similar to the kind of figures used in what Gell calls 'volt sorcery' (ibid.: 103–4),[14] where the victim is both the prototype and the person against who the action is directed. Through the marionettes, the leaders become involuntary agents controlled by the activist. In this sense, the marionettes can be understood as one way that activists seek to abduct the agency and power of world leaders.

Activists clad in animal costumes or who carry huge papier mâché figures of endangered species are also involved in an act of mimicry, but in this case of an animal. The mimicry involves an abduction of their agency, which becomes acquired by activists. The animal figures are animated in various ways – the puppets used in demonstrations are usually hollow, have some human features and huge eyes, which allows for an optical oscillation by which the union between puppet and observer can be achieved (see ibid.: 116–17). The animal figure becomes, so to speak, an extension, or a ritual magnification, of the person carrying it (cf. Strathern 2004). This comes about through the human-like qualities of the puppet, and the social interaction with it, which in the case of activists is expressed not only during its construction, but also in attempts to protect it from the police.

The bolt cutter is not turned into a social person through the exchange of glances, but it is clearly perceived as an agentive entity that acts back on the activists during an action. In the context of the Reclaim Power action aimed at entering the Climate Summit area, one activist commented that 'the bolt cutter was making a request', another activist thought it was a good thing to carry along because 'it is raising people's spirits' and is 'prompting us to take action'. In this way, the bolt cutter acquires intentionality, and might also incite people to follow a certain course of action, but simultaneously this communication about the goals of an action takes place at a safe distance from individuals (as the prosecutor's problems in the case against Kara reveal). Contrary to Maeckelbergh's contention, the bolt cutter's incitement to action can, alongside meetings, be perceived as an example of how activists are not always the sole authors of their own actions (cf. Strathern 1988: 156–57).[15]

Both the activists and the police abduct agency from puppets, and part of the agency can be attributed to their role in the relational texture between activists and police. Activists are eager to protect and hide their puppets, and as evidenced in Graeber's ethnography of the alterglobalization movement in North America (Graeber 2009: 72), where to hide them and the best way to protect them are considered huge problems. Before a major action, the police usually take pre-emptive measures to seize puppets together with banners, tools and other works of art. Usually this is justified to the public with reference to the probable existence of weapons and the threat of violence during actions.

At the Climate Summit in Copenhagen, the police also ransacked the place where many Left radical activists converged to meet and/or sleep, much to their surprise and irritation. The police were uninterested in searching and checking the identity of those present, but they confiscated tools, banners, paint and a number of so-called 'warrior bikes' (homemade bikes with inventive features) that were classified as weapons. In the case of Copenhagen they did not, however, find and seize the giant bolt cutter, but only the drawings in Kara's notebook.

Police actions against harmless objects and puppets give rise to a lot of speculation among activists about the police. Graeber (2009) refers to activists in North America pondering why the puppets are important to the police. Some of his interlocutors conclude that the puppets remind police officers of the fact that they are puppets themselves; some assume that puppets are seen as disorderly, and that the police do not like that; and still others think that the police believe that there might be bombs inside the puppets (ibid.: 497). My interlocutors reached similar conclusions, but also simply took it as police harassment. Graeber goes further, concluding that the police do not like puppets because it makes them lose 'the power to define the situation' (ibid.: 504).

In an interview with the superintendent of police responsible for the overall police operation during COP 15, the importance of pre-emptive strikes in order to seize the objects being prepared for the demonstrations and actions was readily admitted. He explained that the confiscation of objects 'produced insecurity' among activists, and that this helped the police produce security in the streets. The possession of puppets by activists and police alike can thus be understood as a way to extend or enlarge agency. When the police seize puppets, they physically abduct (in the traditional sense of the word) parts of the activists' distributed persons, and thereby diminish the agency of a demonstration or action. From my perspective, therefore, the acute interest in puppets is less a struggle over meaning, and more a way to alter a social relationship through the acquisition of (magical) power.

In sum, activists have a rather peculiar way of dealing with the near future, which entails the avoidance of connections between single persons, goals and intentions, which the police do everything to restore. Instead, the personhood of activists is distributed among, and intentions temporarily stored in, concrete figures such as puppets, or in other determinate forms such as the formalized decision-making procedures of a meeting, such as the 'twinkling' of hands. Sometimes these figures are able to initiate a series of events in their vicinity.

Nevertheless, there still seems to be a reasonable question about how people come to know what must be done during an action. We have already seen that activists abduct intentions from puppets, as well as from posters, colour codes of blocs and expressions concerning the tactic or style of an action (which I shall come back to in Chapter 5). These are all ways in which activists get an idea about the intentions of an action or protest event. It seems reasonable to assume that this may give rise to misunderstandings, and indeed sometimes it does,[16] but usually the protests unfold as fairly well-coordinated performances. In order to understand how this comes about we need to turn to other elements involved in the preparation of actions, namely action training as well as the last coordination that takes place within affinity groups immediately before an action or protest event. In the following, I return to Strasbourg and the action training that took place in the protest camp. I then present an ethnographic description of an affinity group meeting in the context of a direct action in Denmark aimed at shutting down a refugee retention centre. Even though the two are drawn from different preparation processes, in their different ways they tell us something about how intentions are synchronized through different (bodily) techniques, while exact goals and individual intentions remain indeterminate.

The Synchronization of Intentions during Action Training

On a small field outside the anti-NATO village, approximately 6 kilometres south of the city of Strasbourg, I participate in the last round of training aimed at preparing me and approximately forty other activists for the planned blockade of the NATO summit the following day. The trainer is an experienced activist from Germany who has already conducted two similar training sessions every day of the week preceding the protests. The training consists of making us run through a range of methods for establishing an effective blockade, ways of delaying an arrest, methods for democratic decision making under pressure and, not least, how to handle the accessories of the riot police such as tear gas, concussion grenades and pepper spray, which we are likely to face the following day. This preparation, it is explained, 'is aimed at avoiding panic; it will enable us to stay calm and maintain control of the situation'.

First we do 'an action focus exercise', as the trainer calls it. It is emphasized that the police are human beings, and that we should respect their dignity. According to the trainer, this implies not attacking the police, not even verbally, and always staying calm. 'By not running', the trainer explains, 'we show that we are in control of the situation'. I recall a situation about six months earlier where I was running like crazy with tear gas pumping in and out of my lungs. What he says makes sense, but still I instruct four students, who have accompanied me into the field to study camp life, to run if need be. Questions are raised from the group about the legitimacy of self-defence if we are 'attacked' by the police, and about how to react to other activists employing violence. The trainer does not reply directly to the questions, but reminds us of the mass blockade in Heiligendamm: 'we focused on the gaps [between police officers], not on the police. Our tactic is to get between them and around them', he says. Afterwards, we do some physical exercises that teach us to do exactly that. First, we try 'swarming', that is running forward in small groups, taking advantage of the gaps between the people playing the role of police officers, or in various ways trying to get around them. Second, we try making a sitting blockade by locking our arms together. We are taught not to resist an arrest, but encouraged to make our bodies heavy to complicate and delay the work of the police. Then we talk about affinity groups and practice concrete exercises in consensus decision making under time and physical constraints.

During the training session, a military helicopter keeps circling over our heads; it makes it difficult to hear what people are saying, and the constant flapping sound of the rotor blades produces bodily stress. A young man dressed in black, with a German accent, comes running to our group. He explains that the clowns, a group of activists belonging to the Clandestine Insurgent Rebel Clown Army, have been attacked by police in the city centre while they were setting up a 'pink zone' – analogous to the red zone of the security forces – and making a joke of doing identity checks on people in the street. In an overexcited voice he continues explaining that the clowns were met by German water cannons, and when they stripped naked to 'take a shower', apparently to make fun of the situation, they were sprayed with tear gas. 'And now they [the police] are attacking the camp', he finishes. Hearing of this, it occurs to me that our blockade training is not the only training going on in and around the camp/village. For days, the more confrontational strand of the camp has been staging actual confrontations with the police in the immediate vicinity as a kind of 'warming up' for actions on Saturday, when the heads of state come to town.

Activists, and particularly my Revolt interlocutors, constantly fear a police attack on the camp. Clashes have already taken place twice over the previous days, leading to barricades in the street and large balls of straw placed on the fields surrounding the camp being set on fire. Today, our training session falls apart as people start preparing for a confrontation to protest against the repression of the clowns and in order to defend the camp. At the blockade training, the German trainer asks people to stay on for a few more minutes, and uses the opportunity to remind everyone to think of the police officers as human beings. 'Remember to look at the gaps, not at the police', he shouts over the sound of the concussion grenades that the police are throwing just outside the main entrance to the camp.

On the street, activists, who have all changed into black clothes and masked their faces with hoods or bandanas, set fire to the barricades that had been built earlier; the police's advance is met with several more or less coordinated waves of running activists hurling stones at them. The police respond with barrages of tear gas. Behind the line, I talk to Jos from the Netherlands, who has participated in several summit protests, and arrived ten days before to help build the camp. Jos shrugs his shoulders as he tries to explain what is going on: 'You know, we need to defend the camp, but the timing is not right. We should save our energy for tomorrow'.

The defence of the tent village was just a prelude to the widespread rioting of the following day. The incidents reflect the fact that a lot of activities anticipate or take place in the shadow of a larger summit event, not only planning and training, but also the creation of other kinds of temporary interstices, such as the camp/village itself, outside the control of the authorities. Quite a lot of effort had gone into constructing the village, and upon arrival I was welcomed by a sign announcing, 'Welcome to a different world', accompanied by a huge skeleton puppet in a NATO battle helmet. As the summit approached, the village grew to around four to five thousand inhabitants from all over Europe. The camp was in itself a place for experimentation, with consensus decision making and self organization, and run according to a 'do it yourself' principle (McKay 1998), which entailed taking responsibility towards the community and engaging in solving the practical and organizational problems at hand (Robinson 2008: 234). The camp was grouped into several sections, so-called barrios, and the affinity groups inhabiting each barrio organized themselves to take care of refuse disposal, alcohol consumption and fire prevention and control; they also aimed to create consensus about social rules and meeting frequencies, as well as organize participation in the daily meetings about overall camp matters. Food for the entire camp was prepared three times a day by voluntary soup kitchens that travel from one summit or activist gathering to the next, feeding thousands of activists with only a rudimentary infrastructure. Besides the barrios and the kitchens, the camp infrastructure consists of several large tents, where spokes-council meetings are held every morning and evening, and a media centre with internet connection, as well as toilets and showers. On a nearby field, two stages have been put up offering music in the evenings. The physical layout and organizational setup was not only an attempt at practising here-and-now anarchist ideas about horizontality and diversity, but the meetings and daily meals were also – as the sign at the entrance expressed – a space for synchronizing the arriving activists to 'live in the same world at the same time'.

The various small incidents and clashes with the police throughout the week to defend the camp can be thought of as a kind of training. Relatively simple transmissions of 'techniques of the body' (Mauss

1992) were involved in the repeated clashes with the police, as well as in the blockade training. The transmission occurred both by way of the imitation of the actions of others and through education, that is, experienced people drilling fellow activists and correcting their postures (cf. ibid.: 458–59). In the context of these various forms of training, my argument is that the transmission of bodily techniques facilitates a bodily synchronization among participants.

In a study of a New Age community in Israel, Iddo Tavory (2007) has looked at experiences of synchronization in ritual interaction. The ethnographic focus of the analysis is a food circle celebrated every day prior to the shared meals at their summer camp. During the daily rituals, Tavory argues, bodies are aligned to one another through the imitation of postures and synchronized singing 'umming' sounds while participants all focus on the same object (their inner self). By drawing on Randall Collins's theory of the Interaction-Ritual-Chain, Tavory argues that synchronization depends on three techniques, namely focusing exercises, physical proximity and control of the social ambience. Building on Durkheim and Collins, Tavory proposes looking at ritual interaction as the basis of affective solidarity, and consequently training is described as a detachment from the burden of selfhood.

Tavory's findings are only partially helpful for my own inquiry. As I argued in Chapter 2, Left radical activists are less concerned about their inner self and much more about the form of their social relations. Being an activist implies that one is always already a relational entity, insofar as it is something a person becomes by being enmeshed in common action. In my view, moreover, bodily training is less concerned with producing affective solidarity than with producing a synchronization of bodily time, which I understand simply as reaching a concurrence in time. This said, I find Tavory's careful documentation of the techniques employed useful for understanding the synchronization involved in action training. Firstly, the training at the camp in Strasbourg involved two kinds of focusing exercises: one was the shared focus on the advancing police officers, and the other was the focus on the gaps between them. Secondly, there were different physical exercises to be learnt, for example how to move in a synchronized manner while hurling stones at the police (something which is necessary to avoid hitting a fellow activist), or the physical exercises practised during blockade training, such as how to make blockades by braiding body parts together, making it difficult for the police to wrest one person away from another while the activists, simultaneously, avoid and minimize injuries and fractures. Lastly, there was the production of ambience. In Strasbourg, the constant rumours and circulating camp guards, which I return to in the next chapter, produced a sense of being under constant threat from the police, which was heightened by recurrent clashes with the police, sound waves from the circling helicopters and the shock waves from concussion grenades.

Thus, I understand synchronization as the creation of a bodily concurrence in time, and this disposition does not require verbal communication of intentions and plans. The training concerns timing and transmits a series of bodily techniques that, when successful, produces a kind of bodily synchronization, that is, a bodily concurrence in time, which ties into a shared sense of the task and possible hazards ahead, a feel for the appropriate tactic to be employed and basic trust in one another.

Keeping Intentions Indeterminate

By examining the working of an affinity group a few days before an action, I hope to be able to complement this understanding of synchronization with how intentions are kept indeterminate. The example is not drawn from Strasbourg, where I did not participate in a discrete affinity group, but in the work of Revolt's local planning group and medical team. The situation we shall now turn to is drawn from the planning of an action in Denmark aimed at shutting down a refugee retention centre, Sandholm, north of Copenhagen (to which, along with Strasbourg, we shall return again in Chapter 5 for a detailed analysis of the actions).

The affinity group that we meet here is largely made up of women who got to know each other during the planning of a queer-feminist bloc during the mass action G13 aimed at squatting a new social centre in Copenhagen in October 2007 (see Chapter 2). The participants in the group are students and artisans (several of whom have also been part of Globale Rødder), members of various feminist groups, and some people who lived in the same housing co-op as Aske.

Emma has called for an affinity group meeting to coordinate our participation in an action to shut down a refugee retention centre a few days later. It had been announced that the goal of the action is to cut down the fence around the centre, thereby showing that it is possible to act against the restrictive (and racist) asylum policies employed by the Danish state. Our all-female group had been asked to carry the front banner of the demonstration from a meeting point nearby Allerød Station up to the retention centre. From our participation in previous planning meetings, we knew that upon arrival the participants could either stay in the demonstration or try to make their way to the fence in smaller groups. The meeting focused on deciding what we wanted to do, though part of the group – namely those planning to be involved in the action – maintained an indeterminate stance, as will become evident below.

The meeting was held in a small TV-room in a collective in Copenhagen. Besides the television, the room is only furnished with a broad bench along the wall, covered with pillows, and a round coffee table in the centre of the room. Eleven people have turned up for the meeting and Emma serves tea to everybody. The participants in the group are between the ages of 24 and 32; they have been in political actions together for some time, and several are close personal friends. Almost everybody present took part in the feminist yellow bloc at the successful G13 action, and this makes up a powerful backdrop for the present action and the expectation of being able to do things together.

Emma, who has been in contact with the organizers, explains the matter about the front banner, which is usually carried by the first line of demonstrators and which the organizers wish us to carry, but Freja cuts her off to comment that the action group wants just women at the front because it looks better in the media. We laugh while Emma tries to get the discussion back on track by affirming that it is also a good idea to have people in the front of the demonstration who know each other well. It makes it possible to make quick decisions, she argues. Her presentation kicks off a series of questions: What is the style of the demonstration? How should we react if the police stop us – should we push against them, stand still or try to run around them? What should we do when we arrive? Emma explains to the rest of the group that the police will presumably let us reach the retention centre, but that they are erecting an extra fence. The idea is that the front banner should stop right in front of them (the police) and hence stay with the demonstration. 'Okay', Julie says, 'so we have to be the safe heaven when the affinity groups break off from the demonstration?' Several people nod.

We call up Magnus from the action coordination group, who is up scouting at the retention centre. Julie asks if there is 'an ethical codex', as she phrases it, or what the style of the demonstration will be. Will people be masked? Magnus misunderstands the question, believing that we want to cover our faces even though it is illegal to do so during demonstrations in Denmark. He offers us some leftover masks resembling the Danish Minister of Integration, Birthe Rønn Hornbæk. Emma explains that there is no codex, but a style – 'Which tells you what you *can* do', interrupts a girl called Little Emma, making a wry face. Magnus explains on the phone that the demonstration should be family friendly, but upon arrival different groups can break out in order to do their own thing.

After this clarification of the ethical underpinnings of the action, we go round the group so everybody can express what they feel. Everyone agrees to having the front banner and to push up against a police line if need be. Emma does not want to be arrested, so she offers to be a 'runner' who takes care of communication between the front banner and the truck accompanying the action. In our affinity group, about five people (including myself) also consider taking part in the direct action, so we decide to divide our affinity group into two parts that will take turns at carrying the banner. By doing so, we can make sure that the five people who might want to take part in the action are free to run off when we reach the retention centre, while the rest stay behind at the front of the demonstration. We talk for a while about 'success criteria' and how to make it a great day 'even if we do not manage to cut down the fence'. Freja says that she believes it will be a success in any case, 'because we will manage to show with our bodies and voices that it is possible to take action against the retention of people'. Sofie mocks her, 'Uh-huh, the body is our medium'. 'Yes', Freja says, 'that was exactly what I was trying to say'. We all laugh at this cliché about 'the body as medium', though it does undeniably reflect the importance of the body in Left radical politics. Sofie offers to buy cloth to make scarves in the same colour for everybody carrying the banner. 'That way we can recognize each other along the way', she says.

The meeting has lasted about an hour, and some people leave. The five of us who consider participating in the action – Julie, Sofie, Little Emma, her friend Maja and me – stay behind. We go around the group again to discuss 'how far we are willing to go'. This is mostly phrased in terms of willingness to get arrested, which implicitly also involves a willingness to enter into confrontation with the police. We agree that we are willing to be arrested unless it seems to be 'complete suicide', a phrasing that is used for someone running into the arms of the police alone, and without producing any effect. Little Emma underlines the point that we do not need to take a decision, but can wait to see how we feel when the demonstration arrives at the retention centre. Indeed, we do not decide on what to do, but only that we will 'run together' and try to 'come as close as possible', taking the final decision when we are there. Little Emma says she will bring some rope, which can be used to pull down the fence.

Our discussion illustrates how each affinity group is empowered to make their own decisions about how they wish to participate in an action, which often implies that nothing specific is decided until the last moment, apart from what one is not willing to do. This form of organizing allows for great flexibility – the participants can make ongoing adaptations to their tactics during actions – though a possible negative consequence is that even core organizers do not have a complete overview of the participants' willingness to take part, or what is often referred to as the 'energy of the day'. Given this flexibility of self-organization in practice, many activists view affinity groups as a model for how to organize broader networks and other aspects of political life (cf. Juris 2008: 34–35).

What was striking about this and other affinity group meetings is that no plans are fixed, even if the action is only a few days away, and that they never do become fixed. The first time the discussion goes round the group leads to a splitting of the group into those ready to participate in the more free-form action and those who are not. The second round synchronizes our intentions to some extent, as a group, though individual intentions are still vague and indeterminate. If intentions are narrowly understood as agents' determination to act in a certain way in the near future, the participants in this particular meeting cannot be perceived as fully intentional beings. The indeterminate nature of their intentions is not only a question of avoiding possible police repression, though that is still relevant, but also reflects a way of going about social change whereby it does not rely on predetermined possibilities for the future, but rather entails a constant production of indeterminacy.[17] The indeterminacy of the participants within the affinity group should hence not be understood as a lack of ability to plan for the near future, nor solely as fear of being detected by the police, but as a way to keep themselves open and ready for what is not yet there (see also Miyazaki 2004).

Figuration

Meetings might be the single most important space for the preparation of protest actions, as Maeckelbergh has convincingly argued, but they are far from the only form that preparation takes. Building camps, action training, affinity group coordination and the production of objects for protests such as banners and puppets are other important forms of preparation. The present chapter has sought to illuminate the particular way that intentions play out in the context of action planning, so that single persons remain divorced from intentions, while these intentions come to pertain to the relational space of the meeting. In meetings, intentions are elicited via a skilful form of consensus decision-making. Intentions are, moreover, distributed to non-human forms such as puppets that sometimes cause events to happen in the vicinity of persons (Gell 1998: 101). Puppets are one such form that intentions take which, at least temporarily, bracket the intentions of single persons. While the police and activists alike abduct agency from these forms, intentions are hard to ascribe to single persons, as the court case against Kara after the Climate Summit in Copenhagen aptly illustrates. Instead of thinking of intentions as a determination to act in a certain way to obtain determined ends, what is striking here is how intentions obtain, and are mediated by, form.

Taking my point of departure in Maeckelbergh's analysis of what she calls the alterglobalization movement's prefigurative meeting practices, I have proposed that we think of the form given to intentions as 'figurations'. The concept of prefiguration implies anticipation and a foreshadowing of the future, not least because the present is, as in Maeckelbergh's analysis, tied to the future by way of 'process' and strategy (see also Maeckelbergh 2011). This implies that prefiguration becomes a progressive realization of future possibilities or of intentions for the near and distant future.

My notion of figuration is not tied in any straightforward way to the future, but is marked and defined by indeterminacy. While intentions are not communicated verbally, due to fear of repression and in accordance with the security culture among activists, they are distributed and transposed between bodies through different techniques that result in bodies and intentions becoming synchronized without belonging to single persons. In a sense, figuration emerges out of the inherent tension involved in giving determinate form to that which is indeterminate.

Notes

1. According to Gell, in Piercian semiotics, 'abduction' refers to the inference of meaning from signs. This implies that through abduction we form an idea about the intentions of others (Gell 1998: 14–15).
2. Indymedia (independent media centers or IMC) emerged in the context of the protests against the WTO meeting in Seattle in 1999 as a global network of activist-journalists. Activists in cities all over the world have established indymedia centres. Indymedia reports on a range of political and social issues, and provides non-corporate reports from direct actions and summit protests (Juris 2008: 13).
3. The Schengen agreement was signed by five members of the European Community in 1985, and was ratified by all member countries with/through the Amsterdam Treaty in 1997. The agreement involves the suspension of systematic border controls between participating countries.
4. Red zones are areas that are closed, off-limits to protesters. During the NATO summit, the entire inner city areas of Strasbourg and Kehl were declared red zones and the police guarded all access routes. This was apparently done to avoid confrontations around the fence surrounding the summit area – as seen, for example, during several G8 meetings in Europe – but also implied assigning a large part of the police forces to guard the perimeter of the entire inner city. The zoning reflects a spatial approach to security (for more on this see Chapter 4).

5. PGP stands for 'pretty good privacy' and is a data encryption and decryption computer program developed by Phil Zimmermann in the early 1990s.
6. On Harry's double life, see 'Undercover Police: Officer B Identified as Mark Jacobs', *Guardian*, 19 January 2011, and 'Fine Line between Undercover Observer and Agent Provocateur', *Guardian*, 10 January 2011.
7. A distinction between ideal and practice is not particularly conducive in this context, because the practical experimentation with non-hierarchical forms of organizing is (in itself) the ideology (Graeber 2002: 70; Juris 2008: 229). A meeting cannot be seen as either idea or practice, but is both at the same time. Nevertheless, embedded value hierarchies are at play even in experimentation with non-hierarchical forms of organizing and consensus decision making (Bruun et al. 2011).
8. Maeckelbergh's discarding of identity politics as a meaningful analytical perspective for understanding the alterglobalization movement has been criticized by Catherine Eschle (2011), who has drawn attention to how various identity projects coexist within the alterglobalization movement, which is for the same reason also sometimes referred to as a 'movement of movements'.
9. Flux, flow and process are the dominant metaphors in anthropology for describing time (Hodges 2008; Robbins 2007b). I do not challenge the description of time as process among actors within the European Social Forum, but I have not found that this is the main or only experience of time among Left radical activists.
10. Following Bourdieu, Maeckelbergh argues that individuals have strategies, and to 'substitute strategy for rule [in complexity theory] is to reintroduce time, with its rhythm, its orientation, its irreversibility' (Bourdieu, in Maeckelbergh 2009: 214). In drawing on Bourdieu, Maeckelbergh reinforces her description of movement actors as actors of conscious intent.
11. These figurations are neither a social organization or a group, nor an expression of an ideology, but a holographic instantiation (Wagner 1991: 166); that is, a three-dimensional picture implying a resonance between what we conventionally think of as the present and the future, but which are co-present bodily perspectives (a point I return to in Chapter 5).
12. This seizing of power by way of ephemeral materials is contrasted with the destruction of property often involved in anarchist and other Left radical actions. In destroying the property of banks and other large corporate businesses, something that seems solid is shown to be inherently fragile. According to Graeber, both puppets and property destruction are aimed at striking the popular imagination in order to make visible the vulnerability of 'the system' (Graeber 2009: 493).
13. Or put differently, the god is the prototype, that is, the entity held by abduction to be represented in the index.
14. Volt sorcery, according to Gell, is the practice of harming persons through damage done to a representation in their likeness. This is possible because the victim's distributed person is tied up with the index or representation (Gell 1998: 103–4).
15. Other non-human actors, particularly fire and graffiti, could in a similar way be considered as temporary 'stand-ins' for people. Both fire and graffiti sometimes become (secondary) actors initiating a sequence of causal events. A tag is the simplest form of graffiti that involves spray painting signatures on walls or other property. Tagging can, analogous to puppets and fire, be considered a way the graffitist distributes their person.
16. Some activist friends often retell the story about their trip to the World Bank protests in Prague. They had organized several buses from Copenhagen, but even though

they had agreed to stay out of (activist initiated) clashes with the police, they nevertheless ended up in the wrong bloc and unwittingly, became participants in a riot.
17. The philosopher Ernst Bloch has described indeterminacy as the driving force wherein unfulfilled hopes from the past are reoriented towards the future (Bloch, in Miyazaki 2004: 69–70).

4

'We Are Humans, What Are You?'

Securitization, Unpredictability and Enemy-Becoming

In an interview approximately six months after the Climate Summit in Copenhagen in December 2009, the chief of operations of the Danish police, Morten Larsen, who had been responsible for planning the policing of the event, explained to me that in his view the demonstrations and actions had been the most unpredictable element in the entire security planning:

> The part about demonstrations is completely unpredictable because you have no idea what kind of people it is who are coming to Copenhagen. What is their agenda exactly? What happens? How many people will show up at the large demonstration? When they said 100,000 we were killing ourselves with laughter ... But that was what showed up. I have no idea where they picked them up.

What the officer is saying reiterates a commonly held view concerning the alterglobalization movement, namely that it has emerged as if from nowhere (cf. della Porta 2007; Eschle 2005; Juris 2008; Osterweil 2005), implying that it appears and disappears at different points in time. In light of this unpredictability on the side of the protesters, Larsen suggested that it was also crucial for the police operation to defy prediction. In order to do this, he explained, the creation of insecurity among protesters has become an integral part of the police effort to maintain public security during summit events. The present chapter will address this particular configuration of security and insecurity, and examine the relationship between activists and the police with a particular emphasis on how they relate to and make sense of each other. Throughout the chapter the focus will shift between the police and activists, revealing the intersecting temporalities of security. This also shows how enmity is a transformational and temporal phenomenon.

By way of introduction, it is important to underline that the police seldom refer to activists as enemies, but use the terms opponents, troublemakers, threats, violent offenders or simply the black bloc, which connotes all of the characteristics just mentioned. Activists, though, sometimes talk of the police as enemies, and from time to time wonder about their humanity. I look at this relationship from the perspective of enmity because it enables me to enter into dialogue with both the 'securitization theory' of the Copenhagen School in international relations (Buzan et al. 1998; Wæver 1995) and Viveiros de Castro's study of enmity among the Araweté in the Brazilian Amazon (Viveiros de Castro 1992: 286–87, 303–4; 2004); the latter will enable me to expose the fundamental uncertainty about the nature of the 'other' that exists between activists and the police, and to look at how 'the enemy' is something that one becomes. These are obviously quite incongruent sources of inspiration, but they allow me to grasp both the relational nature of enmity as well as the bodily transformability inherent in it.

In this chapter I first examine the host of security initiatives surrounding major events launched by the European Union since 2001. After this first look at the policy level, the chapter will proceed by describing the concrete security measures employed and the policing of dissent (della Porta and Reiter 1999; Fernandez 2008)[1] at the Climate Summit in Copenhagen, at which were gathered approximately 140 participating heads of state, and the similarities and differences between this operation and that of the French police in the context of NATO sixtieth-anniversary summit in Strasbourg in April 2009.

Drawing on insights of the Copenhagen School (Buzan et al. 1998; Wæver 1995), the chapter addresses how certain issues and groups are cast as existential threats, which legitimizes the employment of extra-political measures. In securitization theory, security is understood as a speech act, which implies that the act of securitization is not necessarily an accurate representation of the world. Rather, securitization as a speech act is an act on the world with real effects (cf. Butler 1999; Kapferer 2005; Keane 2006). When a securitizing actor successfully manages to define something as a threat, which requires the acceptance of a broader audience or public, the issue or group gets displaced into the extra-political realm (Wæver 1995: 55). In focusing on existential threats, the theory echoes Carl Schmitt's emphasis on politics as emergency (Williams 2003: 515), and is underpinned by his understanding of the political as antagonism between friends and enemies (Schmitt 2006: 26; Williams 2003: 523).

The chapter looks at what happens when activists move from the category of 'the young' (see Chapter 2) to the category of 'security threat'. I explore the enmity between activists and the police, and the remarkable symmetry in the manner in which they see each other. With a point of departure in the shared concern for the unpredictability of the other, I show that the resultant enmity is not a simple antagonism; it is this reciprocal sense of unpredictability. Rendering oneself unpredictable occasions enmity.

In this light, the chapter takes issue with the concept of enmity that underpins securitization theory, which it is argued underexposes the transformability of the relation. Through empirical analysis, I show that whether a person appears as an enemy or not is highly contingent upon the abduction of meaning from signs (such as bodies or things), and the particular social relationship they are enmeshed in (Gell 1998: 123; Viveiros de Castro 2004: 479). Following this, enmity in the context under study must be considered a social relation, and a temporary phenomenon mainly tied to particular events.

The Enemy Within

After the Prague World Bank summit in 2000, street protests synchronized with international meetings have become a familiar occurrence in Europe. During the so-called 'summer of resistance' in 2001, clashes at the G8 meeting in Genoa proved fatal when a protester was shot and killed by the police amid violent clashes. Alarmed by the spread of protests and the escalating violence, corresponding in time with the expectation that large events were probable terrorist targets, it proved necessary for European authorities to address security around major political events.

In 2001, the Council of the European Union launched a security handbook for the use of police authorities at international events. The scope of the handbook, which was revised in 2006, is public order and counter-terrorism in relation to all major international events (CEU 2006). The handbook covers key subjects such as exchange of intelligence prior to an event, operational and tactical planning, technical solutions such as fencing and zoning and, finally, how the police can develop an offensive media strategy. The objective of a security operation is defined as follows: 'Maintaining law and order and providing security within the territory of a Member State is a national responsibility and prerogative, which must always be a key consideration of any international co-operation on security at international events' (ibid.: 6). Though securitization studies has hitherto mainly concerned itself with international security, it can reasonably be argued that internal and external security are merging through the linking of issues such as terrorism, immigration, organized crime and protests (see also Buzan et al. 1998: 182). The handbook emphasizes that policing protests is no longer considered to be a national matter alone, but the concern of supra-national entities such as the European Union (cf. della Porta 2008: 225). What is significant about the handbook is that it conveys an image of a present state of law and order, and in order to ensure the maintenance of this it can prove necessary to employ extraordinary measures.[2]

The major part of the EU security handbook is concerned with procedures for 'risk analysis' and 'information sharing', and hence with the problem of how and when to identify a threat. According to the procedure described in the handbook, the appointed Europol (the EU's law enforcement agency that handles criminal intelligence)[3] liaison officers – specially appointed police officers in all member countries who have access to their home country's databases – must provide their counterpart in the organizing state with a 'permanent risk analysis' of individuals and groups expected to travel to an event, and who are deemed to pose 'a potential threat' to the maintenance of public law and order (CEU 2006: 11). This implies that relatively abstract threats are translated into a concern for identifying threatening individuals and groups.

In the wake of the release of the EU handbook, a host of other initiatives were launched that simultaneously internationalized, centralized and professionalized previous practices. In 2003, the United Nations Interregional Crime and Justice Research Institute (UNICRI) established the International Permanent Observatory on Security during Major Events (IPO) in Italy. The aim of the IPO is to provide expert assistance to member states to maintain security at G8 summits, the Olympic Games, Expos and other large events.[4] In 2004, the UNICRI and Europol initiated a programme called EU-SEC, under the auspices of the IPO, in order to coordinate national research on security. This programme was extended as EU-SEC II, aimed at harmonizing research policy on security, and developing efficient 'security tools' through public–private partnerships.

Recognizing that European police forces employ markedly different strategies for handling such events, the EU also established CEPOL (the European Police College) in 2005, to bring together senior police officers and encourage cross-border cooperation, exchange best practices and provide training on issues such as public order and crowd management, counter-terrorism, human trafficking and organized crime.[5] The exchange of experiences between senior staff is, according to my police interlocutors, one of the most fruitful elements of the programme. Prior to the summit in Copenhagen, senior Danish police had accompanied other European police forces at summit events, most notably during the G8 summit in Heiligendamm/Rostock in 2007, where they had gained not only a view of the civil disobedience tactics employed to blockade the summit venue, but also of the black bloc riots in Rostock. Common measures within the EU, in other words, concern both how activists are defined and identified, as well as the means by which they are handled by the police.

Within the framework of the EU, policy makers' attention is not only directed towards the improvement of the ability of the police to maintain law and order during major events, and towards streamlining existing channels of intelligence, but also concerns the capacity to look ahead and anticipate new threats and technical possibilities. To handle new threats, a self-announced Future Group established itself in 2007. The group, comprised of selected ministers of justice and home affairs, defined 'the blurring' of internal/external security concerns, and the opportunities and challenges of the 'digital tsunami' as the major security-related tasks ahead of the EU. The digital tsunami was a metaphor for the almost 'limitless amount of potentially useful information' on EU citizens, which can be made available between member states by way of 'automated data analysis' and common databases (Future Group 2008: 41; see also Bunyan 2008: 27).

The report of the Future Group recommends far-reaching changes in the EU's security policy to handle potential security threats posed by migrants, terrorists, organized criminals and political dissidents. In this light, the recommendations range from assigning more authority to Europol and establishing a common border police – that is, to grant certain agencies the possibility of operating more freely across the EU (cf. Buzan et al. 1998: 182) – to registration of all travel within the EU and the development of a 'holistic' information management system, which can not only hold more data on all citizens,[6] but which is also accessible to police from all member countries (Bunyan 2008: 30–38). Based on increased data collection and retention, the Future Group recommends investing in technologies that can analyse large quantities of real-time digital data (so-called Big Data) to allow 'proactive protection' (Future Group 2008: 41). This should allow the police to detain not only terrorism suspects and illegal immigrants, but also 'violent travelling offenders' in connection with major events. Many of the group's recommendations were integrated into the Stockholm Programme approved during Sweden's EU presidency in 2009.

The Stockholm Programme describes the European Union as an 'area of freedom, security, and justice' (CEU 2009: 3) and hence upholds the idea that law and order must be provided for the citizens by the (European) state. These various policy documents reveal how measures that were previously characterized as extra-ordinary and exceptional have become the rule in the aftermath of the 11 September 2001 terrorist attacks, and in light of increased public and political resistance to migration, as well as worries about the growing expression of dissent during summits on European territory. The new measures of control and surveillance are not only directed against the known offender, but against all citizens who may potentially turn into threats. As Nicolas Rose has rightly pointed out, it is characteristic of this new logic of control that it does not operate by disciplining, moralizing or resocializing anti-social subjects, but aims at mapping out the conduct of the entire population at a greater level of detail in order to act pre-emptively and reduce the probability of undesirable events (Rose 1999: 235–40).

Underlying the EU's security policies is thus a particular, and somewhat peculiar, future-oriented logic. On the one hand, a picture of a present state of perfect law and order is transmitted – an area of freedom and justice – which through careful operational planning, continual risk assessment and identification of enemies must be extended into the future. The keywords here are 'potentiality' and 'pre-emptive measures', or put differently, that in principle, everyone constitutes a potential threat. On the other hand, particular groups are cast as existential threats to European security and democratic culture, particularly terrorists and migrants, but also protesters.

The justification for the use of force against distinct groups and individuals is that this helps safeguard democracy and the governing authority of the international system, as well as ensuring law and order for the safety of the individual citizen (cf. Buzan et al. 1998: 182). In the EU policy documents it is particularly migrants, possible terrorists and protestors who are cast as threats, and in public discourse they are often represented as wilful 'others' who are known to hide out among, and periodically become indistinguishable from, 'normal' law-abiding people. In sum, the various reports convey a picture of relatively vague and intangible threats, which can only be identified through the increased sharing of intelligence, as they may only reveal themselves potentially or occasionally.

It hardly comes as a surprise that this definition of threat is not in keeping with the political views of Left radical activists. Rather, they question the normality of normal politics, that is, the idea of a present state of affairs governed by law and order. 'When injustice is law, resistance is duty', as a popular slogan among activists has it. This slogan and the message it conveys is a direct continuation of the political cosmology described: activists see the world as fundamentally unjust, and summits are considered to be particular moments where the evil forces of capitalism convene and materialize in bodily form. In this light, activists could be said to perform an inverse securitizing move (see Holbraad and Pedersen 2013), whereby heads of state and their armed protectors are defined as existential threats.

'Enemies disagree about what world they inhabit', Latour has said, paraphrasing Viveiros de Castro's theorization of Amerindian perspectivism and enmity among the Araweté (Latour 2004: 453; Viveiros de Castro 1992, 1998, 2004). This implies that they are located within each other's field of vision, but what they see may differ greatly. Exactly how that plays out is the subject of the following, where we shall return to Strasbourg and Copenhagen in order to follow the efforts of the police to identify and handle the alleged threat posed by protesters. I show that threats are individualized, and that the police seek to equate threats with concrete persons. This view comes up against difficulties when the police seek to tie intentions to persons and come to realize the highly transformational nature of the activist.

Distancing Threats, Identifying Enemies

Since 1996, the Danish police have developed a 'mobile-tactical concept of operation' (*mobiltaktisk indsatskoncept*) for handling large demonstrations and other forms of civil unrest. The concept is based on highly flexible and mobile police units, and the use of vehicles for tactical purposes, for example as barriers or shields for police officers on foot, for crowd diversion, to pressure protesters or produce an 'optical lead' to guide processions of demonstrators in a desired direction. Moreover, the vehicles can be used either for 'pending' patrolling, where the police simply keep in the background, or in a 'show of force', where headlights and sirens are employed to produce a forceful and overwhelming presence (Vittrup 2002: 116–17, 141–42).[7]

This new tactical concept, which was developed as a response to almost symmetrical confrontations during the 1980s and early 1990s, described in the Introduction, shows that the Danish police force had to learn a whole new set of operational techniques for crowd management, which was subsequently employed and refined over the years. Morten Larsen, who headed the police operation during the Copenhagen Climate Summit, has participated in the development of this tactical concept, as well as in the running of major security operations in Denmark over almost a decade. After the 2007 decision to hold the Climate Summit in Copenhagen, he visited Seville and Rostock among other cities to learn from the experiences of other police forces. The use of armoured vehicles (*sikrede indsatsvogne*) and plain-clothes arrest groups – used to point out and arrest so-called 'aggressive and leading elements' – had been copied directly from Holland early on, but after his travels Larsen adapted an organizational model used by Spanish police in Seville to the task in Copenhagen. During the preparations, a wealth of contacts with police authorities in other countries were drawn on for helicopter pilots, police-dog handlers, additional vehicles and other equipment. EU initiatives proved useful on the practical plane. The Danish police force is smaller than those of other European states, but it prides itself on the fact that Denmark needed less than a third of number of officers employed by France and Germany during the NATO summits in Strasbourg and Baden-Baden to keep Copenhagen safe during the Climate Summit in 2009.[8] To achieve this, Danish police officers had all received event-focused training, which involved role-playing of riots and confrontations, and enabled them to perform different functions. As a consequence, they could be deployed flexibly throughout the city.

In Strasbourg, the police opted for a tactic of spatial control that can be best described as an attempt at distancing threats. In light of the experience of previous summits – Genoa in 2001 and Heiligendamm in 2007 – where enormous fences around the red zones of the summit venue became sites of confrontations, the police authorities in Strasbourg decided to take advantage of the topography of the city, in particular the fact that the inner city is only accessible by crossing a limited number of bridges, to shut the historic city centre off from protesters. The day before the summit, streets were empty, shops were closed, all public transportation was cancelled and special summit passes were issued to local inhabitants allowing them to move to and from their homes. Everybody moving in the street had to undergo repeated identity and bag checks by the approximately 10,000 officers deployed in the streets. As part of this plan of obtaining spatial control by creating distance, the protest camp, which I described in Chapter 3, was located 6 kilometres south of the city centre. Moreover, the Schengen agreement was temporarily suspended, thereby hindering approximately 10,000 protestors from entering France, who then concentrated at the border, the result of which will be described in Chapter 5. The operational tactic turned the inner city into a 'zone of exception' controlled by the police, while the areas around the cordon, which were not so heavily policed, turned into veritable war zones partially controlled by activists.

By contrast, the tactical concept employed in Copenhagen was built around the flexible deployment of police forces, but also the avoidance of a red zone. Instead, the focus was on producing a psychological impact. According to Larsen, the key was to be unpredictable and generate insecurity among 'the opponents', and it then became possible to gain the initiative and define the time and place of police intervention. This implies, among other things, a readiness to move when the opponent is weak or resting (see Vittrup 2002: 74–75, 331–32).[9] This was complemented with the legal right to undertake searches and the preventive arrest of 'leading elements' and other persons who the police considered likely to pose a 'potential threat' to public order.

In order to understand how the Danish police identify and relate to their opponents, I seek below to clarify their two-pronged approach: the police seek to make themselves visible and enter into dialogue with activists, while simultaneously striving to make activists unsure of the police's presence and intentions.

During the Climate Summit, the Danish police did not succeed in establishing a continual dialogue with Left radical activists as they had done at the EU summit in Copenhagen in 2002. At that time, the Danish EU presidency had established an 'anti-violence secretariat', staffed with people who were sympathetic to the activist cause and able to establish and mediate in a dialogue between the parties. In Larsen's view, the police had at the time managed to 'embrace them with love', which involved remembering people's names and referring to them as 'intelligent young people', as well as crafting agreements that were roughly respected by both sides. At the time, the police also seemed able, or willing, to distinguish between acts of civil disobedience and sheer violence.

However, Left radical activists had become more observant and wary when the police tried to repeat this employment of 'soft power' (Fernandez 2008) in 2009, and the historical situation too was somewhat different. In 2002, most activists were eager to de-escalate conflict in the streets, and seek out new forms of action to avoid a repetition of Göteborg and Genoa in 2001. In 2009, the implacability was noticeable on both sides after the conflict over Ungdomshuset. Danish activists were aware and confident of their strength in the street, and experienced at enduring a lot of tear gas. On the police side, the chief of operations contended that he was not willing to negotiate with activists about what could and could not be allowed. Though an attempt was made to establish a forum for dialogue between the police and climate activists, the activists judged this to be a purely pro forma initiative, which would have little real impact on the police's conduct during the protests.

A new initiative of the police at the time of the summit was the so-called 'dialogue police', who flanked the demonstrations; besides this, the police depended on surveillance and searches to uncover activists' intentions and plans. In the week prior to the summit, known activists were stopped and questioned in the street, and several activists reported receiving 'threatening visits to their homes'. Moreover, the police raided the largest convergence centres (meeting hubs) and sleeping places.[10] People were pulled out of their sleeping bags at night, handcuffed and placed in so-called *futtog* (literally a childish word for train, but in police jargon the word is used when people are handcuffed and seated in line). Internationally, the tactic of raiding convergence centres and sleeping places, for example to confiscate puppets and banners, is frequently employed, such as in Prague, Genoa, Göteborg and Gleneagles (see also Fernandez 2008; Graeber 2009; Juris 2008). In a Danish context, the searches were later declared to have been illegal, though the police argued in the media that they had found potential weapons such as paint, fluorescent tubes and 'warrior bikes'.

Unlike the NATO summit in Strasbourg, where the entire inner city was declared a red zone and sealed off to protesters, in principle the police let everybody move around Copenhagen freely, while only the summit venue at the Bella Centre on the outskirts of the city was off limits to protesters. In Strasbourg, the police performed bag and body searches on everybody entering or moving through the inner city (the intensity of these varied, however, according to the extent to which a person conformed to a stereotypical image of the radical activist). The Danish police were visibly present throughout the city via sector patrols. According to my police interlocutors, the logic behind these sector patrols was to make the police presence more visible, while also keeping an eye out for irregularities. As one junior police officer explained:

> To do sector patrolling is really fun and exciting. Something happens. When you drive a sector patrol you have to keep an eye out for what happens. Is somebody gathering some place? Is there a huge pile of cobblestones somewhere, ready to make an ambush on ... We look for things that diverge from the normal picture, like things that are not normal, something lying different from what it used to, or people, right? You know the different types around town, so if there is a kind of person where they don't tend to be, small things.

These remarks once again show that the police perceive law and order as the normal state of affairs, with reference to which they must identify deviations. Hence, when doing sector patrols, police officers seek to interpret and abduct agency from signs (cf. Gell 1998) encountered in public space.

The police base their actions on a belief that people's intentions should always be doubted, and sometimes on internal agreement on who to pin down as troublemakers – even before an actual crime is committed. The police differentiate between so-called 'peaceful demonstrators', who are seen as attending a demonstration to express their point of view, and so-called troublemakers (a category often used interchangeably with the black bloc and previous offenders), who are 'just there to make trouble'. According to the junior officer I interviewed, it is not possible to talk to the black bloc as their only motive is to make trouble and seek confrontation with the police. In response to the question whether he could identify a meaning or a reason behind their acts, he contended that 'there is nothing deeper in that' (i.e. in what they do). Troublemakers are, from this perspective, devoid of rationale and in need of correction. At the same time, however, they are characterized as wilful choosers of their acts or, in other words, individuals who have intentions about where and when to make trouble, which must be deciphered.

Troublemakers can be either known or unknown to the police, but the police can spot potential offenders by their clothing (an unspecified kind of 'uniform') or the way they walk. Technically, the police work with some 'archetypes' that, according to Morten Larsen, give police officers 'a good picture' of what they are looking for. In practice, however, acting upon these archetypes and trying to take pre-emptive action was not so easy in light of the known fact that black bloc activists may not always appear as the black bloc: they can blend in with the crowd, or change their clothes after an action, which would render troublemakers indiscernible from peaceful protesters. To handle the paradox between their perception of a certain section of protesters as troublemakers who can be recognized by way of their bodily characteristics and signs in the urban landscape, and the knowledge that the same troublemakers may change form, the police had to resort to ongoing surveillance, patrols and searches.

When not undertaking sector patrolling, a large group of police officers worked as so-called dialogue police 'with a soft hat and a yellow waistcoat', as the junior officer phrased it, worn on top of a riot uniform. According to Larsen, the idea was 'to get out of the cars and get at eye level' with the demonstrators. This was perceived as one way to prevent violence, because it was thought that protesters would find it more difficult to attack someone who had walked next to them, and on the other hand it was a measure that would allow the police to spot individual troublemakers *in media res*. An officer explained his experience of the dialogue initiative in this way:

> It had to be confidence-building that we were there, but on the other hand you could also feel that some found it very provocative. We tried to explain that, like, it could be to protect them from a counter-demonstration or to spot single troublemakers or elements of [the] black bloc who could throw stones or some of their homemade bombs, and all that. So we were there, really, to make sure that they could continue their demonstration … It was also connected with many good experiences, because many of those … of the protestors were really, really nice to talk to, and they were very interested – they were not really used to the police being someone who speaks.

The police officer had thus gained a positive impression of the large majority of demonstrators, and expressed his support for citizens' legal right to demonstrate. To the police, the dialogue initiative was, in other words, a way to separate the sheep from the goats along the way, while also seeking to avoid a confrontation with demonstrators. The dialogue aimed at de-escalating impending conflicts, while also solving the difficulty the police had in actually identifying – spotting – those perceived as irreconcilable troublemakers.

The same police officer explained that it is sometimes necessary to 'change roles' along the way. If the dialogue police became aware of an approaching or already committed offence, they could either call on other officers to handle the problem, or they could 'put on a different hat', as he phrased it. This particular officer had, for example, judged this role change to be necessary at the 16 December Reclaim Power action briefly described in the Introduction; that is, a need to replace the soft police cap with the hard riot helmet. This happened when activists from the so-called bike bloc dropped inflatable mattresses into a small stream surrounding the Bella Centre and paddled into the summit area while fellow activists blocked the way of the police with their homemade warrior bikes. The police officer had first tried to talk to them, but when the activists refused to draw back, the police officer said 'they [the police] had to put on a different hat' and 'do it our way'. On their side, activists are alert to this role switching. It showed that the police were as inconstant or mutable to the protesters, as the protesters were to the police.[11]

The police also used plain-clothes officers.[12] This can be perceived as another way of switching roles, which plays on the same logic of visibility/invisibility that, according to the police, characterizes the black bloc. Larsen explains:

> It is pure psychology that we use them [plain–clothes officers]. They drive in police cars, but when they get out you cannot recognize them anymore. The participants in a demonstration always focus on the uniformed [police] because they can see them. Sometimes, if there is a special atmosphere, then we want to create extra insecurity among the participants. We do that by picking them up. It has a fantastic psychological effect ... But we got a bit scared of using them too close to the demonstrations during the EU presidency, because it created really bad press.

Plain-clothes police are used in crowds, and they also make arrests both before and after an action because of the insecurity it generates. While the police sometimes appear as a person with a soft hat and someone 'who speaks', as the officer put it, at other times they are the ones who blend in and become indiscernible from the crowd. Yet, the police force is also concerned about its own image in public, which sometimes leads to a more cautious use of plain-clothes police. Media reactions to police measures are used to take bearings, as had happened, for example, in the context of the EU summit in Copenhagen in 2002, where police officers acted as agents provocateurs.[13] Plain-clothes police are, in other words, a powerful tool in operational tactics that can best be described as the creation of security through insecurity.

In sum, in spite of increased cross-border cooperation around security for major events, the various national police forces of the EU still have different operational tactics for handling demonstrators and Left radical activists. The Danish police have developed a relatively sophisticated operational concept that rests on performative unpredictability, role changes and disguises in the hope of spotting and catching equally unpredictable and evasive troublemakers who are also known to change their bodily appearance. It is against this background that I now return to the activists to consider their view of the police, and the surprising symmetry between how they see and relate to each other.

We Are Humans, What Are You?

There are numerous stories in circulation among activists about police infiltration, surveillance and repression. The stories convey a picture of the police as unaccountable, cunning turncoats who at one moment act friendly, only to arrest you the next. Stories about particular incidents serve to socialize and educate fellow activists about the nature of the police (see also Christensen 2009), and how to deal not only with surveillance and infiltration, but also with their unpredictability. Here, I briefly describe three situations, which illustrate how activists speculate not only about the police's intentions and plans, but also about their status as human beings, as points of departure for the more concrete security measures that activists employ, which are aimed at handling unpredictable 'attacks'.

In the week ahead of the Climate Summit in Copenhagen, activists were busy preparing the sleeping arrangements for international activists. In the south harbour, at a place named Teglholmen, a group of activists had rented some closed-down factory buildings, which could host several thousand people. To prepare the buildings, activists had to not only clean them and put in kitchen and toilet facilities, but also meet the requirements of the fire department, which involved building several new fire exits. The activists worked hard and were in frequent contact with both the fire and police authorities, but nevertheless they increasingly reported being stopped and searched by police when cycling to and from the area. More worryingly to those involved, activists were also followed by slowly driven cars, which produced fears about being out alone, particularly at night. The hard work finally resulted in the fire department's approval of the buildings as suitable sleeping facilities. Yet, a few days before activists from abroad were to arrive, the police raided the place at night. Activists were woken up and handcuffed, while the police searched the premises. When asked about the reason, the police argued that this was to check if the directions of the fire department had been followed.

The fact that this searching was later ruled unlawful is not the issue here; what is, is the effect it produced among activists: within a few hours the news was out, and activists spent the next day speculating about the police's intentions, trying to make some sense of what had occurred. Was it mere coincidence or a mistake, as some activists seemed to believe? One activist argued forcefully that he trusted his police contact, who might not have been aware that the fire department had approved the changes made at the sleeping place. Some saw it simply as harassment and shrugged it off, while others argued that the police had actually been there to put up microphones and surveillance cameras before the arrival of Climate Summit protestors.

A second situation took place in the camp in Strasbourg one Thursday morning. I was sitting on the grass outside the reception tent with my Danish research assistant, going through our fieldnotes. Jos, a Dutch activist, came running to us, visibly excited. He quickly explained to us that he had heard that the police had changed the programme of the official summit, so that the events that were to take place the following day (Friday) had been moved from Baden-Baden in Germany to Strasbourg, while the official meeting scheduled for Saturday in Strasbourg had been moved to Baden-Baden. 'We have been tricked by this change of plan', he said, 'and our protests planned for Saturday will be in vain'. On being questioned about the certainty of this information, he explained that some journalists had confirmed it. He quickly ran on only to return half an hour later to say it was just another rumour.

The two situations drive home the point that police tactics have an effect not only by causing insecurity and labelling activists as potential troublemakers, but also in generating an image among activists of the police as unpredictable turncoats. In Chapter 3, I described how the action trainer in the camp in Strasbourg repeatedly reminded participants of the humanity of the police, while also stressing the importance of keeping cool when around them so that they do not react unexpectedly or resort to violence in order to handle the situation. In the context of mass direct actions, activists often depict the police this way, namely as someone who turns to violence if somehow provoked or scared. It is said to be advisable not to look them in the eye, but to talk to them in a calm and firm voice. The view of the police as unpredictable and dangerous is not restricted to the preparatory phase, but also holds for actions, as the next situation illustrates.

At the Reclaim Power action at the Bella Centre in Copenhagen, activists pushed against the police line to get over the fence around the summit area (described in the Introduction). After the first three pushes there was a brief pause. One activist took advantage of the pause to find a gap in the police line and climbed onto the rooftop of a police van that served as barricade in front of the fence. He turned towards the crowd and gestured for people to follow him. From behind him, a police officer in riot gear approached with his baton drawn and hit the activist over the head and shoulders, and, before pushing him back down into the crowd, his face was pepper-sprayed. Among the several thousand people gathered below a measured chant emerged, 'We are humans, what are you? We are humans, what are you?' that was repeated for several minutes. After the action, a female activist told me of her encounter with the police:

> At the fence when we pushed against the police line, I happened to stand close by a very young cop. He was really scared and extremely aggressive. He stood there holding his pepper spray at arm's length, and just screamed at us. I was really worried that he could pull the others along. I tried to talk to him, to call him back, but he was completely off.

As already mentioned, stories like the one above often serve to educate fellow activists about how to handle the police. But the last situation is also rather puzzling: What kind of beings are the police depicted as?

The stories do not only convey a picture of an unaccountable police who may resort to either trickery or violence to get the upper hand in a situation, but activists also often seriously doubt their humanity. In the context of the conflict over Ungdomshuset, I had talked to Katrine (see Chapter 2) about the legitimacy of different means of protest in the street, and how the police become cast as enemies. She said:

> Of course nobody believes that a bomb is okay. The boundaries [of what is acceptable] are read between the lines: not people, but materials [property], and pansere [police in riot uniform] who – at least to some people – are not really humans, at least not in this context. They [the police] are definitely an army who is the enemy, right?

Among activists, the police have many names. In English they are called pigs; a cop is someone who catches, snatches or takes hold of something.[14] In Danish, a police officer is called a *panser*, the term also used by Katrine, which refers to the armoured, impenetrable clothing of the police. So, whereas the police-as-pig is often depicted as an animal in a human (uni)form, the word *panser*, in contrast, refers to humans with a particular protective surface or clothing, which makes them appear non-human.

While the police's humanity is doubted, and dismissed in some contexts or situations, in which they are instead cast as enemies, the situation is starkly different from that which, according to older Danish activists, existed between police and squatters in Copenhagen in the 1980s. At that time, squatters and the police always considered each other as enemies who would beat the other party up when encountering the other unaccompanied in the street. Today, this view of the police has changed somewhat, and many activists do not mind calling up the police if they have been robbed or are victims of a burglary, and harming single persons, and also police officers, is largely unacceptable. The enmity is far more situational and performative, tied to particular events, which means that police move in and out of the enemy category.

What the various names and the chant point to is that both parties see the other as transformational beings who may assume different bodily forms and clothing. The body surfaces of both the police and activists – the use of hats and waistcoats or of black clothes – are read carefully to figure out who or what someone is, and what their intentions might be. In addition to this transformability of the police, they are known by activists to be co-present – for example through surveillance technology and as undercover agents – even when not visibly or physically there (an example of the police's distributed agency). To activists, the police are, in other words, a certain kind of evasive enemy that does not necessarily retain its form. The police look at activists in a similar vein, but still expect to be able to identify an individual intentional agent below the shape-shifting. In the face of this, activists have developed their own security measures.

All That Is Solid Melts into Air

Security culture is the term that activists use about protective measures to counter police surveillance and infiltration. In Chapter 3 I described how the security culture involves what may be discussed, where and with whom (Robinson 2008: 232), and how activists find ways to plan actions without intentions being attributable to single persons. What I wish to do here is describe what activist security measures are like when the enemy is a transformational being. In the following we turn to some concrete examples involving both the 'art of hiding' in a given environment (Povinelli 2011: 30) and mimicry, where imitation becomes a means of disguise. This often takes place even though activists have nothing incriminating to hide.

In the anti-NATO camp/village in Strasbourg, activists developed a highly spatial approach to security, thereby mimicking the police. Even while the camp was under construction, voluntary activists would patrol the perimeter of the village, even though it was only an open field, on the lookout for police and fascists, who were considered the two most likely attackers. This took place under the guidance of the Mohawk-man who, at the preparatory meeting, had been preoccupied with the identification of spies. As the summit drew closer and more people arrived, huge straw balls were placed on the four access roads to the camp. These served as permanent lookout points, which could also be set on fire if an enemy should approach. Bottles and stones were gathered in heaps in order to defend the camp. In addition to this, two cars patrolled the adjoining neighbourhood, and both the control posts and the patrolling cars were in walkie-talkie contact with the base camp inside the village from where the entire camp could be roused by a megaphone connected to a loudspeaker.

These spatial security measures could only protect the village from threats from the outside. To counter the activities of possible undercover agents within the camp, activists were very cautious about giving out personal information, and largely unwilling to reveal anything specific about their background, motivation and plans. Anthropological inquiries about things that were not considered practical matters were politely declined. Even bragging was seldom a source of information, and mistrust and paranoia were widespread. To counter threats from the inside – that is, police infiltration or police agents within their own ranks – activists distanced themselves from one another. Some activists were aware that this in itself threatened to turn the milieu in on itself, making it impenetrable to their own people (cf. Robinson 2008).[15] Katrine spoke at one point of the effects of paranoia on the activist milieu in Copenhagen:

> A paranoia trip is often completely justifiable; to keep [one's] cards close to one's chest. But it is also in conflict with what we are aiming at … [After the eviction of people from Ungdomshuset] things were closed, and there will be internal strife to open things up again. Some people have got into the habit of keeping their cards close to their chest and being paranoid. It is completely justifiable, but it is also a dangerous habit to acquire. It is dangerous if it becomes normal in a milieu because then it [the milieu] will die.

Recalling my prior analysis concerning dead time, which was associated with the apathy arising from the experience of being alone, the paranoia that Katrine is talking about – and which was very real in the camp in Strasbourg – has the effect of singling people out, and distancing them from one another, and minimizing the success of direct actions (Fernandez 2008: 112). Paranoia is dangerous, because it becomes impossible to do things together, and it is quite telling that this is associated with the death of the activist milieu.

In Copenhagen, activists' sleeping places, convergence centres and meeting places were distributed throughout the city, though they were mainly concentrated in Nørrebro and Christiania. This obviously impeded a spatial approach to security similar to the one employed in Strasbourg. Instead, activists developed an emergency communication system to alert each other to dangers from the police. Although the system was first envisioned as being organized around a computer hub, to avoid the possibility that someone using a phone could be accused of inciting violence, this had to be given up due to time constraints. A separate phone system connecting sleeping places, convergence centres, information points, legal aid centres and, not least, the media centre, was set up. While the police were quite obviously considered an enemy that might attack at any given moment, it was agreed that they were not to be considered a threat that activists could and should react to at all times by calling an emergency. A raid on accommodation spaces, the arrest or injuring of coordinators, targeted arrests (of spokespersons, for example) or the setting up of stop-and-search points at new spots in the city were considered worthy of the 'emergency' label.

These issues were discussed at a meeting where people removed the batteries from their phones to avoid interception, and participants impressed each other with the need to avoid unnecessary panic and rumour mongering. As one participant phrased it, there is not much reason to 'cry wolf' if nothing can be done about it. It was agreed that the system should only be used when many people needed to know something at the same time, and a cautionary message was issued to only distribute information and not to call for action as the insecurity of the system could have legal consequences for those involved.

Prior to the Climate Summit, the police's whereabouts and interventions were not issues that activists were concerned about all the time. It was not considered a top priority until the police began searching sleeping places and arresting those they suspected of being 'leading elements'. The police's approach seemed arbitrary and odd, reflecting the error of expecting activists to be organized in a hierarchy similar to that of their own organization. And while obviously frightening to the targeted people, it was not expected to influence the overall development of protests, which depended on the activities of affinity groups. So even though arrests did not significantly influence the protests, they had the effect of turning the police into an enemy. Moreover, the emergency system in itself contributed to constituting the police as a particular kind of hidden, invisible enemy that activists should keep an eye out for because they could suddenly appear and become visible, tangible threats.

The attentive reader has probably already come to understand the curious symmetry at play here. What I have sought to convey is the idea that activists and the police not only securitize each other, but that they equally see each other as largely unpredictable and evasive beings whose intentions, moreover, are hard to establish. Their bodily transformability is quite literally tied to the change of clothing and bodily appearance. This transformability is linked with the expectation that the 'other' might be present without being visible, and with an uncertainty about when the other will make their (performative) appearance. Hence, the temporary enmity between activists and the police depends upon both the unpredictability and the constant shape-shifting of the parties.

In his work on enmity among the Araweté in the Brazilian Amazon, Viveiros de Castro draws an analogy between eating and enmity. Put simply, this analogy implies that a person who eats an enemy becomes an enemy. It is not a matter of assimilating the enemy's power, but literally of incorporating the other. Thereby the eater of human flesh becomes the enemy (Viveiros de Castro 1992: 286, 303) and comes to take up their bodily point of view. Obviously, neither activists nor the police are cannibals, or eat each other in any straightforward sense, but Amazonian ideas of enmity are good to think with because they elucidate the relational and bodily side of the matter. Analogous to the particular way in which vegan activists absorb values and transform their bodies through eating, security practices also entail bodily transformability (in various ways of appearing and disappearing) and this has real implications for how others become enemies. Moreover, the police infiltration of activist planning meetings does not only result in the minimization of success (Fernandez 2008: 112), but it also pushes activists to constant invention and reinvention of forms of action.

I will illustrate this point with a historical example. The Italian Tute Bianche activists adopted the metaphor of the spectre as self-representation in the late 1990s. Tute Bianche means 'white overalls', and the name was born as an ironic reference to the 'ghosts' of urban conflicts in Italy. The mayor of the city publicly announced, in the context of the eviction of a squatted social centre in Milan, 'From now on squatters will be no more than ghosts wandering about in the city!' (Bui 2001: 5). In reply, activists from the Ya Basta network,[16] influenced by the Italian autonomist movement (Hardt and Negri 2000, 2004; Juris 2008), started wearing chemical-proof white jumpsuits, elaborate forms of padding, foam armour and helmets at demonstrations and direct actions. Tute Bianche described themselves as 'a ghost army' bent on developing a new language of direct action (Bui 2001). When in the street, the elaborate white clothing marked a visibly distinct style compared to black blocs. By way of their padded bodies, activists entered into a spectacularly confrontational yet non-violent style of action when clashing with the police. In so doing, they epitomized the activist dictum referred to earlier, that 'the body is the medium' for manifesting political dissent. To activists, this does not just mean that the body makes an otherwise invisible conflict or relation of enmity appear (cf. Strathern 1988: 277–78), but also that the body can become a figuration of 'a different world'.

The Tute Bianche outfit was influential among Left radicals activists due to its deliberate experimentation with modes of protest and styles of confrontation with the police. This ghost army continuously re-emerged during international summits in Europe to engage in 'non-violent rioting', as they called it, and the (symbolic) transgression of red zones around summit areas under intense media coverage. The tactics of the Tute Bianche reached their climax during the anti-G8 meeting in Genoa, Italy, in July 2001. Ironically enough, the participants decided to take off their white overalls just before the summit, because the clothing had become 'an identitary feature' (sic), that was both an essential characteristic and a way to identify them, giving them an undesirable position as a vanguard within the movement and thus exposing them to police repression (Bui 2001; Juris 2005, 2008). Shortly after the Genoa summit, the Tute Bianche dissolved itself, but re-emerged as the Disobedienti, now placing more emphasis on engagement in local autonomist struggles around social centres and on broadening disobedience to 'all aspects of life'. The forms of protest first launched by the Tute Bianche were carried on and transformed by other groups of activists such as Globale Rødder in Denmark, Globalisering Underifrån in Sweden, the Wombles in the UK and Ya Basta in New York (see also Graeber 2009). The Tute Bianche did, in other words, emerge as a visible ghost, but returned to the shadows when security measures, policing of the movement and legal persecution became too intense.

Like the Tute Bianche, many Left radical activists, whether or not engaged in the radical strain of the alterglobalization movement, often conceal their views and intentions. Being visible is seen as inviting police repression. Hence, contrary to Marx and Engels's evocation of the spectre in *The Communist Manifesto*, which is used to argue that communists should 'exorcise' their own force and move to the visible realm by way of publishing their views (Marx and Engels 2002: 218), Left radical activists seek to remain indiscernible and carve out camouflaged spaces of their own, such as Ungdomshuset or Utkanten in Malmö.[17] The adoption by activists of what we might call mimetic disguise is hence not completely independent of the way that the police are seen to disguise their intentions and convey an impression of lacking a fixed form. This mimetic disguise, camouflaging oneself by taking on a form similar to the opponent, relies on something like a hall of mirrors between the activists and the police. In my view, therefore, there is no reason not to take seriously the metaphor of the spectre as evoked by the Tute Bianche.

In sum, there is a remarkable symmetry between the way activists and the police see and relate to each other despite the fact that they have different ideas about what constitutes a secure world and the temporal outlook on its realization (Krøijer 2013). The symmetry does not entail that the security culture of activists could or should be perceived as a direct consequence of or an adaptation to the securitizing acts performed by the police and other authorities, such as the European Union. Sociologists concerned with repertoires of action argue that the relationship between activists and the police 'follows a reciprocal process of innovation and adaptation, with each side responding to the other' (Tilly, cited in della Porta 2008: 222) – equipment is upgraded, training specialized and new tactics developed. Yet, there seems to be more at stake here than mutual influence and adaptation. Activists and the police securitize each other, while also employing some of the same categories to describe the 'other': unpredictable opponents, threats and wilful enemies. Whereas activists and police largely see the world and the 'other' in the same way (that is, through the same cultural categories, we might say), *what* they see is different, to paraphrase Viveiros de Castro (2004: 471).

The EU securitization of summit events has cast protesters as threats to democracy and the authority of the international system, as well as to public law and order. But enemies materialize only potentially and occasionally. To counter the threat posed by protesters, the police count on prediction (in the form of surveillance and risk analysis) and proactive protection (in the form of red zones and fences, sector patrols and plain-clothes officers, searches and pre-emptive arrests). All this notwithstanding, the police have difficulty identifying the threat particularly because they try to tie intentions to individual human beings. The police come to perceive activists as transformational beings who change their clothing, evaporate into a crowd or remain camouflaged for long periods of time. Agency is abducted from small and material signs in the urban landscape, from activists' bodily attributes, clothing and movements. And their attempts are often in vain.

Activists are equally attentive towards the police's gestures. They see the police as dangerous beings because of their bodily metamorphosis, that is, their ability to put on different hats, change roles and work in disguise, and to be present when they are not really there. Activists do not only believe that the police can become non-human entities, become devoid of compassion, but also that they can be 'called back', that is, be made to return from this state of being. The conclusion that can be reached from this is that even in a presumably modern European context enemies do not necessarily retain their form.

If we recognize enemies as both transformational and relational beings, which means that on the one hand the enemy does not necessarily retain its form, and on the other we presume that human relations are always also internal relationships (Wagner 1991: 159), self and other are tied together in a more complex relationship than that suggested by Schmitt's simple antagonism between friend and enemy, which forms the basis of the Copenhagen School's 'securitization theory' in international relations (Buzan et al. 1998; Wæver 1995). My ethnography has illuminated how enmity is a social relation, but one that has a special temporality to it. In the present context, enmity is mainly concentrated around particular events, after which relations of enmity tend to abate. How this enemy-becoming plays out during bodily confrontations will be discussed in the next chapter.

Acknowledgements

An earlier version of this chapter was published in M. Holbraad and M.A. Pederson (eds), *Times of Security: Ethnographies of Fear, Protest and the Future* (Routledge, 2013).

Notes

1. Whereas della Porta and Reiter (1999) use the concept 'repression of protest', Fernandez talks of the 'social control of dissent' (Fernandez 2008: 9) in order to include both overt tactics of physical repression, detainment and so on and more soft forms of control, such as legal regulation, negotiation with protestors and forms of self-monitoring (ibid.: 8–19).
2. One such extraordinary measure in the context of summit protests is the suspension of the Schengen agreement in order to prevent certain protesters from moving freely within the EU; others are the use of preventive arrests and, more rarely, the use of undercover agents who infiltrate the movement, all of which I have observed first hand (on these issues, see 'Fine Line between Undercover Observer and Agent Provocateur', *Guardian*, 10 January 2011; 'Undercover Police: Officer A Named as Lynn Watson', *Guardian*, 16 January 2011; 'Undercover Police: Officer B Identified as Mark Jacobs', *Guardian*, 19 January 2011).
3. Europol's aim is to improve cooperation between EU member states. The establishment of Europol was agreed in the Treaty on European Union of 7 February 1992. See the Europol website: www.europol.europa.eu/. Last accessed 30 December 2014.
4. See the UNICRI and IPO website: www.lab.unicri.it/ipo.html. Last accessed 15.04.2011.
5. See the CEPOL website: www.cepol.europa.eu/. Last accessed 30 December 2014.
6. The existing legislation concerns the data retention from the internet and telecommunications, as well as the collection of biometric data (fingerprints) when citizens apply for an EU passport (Bunyan 2008: 4). In relation to the Preum Treaty (or Preum Convention) on cross-border cooperation, it was decided that a common information system could file DNA, fingerprints, vehicle registration and identity card numbers on all EU citizens. The Future Group mentions an additional list of forty-nine sets of relevant information (Future Group 2008: 44).
7. The idea behind a show of force, which is described by Vittrup as a last resort, is that 'the demonstration of strength must be so overwhelming that no potential troublemaker has the ability or will to turn against the police' (Vittrup 2002: 116–17).
8. The NATO summit in Baden-Baden and Strasbourg on 3–4 April 2009 represented an exception to the rule established in 2001 of locating summits in inaccessible places. Not only did the NATO summit take place in two cities, but it also required the transfer of delegates from one city to another.
9. The street battles and the police tactics in the days following the eviction of Ungdomshuset in Copenhagen are examples of the police's employment of this kind of guerrilla tactics. Activists gained the advantage in the street by operating in small flexible groups, while the police, for its part, moved while activists slept; for example, the eviction of protesters from Ungdomshuset and most house searches were carried out in the early hours of the morning.

10. The searches without a warrant took places at Teglholmen, Bolschefabrikken and Ragnhildsgade, the first allegedly to check if the fire regulations were observed and the latter two to search for weapons.
11. For this reason, the dialogue police in Sweden are not supposed to switch roles, whereas Danish dialogue police do not have such restrictions.
12. The use of plain-clothes police officers during protests has been reported in a range of other countries (see Juris 2008; Graeber 2009). Among activists they are known to act as agents provocateurs who incite violence by leading the way, for example by being the first to throw stones or bottles at uniformed police officers and/or inciting others to do so. For this reason, and because they are used to identify people for arrest, activists are always on the lookout for plain-clothes officers, who are then asked to leave a demonstration.
13. During a demonstration organized by the Anarchist Federation on 14 December 2002 (during the EU summit in Copenhagen), a handful of Danish police officers were masked and dressed up as protesters, either to incite violence or as part of an attempted mass arrest of protesters for violating the prohibition on wearing masks. The chief police inspector at the time argued that these particular officers had 'acted on their own behalf'. Following this, the officers were convicted in court for violating the law on masking ('Politiet ophævede forbud og anholdt otte maskerede', *Politiken*, 29 March 2004; 'Anarkister skulle anholdes', *Modkraft*, 1 April, 2004; 'Maskeringsforbud underkendt', *Modkraft*, 27 April 2005).
14. *Oxford Advanced Learner's Dictionary* (1995: s.v.).
15. Christine M. Robinson (2008) is one of the few people to have described anarchist security culture, with an empirical focus on a community of anarchists in the US. She describes security measures as a form of resistance; she also sees such measures as a form of 'social glue' that ties the community together, thereby mitigating possible individuating effects that the terrorist label might produce (ibid.: 247). Fernandez (2008: 114), on the other hand, argues that security culture heightens paranoia, thereby threatening to rip communities apart. My findings show that while security procedures and paranoia might strengthen the sense of solidarity and togetherness in smaller groups of activists, who know each other well, they generally contribute to disarticulate people.
16. Ya Basta was originally formed as a solidarity movement with the Zapatista rebellion in Mexico after the first *Encuentro* in Chiapas in 1996. Many Ya Basta activists joined Tute Bianche and transferred some of the ideas encountered among the Zapatista to their struggle for global justice.
17. By remaining in a state of camouflage, Left radical activists hence distinguish themselves from classical Marxists. The Marxists' attempt at bringing the spectre to permanent life, and laying down an image of a utopian society, is perceived by Left radical activists not only as dangerous, but also as totalitarian (cf. Derrida 1994: 30).

A Street Dance in Hyskenstræde

Light rain and darkness. I meet with a couple of activist friends a little after midnight to join an illegal dance in a rainy street in the inner city of Copenhagen. The location has been kept secret, but at 11 PM we receive a text message announcing the place: Hyskenstræde, a narrow side street off Strøget, the largest pedestrian shopping street in Northern Europe. We walk towards the street, and on the way we debate the probability of many people attending, and discuss possible escape routes for when the police show up.

The dance, or Reclaim the Street party as it is called in activist jargon, is part of Undoing the City, a 'festival *on* the city' organized by Left radical activists. For more than two years, activists have been locked into the fight for Ungdomshuset, and a group of activists decided to 'broaden the scope of the conflict' to encompass a more generalized concern about the increasing control and gentrification of urban public space. The network consists of articulate students, experienced activists and artists who wish to combine the analysis of urban development, such as gentrification and urban segregation, with activist interventions for reconquering and redoing (common) space. On the festival flyer the dance is presented as 'an overthrowing ass-shaking [party] to the smell of spray-canny-untidiness in the market place. Cheap bars – mad DJs – open street stylee!'

As a consequence, we have an idea about what to expect. While putting my phone number on a list earlier the same day, Magnus had explained in a voice filled with nervous anticipation that the idea is to 'take back the street' for a couple of hours until the police, at some point, ends the party and restores order. The young activist adds that it is up to people to improvise, but that there will definitely be graffiti and music and disturbances of the usual inner city tidiness.

On the corner of Strøget and Hyskenstræde a truck blocks the road. Large banners are stretched across the street, which lies in darkness as activists have short-circuited the street lighting with bicycle chains. The street is crowded and we dive into the mass. 'The cops are not in sight', my companion says before we join the dancing close to the truck. The music is loud and we are embraced for a long while by the collective joyfulness. Then we set out to find familiar faces and a drink, while most other people at this end of the street are still absorbed by the dancing. The light cannon sends flashing lights along the street, but the glimmering light from the burning oil barrels makes it difficult to recognize and distinguish between people – most are clad in black and the graffitists have their hoods tightly tied around their face. My companion and I hang out for a while near a carrier bike where cheap shots are being sold. Christian, who was one of the first people I interviewed about the G13 protests, comes along and asks if we are enjoying the party. We nod. 'Me too', he says. 'These parties are so energetic. You just have to give it full throttle – it can be over any moment'.

The darkness is filled with frenzied activity: long ladders have been erected over storefronts and the façades of the old houses, and most walls are already scrawled with graffiti, mainly tags but also statements such as 'Capitalism is boring' and 'We harm with charm'. 'They are not going to be happy about this tomorrow', my companion comments. 'It is not that I feel sorry for the shop owners, but I think this is ... [she pauses] ... whatever happened to the police?' We listen for the sound of sirens over the throbbing bass of the music. Only a few police vans were parked down Strøget when we arrived, and nothing happens. The window of a red Peugeot is smashed, but the car is not set on fire here in the narrow street. We decide to leave. From the sound truck we hear the message that the party is over and people break off in smaller groups, drifting into the adjoining streets. Strangely, the police are still not in sight.

The next day there is silence – among activists, but not in the media, of course. The party developed into a smashing of storefronts and further trashing of cars parked in the street. The media call it 'meaningless vandalism' as a result of 'a primitive appetite for destruction'. Only one young activist publicly expresses his feeling of joy when the storefronts were smashed. Apart from this, the newspapers are filled with statements from local inhabitants and shop owners, their shocked questions and disapproval: What was the point? Why a side street to Strøget with small shops, where people are living? Was it spontaneous or organized?

Outside Folkets Hus, another legalized squat in Nørrebro, where the Undoing the City festival has been held over the past two days, people talk in small groups. My companion at the party looks at me; her eyes are dark. 'It got out of hand after we left', she says, 'it seems really stupid. The media have been calling all morning, but the spokesperson disappeared'. Mikkel, one of the organizers of Undoing the City who had formerly been very active organizing social forums, reluctantly comments on the incident. He turns to me, 'You know that a Reclaim the Street party is about taking back the street; there is nothing more to be said, the media have already written their story'. I nod; this is obviously not in any straightforward sense an instance of groups and individuals appearing in public space to gain recognition from the state or the general public. But if not that, what is it an appearance of?

5

'I Used to Run as the Black Bloc'

Style and Perspectivist Time in Protests and Direct Actions

> Mass direct actions are complex performative terrains that produce a dual effect. Externally they are powerful image events ... where diverse activist networks communicate their messages to an audience ... Internally, they constitute platforms where alternative subjectivities are expressed through distinct bodily and spatial techniques, and emotions are generated through ritual conflict.
>
> —Jeffrey Juris, *Networking Futures*

Direct actions have much in common with ritual performances. Protests play with different techniques, such as masks, colour, music and repetition, and employ a number of performative styles to engage participants and engender particular effects (cf. Mitchell 2006; Sjørslev 2007; Sneath et al. 2009: 12). This view is eloquently argued by Jeffrey Juris (2008), in an analysis of alterglobalization activists in Barcelona with a focus on the activists' networking practices. Juris argues that activists' networking practices and abstract political values – such as autonomy, horizontality and diversity of tactics – are physically embodied and hence made experientially real and concrete through mass direct actions. Through description of his participation in protests against the World Bank summit in Prague in 2000, he shows how urban space is occupied by means of different forms of protest, each entailing different 'techniques of the body' (ibid.: 124–25; cf. Mauss 1992).

The present chapter takes as its point of departure Shut Down the Camp, an action aimed at shutting down a refugee retention centre in

Denmark in October 2008, and the protests around NATO's sixtieth-anniversary summit in Strasbourg in 2009. Against this background, I will proceed to the unfolding of the various forms of actions found at protest events organized by Left radical activists.

While sharing Juris's understanding of protests as performative events, as well as agreeing with his insights on the importance of bodily techniques for revealing the raison d'être of protests, my trajectory departs from his in the analysis of these actions: where Juris stresses the expressive qualities of protest – that protests are conceptualized as moments of the bodily expression of underlying subjectivities, perceptions and values – I fix my gaze on the techniques of the body, particularly the collective bodily intensity manifest during confrontations with the police, and the effects elicited in their wake. Behind my choice of emphasis is a scepticism towards making activist values, culture or even cosmology a totalizing and holistic backdrop for the meaning of a protest event (cf. Sneath et al. 2009: 7–8). Instead, I find that protest performances, and the various techniques of the body involved in staging mass protests, have cosmological effects. In continuation of the argument developed in Chapter 1, cosmology is not taken here as an underlying belief system, such as is sometimes assumed in anthropological studies of so-called primitive societies, but as that which falls into place (Willerslev and Pedersen 2010) when a protest performance reconfigures the relationship between active and dead time. In short, cosmology is not an apriorism (prior to experience and action), but an emergent effect of the confrontation between activists and the police. The heart of my argument is that a skilful protest performance, which in the present context is a well-orchestrated moment of bodily confrontation, elucidates the multiple nature of time, and gives rise to the particular relationship between active time and dead time, capitalism and its potential alternatives, that I have described in previous chapters.

To develop this argument, I will revisit the concept of style, originally put forward by the Birmingham School of cultural studies, to make sense of youth culture and radical politics. From the perspective of the Birmingham School, style is played out in the appropriation and transformation of symbolic meanings attached to dress, music, body postures and language that are tied to the construction of an oppositional youth culture (Clarke 2006: 40–45). Juris employs this concept of style, and argues that the actions of so-called black blocs at summit events should be understood as the performance of an oppositional identity (Juris 2008: 181–82). I, however, propose a radically different concept of style, arising from the particular way Danish activists use the word, and seek to extract an anthropological concept of style from the ethnography.[1] Style, among activists, first of all represents a concern with the form's appropriateness, that is, it reveals a situated ethic. This situated ethic is conceptualized as judgements about right and wrong, legitimate and illegitimate actions, which accompany discussions over forms of protest. Inspired by Marilyn Strathern's thoughts on aesthetics (Strathern 1988, 2004), I argue that activists' concept of style reflects an acute attention to the appropriateness, persuasiveness and effectiveness of form (Strathern 2004: 10). Style is a scale for activists to pass judgement on the appropriateness and effectiveness of the forms of action employed for specific situations. Thereby the concept of style is key to approaching persistent debates over violence among activists and among the broader public. Furthermore, this new concept of style overcomes the form/content distinction inherent in most ideas about politics by elucidating that what we conventionally think of as political content or a political message is engendered by form.

Hitherto, looking at protests through a performative lens has often implied understanding them as liminoid phenomena (Juris 2008: 139). The conflation of rites of passage, carnival and political protest is common in anthropological literature (see e.g. Cohen 1980; Ekman 1991; Gluckman 1963; Turner 1982, 1995),[2] and not uncommon among theoretically informed activists (Jordan 2002). However, the model of the ritual process – which divides time into a threefold structure of separation, transition involving a state of liminality, and a phase of reincorporation or redress – suffers from an ontology of linear time. In being structured around the reversal along a temporal axis of order and disorder, rule and exception, the everyday and the festive, the ritual model has fostered a paradigmatic discussion in anthropology about the extent to which these moments of ritual reversal lead to perpetual societal change.

My aim is to offer some elements for rethinking the model of time underlying many studies of protest events by examining activists' mode of being in and engendering time with their bodies; this exposes the ontological partitions of the present and the future to an ethnographically informed critique. In working towards this end, and building on my critique of prefiguration, I will attempt to transpose Viveiros de Castro's theorization of Amerindian perspectivism (Viveiros de Castro 1992, 1998, 2004) to a context of direct action in order to think about the role of the body in engendering time. I will argue that the antinomy between the present and the future can be reconsidered in the context of Left radical activism if we take into account 'the bodily point of view' (Viveiros de Castro 1998) that emerges during confrontations with the police. I advance an idea of a perspectivist model of time, which implies a bodily ability to see different temporal worlds within this one. In the present context, in the moment of confrontation where a collective body of protesters emerges, active time and dead time are coexisting temporal perspectives, where the former is brought into being by a 'good style'.

I begin this chapter by describing protest events based on my fieldnotes, then turn to the issues of forms of action and style, and end with my argument about how actions give rise to a certain temporal bodily point of view. By examining these protest events, which have no immediate chronological connection, and also drawing the street dance in Hyskenstræde into the equation, I not only intend to focus attention on their similarities, but on a particular figuration of time that replicates itself across protest events and other actions, suggesting that 'meaning' is not best derived from a singular event, but from the internal relation between them (cf. Riles 1998).

Shut Down the Camp

When we meet at the train station, Emma quickly summarizes the decisions taken at the affinity group meeting (described in Chapter 3): that we will make up the front bloc which will consist of three chains, how we will react if the police stop us on the way, and that we will take turns at carrying the front banner, so that people wishing to participate in the action can break off from the demonstration as we reach the refugee retention centre, Sandholm. Sofie has bought some orange cloth, but the group has multiplied and we only get a shred each to tie around our heads. Being sympathetic to the cause, I have decided that I am willing to be arrested, a decision also taken in light of the fact that I feel I am in trustworthy company and relatively sure about the terrain and the methods of the police. The style of the demonstration has been talked of as 'family friendly', which implies neither breaking the law nor contemplating a bodily confrontation with the police. The action, which will break off from the demonstration upon arrival at Sandholm, has been defined as confrontational civil disobedience. This means we will push against or put direct physical pressure on police lines without resorting to hitting, kicking, throwing objects or destroying property except for the fence surrounding the retention centre. Through various press releases and interviews, the public had been made aware not only with the date and time of the action, but also with our intended tactics. The press coverage had been fairly positive, but critical voices have also been heard about the possible harm that the action could cause to the psychological well-being of the detained asylum seekers.

On the train, Freja and Jan, who had both been active in Globale Rødder, rehearse their speeches and go over the directions to be given from the sound truck when the demonstration arrives at Sandholm, in order to ensure that the action can be successfully separated from the demonstration. Three youngsters sitting next to us have already put their gloves on, and the most experienced of the group instructs his friends about how to handle tear gas: 'When it stops burning and stinging you will get a clear and purified feeling', he explains. We cannot help laughing because most of us can recognize the sensation (of ritual clearance) after a heavy round of gas. It makes us talk about how the battle around Ungdomshuset has made a much larger group of people familiar with tear gas. Our conversation is soon interrupted by the announcement of problems with the railway signals, and we are informed that the train service is interrupted. We get off at Holte station, some 10 kilometres from our destination. We have been told that buses will be organized by De Danske Statsbaner (DSB), the train operator, but not much happens. We wait and speculate. Emma believes that the police have requested the train company to interrupt the service, but Little Emma argues that it is just bad luck and that the service is frequently interrupted on this route. After an hour, some 700 people have gathered at the square outside the train station and only two buses show up. There are rumours that the police are searching people on the buses, and a group of people starts walking along the road to Allerød, while Mikkel, who I know from the European Social Forum and who was also involved in G13 and the street party in Hyskenstræde, tries to organize some activist-run buses to pick us up. But the train service soon returns to normal, and we arrive at the starting point of the demonstration after a two-hour delay. We quickly get into formation, and Aske shows up to explain the route. He will be maintaining police contact, and is located with Freja and Jan on the sound truck that has been decorated with balloons and the large red and black papier mâché bolt cutter.

It is an unusual demonstration because we walk through forests and open fields without much of an audience. We follow the road through the forest to Sandholm retention centre located about 4 kilometres out of town. It is a sunny autumn day and the wood is clad in brown and yellow, which is colour-coordinated with our banner. Unlike a demonstration in the city, there are only a few bystanders apart from the journalists flocking around the front banner with their cameras, and a police helicopter circles over our heads. Nevertheless, several speeches, rallying cries and music are heard; they are employed to get us in the mood. The first row carrying the front banner also has the role of adjusting the tempo to make sure that there are no gaps in the procession of demonstrators. The internal organization of the demonstration – with functions such as front group, runners, speakers, police liaison and so on – does not differ from what can be found at any other demonstration. Being in the second line, Little Emma, Sofie and I have time to find a name for our affinity group. We decide on 'smashing salmon', after our ugly salmon-coloured head ribbons. After having taken turns with the front banner, we make a stop less than a kilometre from the camp. We are met by Grannies for Asylum (*bedsteforældre for asyl*) and the Front of Socialist Youth (*socialistisk ungdomsfront*), who will also participate in the action. The participants rest on the road and have something to eat. The people on the sound truck use the break to urge the participating activists to make sure that the detainees at the camp do not sustain damage from our action, and we are encouraged to check the map of the area. Before we leave again, Sofie mixes magnesium and water in two spray bottles, an excellent solution for easing the effects of tear gas.

People are getting excited and the pace of the demonstration increases slightly. A runner[3] from the sound truck informs us that the police have put up an extra fence on the lawn in front of the main entrance to the retention centre, but that we should stay on the road and continue to the edge of the fence from where it is possible to run into the open fields surrounding Sandholm. Little Emma, Sofie, Julie and I discuss our tactics. We decide not to run first, but to bide our time. Then the main entrance is ahead of us, and we walk resolutely towards the fence, staying on the road. To our right, where the terrain starts to slope upwards, are the mounted police along with three or four divisions of police on foot. I am reminded of the film *Braveheart* due to the epic line-up, and of Michael Jackson's comment that sometimes fiction seems more real than reality (Jackson 2002). The police appear quite distant and unreal, and the eye is tempted to look for a route through the terrain. But instead of turning up the hill, we continue straight on and wave to a group of asylum seekers inside the fence.

As we reach the intermediary fence made up of metal trestles, a group from behind rushes forward and pushes it over. Simultaneously another group of some 150 to 200 people break off from the main demonstration and follow the lead of three purple flags into the military exercising terrain, north of the retention centre. People yell and cheer, and from the sound truck it is repeated that we should look at the map, take care of each other and avoid getting into violent confrontation with the police. The police posted near the entrance of the centre start moving down the road, but fall behind the activists on the field, who have split into various groups now seeking ways to get round the police in order to reach the fence. About forty activists outsmart the police by running around their line and manage to get to the fence. Little Emma, Sofie and I follow with sprayers and rope, but as we reach the road again we are met by a large group of people fleeing in the other direction. Several people are violently arrested, but Little Emma and I see a young man outrun a police officer in heavy riot gear, who finally trips and rolls over in one of the deep, ploughed furrows in the field. It becomes her favourite story of the day.

Our 'field trip' is interrupted by the whistling sound of tear gas canisters falling all around us. We slowly jog away, and remain calm as the wind on the open field carries most of the gas away. A group tries to make it through to the fence at the further end of the field, while we return towards the demonstration, which is still standing on the main road behind the interim fence. Almost simultaneously, Magnus appears with a purple flag, and Little Emma, Sofie and I follow him across the lawn in front of the main entrance and reach the fence. But the police are better prepared now: they fire tear gas directly at us. I panic and run down wind, against everything I have learned. I collapse inside the cloud, my eyes burn, I cannot breathe and am on the verge of vomiting. Activists lie spread on the field around me.

The stationary demonstration on the road has also been enveloped in a cloud of tear gas, and I see a father with his two-year-old child on his shoulders running while the child cries violently and rubs her face. Emma runs to them and sprays both the child and the father in the face with the magnesium solution. From the sound truck, the main demonstration is asked to withdraw to lessen the impact of tear gas on children and elders. To lessen the urge to vomit, I concentrate wholly on my breathing and on calming myself down. I spray my face with the magnesium solution, and then I slowly walk around spraying the people lying on the ground. 'How beautiful', I think, 'the anthropologist as activist-shaman performing a healing ritual'.

When I find Little Emma again she is fed up. 'This is too chaotic', she complains, and continues: 'This decentralized action thing makes me feel insecure. I like blocs better, like the yellow bloc during G13, where we would stick together in chains. We were like lemmings, and that made me feel strong and not in the least bit scared of the police'. I do not give much thought to how blocs are lemming-like, and how this is associated with bodily strength, but share her sense of exposure. From the sound truck we are asked to gather again to walk back towards the station. We have been here for about an hour and managed to cut down a large section of the fence, but Sofie is not satisfied. 'We cannot go back now', she says grumpily, 'I didn't even get started. We should stay'. Little Emma convinces her that it will be too dangerous to do this kind of free-form action without protection from the main demonstration. We meet Christian, whom I had interviewed the year before about the G13 action. He recounts how he was in a confrontation with the police up on the road, while a large group managed to slip through to the fence. 'The police officers will get a bollocking because we managed to cut the fence', he says with a grin, and hurries on.

We start walking back towards Allerød train station. My group is responsible for carrying the rear banner, which involves making sure that people keep up the pace and that we use our bodies and the banner as a shield to keep the police vans following close behind us. I walk next to Emma and reiterate Little Emma's argument about blocs versus free-form affinity group actions. Emma replies that the idea of this kind of action is that they are much more flexible and create a chaotic situation, which the police have difficulty controlling. 'We have all contributed to that, even though you did not cut down the fence', she says. She believes the action has been a success because we managed to cut down part of the fence, and she will not listen to my complaint that it is 'not really' shutting down the camp.

Our talk is cut short because Julie and Emma have to leave the demonstration to hurry somebody on, who may otherwise get into trouble with the police. When we are near the train station, a group of plain-clothes police officers try to enter the demonstration from the side. They have been filming us from their cars for a while now and are clearly on the lookout for someone to arrest. At first, we manage to push them away, but then about thirty police in riot gear get out of their vans. Julie makes us lock arms and form three chains facing them. I only reach the chest of the riot cop in front of me, and Little Emma and the young women next to me are even shorter. We have not been standing long when they start hitting their way into the crowd. They grab Magnus, but he manages to wrest himself from the police with the help of a couple of friends. The police withdraw, and we continue slowly with our arms locked – that is, in black bloc formation – towards the train station, stopping every time the police draw closer.

People leave on the train for Copenhagen, and we follow after dismantling the sound truck. I feel exhausted, my back is stiff either from fear or from a blow by a police baton, but we decide to go to Folkets Hus for a drink to achieve closure on an eventful day. We hang out at the activist run café and talk the day's events through. Emma's brother is checking the coverage in the media and giving us reports, while the rest of us drink beer and tell stories of the day's events. Little Emma rests on a sofa; she feels dizzy from all the tear gas, but she comes to life again on several occasions to tell the story about the police officer who fell into the ditch while chasing an escaping activist. I am amazed at how the uncertainty we had felt about the success of the action has now turned into a generalized feeling of victory.

Blockade and Riots in Strasbourg

The atmosphere is tense at the evening spokes-council after the day's fighting at the entrance to the camp outside Strasbourg. 'The diversity of tactics' is to be put to the test the next day. Hundreds of people have crowded into a large red and blue circus tent, and now they are sitting on the ground or on bales of hay, talking about the day's events. The aim of the meeting is to discuss the organization of a black bloc in conjunction with the large demonstration being organized by the European peace movement the following day, but Alvin from Interventionistiche Linke is informing people that the police will seal off the whole inner city. He explains that those wanting to take part in the blockade should either leave within a few hours and try to sleep somewhere in the city centre, or walk the 6 to 7 kilometres to town in smaller groups in the early hours of the morning. He also urges people not to get into confrontations with the police. Several activists around me are visibly bothered. They pay no heed to him and his words are clearly lost on most of those gathered.

Before entering the tent, Natalie has explained to me that people are 'pissed off' due to the violent death of a protester during the mostly peaceful London G20 protest a few days before, by the fact that their protest in Strasbourg is being relegated to an industrial zone outside the city centre, and because approximately 5,000 protesters have been held back at the French–German border. For days there have been whispers about alternative targets. Harry had tried to pull me along to some of these meetings, and the day before he had left saying he was to meet up with his affinity group at a border crossing. He never returned. Natalie had told me that there would be riots the following day, but also that she had decided to stay in the camp. At some point during the meeting she shouts at Alvin, 'That is all very fine, but the police have informed us that they will not let us leave the camp until 11 [o'clock], when the summit has started'. I never found out if this was actually true or one of the many rumours that had been circulating all week. Nicola sitting next to me in the hay whispers, 'I love this, now you have to think for yourself'.

Those gathered who wish to participate in the black bloc decide to leave in the early hours of the morning. I am inclined to follow the black bloc, but concerned about my own security and that of the four students I have taken along to study the construction of the camp. After the military helicopters that have been circling over our heads for days, I am worried that the police might finally decide to raid the camp during the night. The freedom embodied in this kind of 'thinking for myself' for a while seems overwhelmingly trying and strenuous. Outside the circus tent people are chatting in smaller groups. Nicola and I decide to start driving my students and a group from Revolt France, who will act as street medics the following day, into the centre in his car. We agree that we can probably find a place to have a few hours' rest at Molodoi, the self-managed social centre in Strasbourg, which has served as convergence centre during the NATO summit.

The streets lie dark and empty. Since yesterday, the streets have been deserted; shops, schools and other institutions are closed, and all public transportation has been suspended. Special summit passes have been issued to local inhabitants, allowing them to move to and from their homes. The first trip goes well, but on our second trip we start getting nervous: we have a creepy feeling of being observed, although we tell each other that we have done nothing wrong. Police officers are posted on the street corners, and in a moment of absent-mindedness Nicola drives the wrong way on a one-way street. We are pulled over. The police search the car itself and us. In the boot they find Nicola's helmet, skater's safety gear and his notebook, and the highest-ranking officer starts turning over the pages with great interest. 'So, you are an organizer', he says to Nicola. Nicola denies it, but is taken into custody. The rest of us are left on the street, and we walk to Molodoi while my notebook burns in my pocket. I am getting very paranoid. Luckily, Nicola and I remembered to exchange personal data (last name and social security number) before we left the camp, and after waiting anxiously for an hour and a half, I call up the legal team to inform them of Nicola's arrest. An hour later, around 2 o'clock in the morning, he is back; he says that he is okay except for having 'his head screwed up by all their questions'. We drink tea before we tiptoe into the upstairs room where sleeping people cover every inch of the floor.

We get up before 7 AM and quickly head to the meeting point for the blockade. As we walk along the quays surrounding Strasbourg's inner city, which is also the perimeter of the red zone, we observe that the police are already guarding the bridges. When we reach Quai des Alpes we see the first groups of the black bloc arriving from the camp. Tear gas already fills the air. Clashes with the police get underway as the groups try to find a crossing point. We watch in silence for a while then decide to move on. We head north and pass the official meeting point of the blockade, which has already been abandoned. We turn west towards the centre following the trail of the pink bloc and a scent of tear gas until we reach the blockading point at the intersection of Avenue des Vosges and Avenue de la Paix. We are stopped and searched repeatedly. These measures are meant for identifying the 'unwanted elements' moving through public space, and everybody walking on the streets has to undergo repeated identity checks and bag searches.

The pink bloc is a colourful gathering, mainly organized around a large samba band; men and women in pink skirts, elaborate hairdos and hats beating their drums. There is also a large group of German clowns, each wearing a hilarious mix of army and clown costume. They march and drill in front of the police line, mimicking their movements, which adds an element of comic suspense to the situation. Only half an hour earlier the police had tried to chase protesters from the pink bloc off the street, and the participating activists were tear gassed while trying to reach the blockading point. Whether they have prevented the delegates of the NATO summit from reaching the conference centre at the Palais de la Musique in time is still uncertain.

We take turns dancing and resting, and Nicola attends to a few people who are feeling queasy from the tear gas. Much to my surprise, I run into both Swedes and Greeks whom I had previously met during the social forum in Malmö, and as the situation has calmed down we have time for a chat. Alvin announces through a megaphone that the summit has been delayed for an hour due to the blockade, but my Greek companion seriously doubts this. 'The blockade has not been sufficiently effective', he says. 'There are plenty of places to get through. The delay was probably caused by Berlusconi, who needed to go to the bathroom'. Seeing how calm the police are, it is obvious we no longer pose a threat to the smooth running of the summit, and at a spokes-council meeting[4] following Alvin's announcement it is decided to pull up stakes and head towards the large demonstration due to start within the hour. First, however, Nicola and I need to prepare to join the confrontations in the harbour area close to the border.

We make a detour back to Molodoi to stock up on medical supplies. When we leave again our bags are stuffed with bandages, cotton wool for broken noses, a few other medicines and six or seven bottles of Maalux, a wonder treatment for heartburn and tear gas. We are both eager to go back to the action and I try to ignore the growing fatigue resulting from a lack of sleep. From a distance we see black smoke rising from the Europe Bridge, normally the busiest border between France and Germany. Close by, the NATO leaders undertook a 'diplomatic footstep' and an official photo session a few hours earlier, and now the border post has been set on fire by protesters. Nicola is wearing an old bike helmet and his skater's safety gear. It is a warm day and he looks at me, smiling: 'The border is burning', he says, 'let's go to war'.

We follow in the direction of the smoke and the sound of the helicopters until we reach Grand Pont, a long bridge connecting the inner city with the harbour area, about 1.5 kilometres from the burning border post. On the way to the bridge we are stopped repeatedly by police officers searching our bags and questioning us about where we have come from, our plans and organizational affiliation. They eagerly go through Nicola's bags, but find nothing.

As we reach Grand Pont, large water cannons and a dozen police vans take up positions at the centre of the bridge. Cement blocks have been placed across the street, covered with plastic and barbwire. Nicola approaches a police officer and asks to be let through in order to provide medical aid to some of the activists on the other side. In a polite but firm voice, the officer informs us that it will not be possible. At the foot of the bridge we meet up with some 300 activists from the pink bloc, who had all participated in the failed attempt to blockade the NATO summit. Some people are taking a rest, some are looking for food and water, while others are eager to cross the bridge either to join a large demonstration convened by the European peace organizations or to participate in clashes with the police, which have been going on since around 7 o'clock that morning. A row of police cars leaves the bridge, and after a spokes-council meeting, the assembled protestors decide to make an attempt to 'open' the bridge.

When we walk onto the bridge, three rows of riot police protected by anti-riot helmets, shields and tactical knee, arm and chest pads obstruct our retreat. For a minute I consider jumping down the steep slope over the side of the bridge to avoid what seems to be an imminent arrest, but I am discouraged by the way a couple of protesters are beaten severely and kicked back into the group when they try to make an escape. The police line moves quickly forward and, aided by portable fences, they push the samba band and everybody else ahead while the drummers struggle to keep time. We are squeezed together in what I later learn is called a 'kettle', police jargon for the temporary imprisonment of protestors. The smell of tear gas reaches us from the other side of the bridge, where around a thousand activists from the black bloc are clashing with the police. In our 'kettle' on the bridge, the samba band keeps playing on against a background of silence. The refrain, 'This is what democracy looks like!' is shouted repeatedly. When it was played at the blockade in the morning, I thought it referred to our control of the street, but now it sounds more like a sarcastic reference to police repression. I talk briefly to Svante from a Swedish anti-military group who is a familiar face from the European Social Forum in Malmö. He explains that he had slept under a bridge that night to participate in the blockade. His affinity group had been planning to head back to the camp, but, he says with a pale smile, 'Now we don't know how it will end up'.

We are herded together ever more tightly and compressed further. The temperature rises in the 'kettle'. People raise their hands and turn the palms towards the police to show their peaceful intentions. I become acutely aware that if someone panics or loses their temper, the situation will turn into either violent confrontation or mass arrest. When the first line is pressed back by the police, it instantly produces a collective wave, rolling back and forth; the rhythmic drumming of the samba band gives us a collective pulse. We have become one body acting together, where a movement in one part instantly exerts an influence on the rest. I am filled with a strong sense of solidarity and togetherness, mixed with fear. Nobody moves or talks. The air is full of a vibrant tension, and I observe the jaw muscle of the nearest policeman turn white as he fixes his gaze somewhere above my head. I am reminded of H.G. Wells's novel *The War of the Worlds* (1898), which describes the conflict between mankind and an alien race (Martians) in a London suburb. Even though the policeman does not exactly resemble the large extraterrestrial octopus-like creature, I still wonder what kind of being hides behind the armour and if we are of the same world. It is a long, terrifying moment of possibility in which I mostly sense our own breathing. After some fifteen minutes the riot police withdraw without a word, and we are allowed to walk away.

People start talking again; we hug and laugh, and some people even start dancing in the street. When I question him, Nicola explains that he has a mixed feeling of relief and power. I share the general feeling of joy, but mixed with anger and a rare sense of strength, which appears rather odd in the situation, given that we did not have the upper hand. I observe a large German water cannon pulling away and feel an instant desire to throw a rock at it. I check with Nicola, who feels that we would probably not get away with it. Someone pops open a red fire hydrant to allow everybody a sip of water. The water pours out on to the warm tarmac, and Svante, who stood next to me in the 'kettle', comments how happy he is that we were able to 'keep calm and control the situation'. A middle-aged German man joins in to tell us that he had spent several hours in his car that morning to reach the protest, and now 'had experienced what he came for'. He rambles on, but I turn away to find out what our next move will be.

After the moment of joyful celebration, we hold another spokes-council meeting at Rue du Grand Pont. About half the group, including half the samba band, decide to return to the camp, while the rest of us want to proceed to the remainder of the demonstration-cum-riot. Several clowns remove their make-up and costumes. The next day, while driving me to the railway station, one of the clowns from Freiburg explains:

> I lost the clown in the 'kettle'. I used to run as the black bloc, but started clowning about four years ago. Clowning is a good way to go into a confrontation, I think. But I got so angry [in the 'kettle'] that I could not continue clowning and handle the situation in a humorous manner. After all the tension, I just felt angry and had to take off the clown.

In this situation it was less the fact that the clown became recognizable to the police as a troublemaker that led to his shape-shifting, than that he saw himself unable to adhere to the style of the pink bloc in a situation that called for other means to be employed.

In the otherwise deserted harbour area, the demonstration of the peace movement has fallen apart and people drift around without direction. Simultaneously, violent confrontations between militant protesters joined by youngsters from the *banlieues*[5] and the riot police continue near the Europe Bridge. The confrontation takes place at a distance and at a slow pace. Small dispersed groups of activists take turns in throwing stones and Molotov cocktails at police officers on foot, who keep their distance and respond with tear gas, concussion grenades and, eventually, a few stones. The activists are ritually clothed in black, with gas masks, helmets and padding in a striking resemblance of the police. Even the bodily movements when attacking and hiding behind their shields are similar and so, I think, is the idea about the need to 'take action' to change the course of events.

At the Europe Bridge activists have set fire to the border post and a nearby Ibis Hotel. Two activists explain that the police have been hosted here, while others seem to think that it has been used for rejected asylum seekers, but in either case the target is considered legitimate. One of my student assistants who had not wished to take part in the blockade had been present near the bridge, and in the evening she described to me how small groups of youngsters had been running around the burning buildings shouting with joy, giving each other the thumbs up. Locals from the nearby *banlieue* had joined in, she explained, plundering a couple of smashed-up petrol stations. The black bloc riots and the property destruction are the incidents broadcasted and reported on in the mainstream media over the following days. 'No Borders' reads the graffiti on the burned-out border control post.

In the late afternoon, people start walking back towards the camp, while others change their clothes to appear like 'regular citizens', which might enable them to pass through the police checkpoints into the city centre. Nicola, I and a few other people walk towards the centre, but to reach Molodoi and Nicola's car we have to pass over one of the bridges, which the police are still guarding. We are repeatedly turned away, though we try to appear as inoffensive as possible. 'Try not looking them in the eye', Nicola advises. I have trouble walking due to large blisters on both my feet, and we are all soon overwhelmed by fatigue. I remember thinking that there is apparently no agreement between activists and the police about when the party is over. At the fourth bridge we change our tactic. I walk up the bridge, approach the police directly and gently ask them to let us through. They check my passport and question Nicola, but it works. When we are well on the other side, Nicola mumbles, 'So, they are humans after all. I told him [the police officer] that I was tired, and he said that he was too'.

When we are back in the car, Nicola describes the day as a great success. 'You can't expect that we can accomplish everything in one day', he says, and continues, 'but we managed to control the street and to create disorder in their planning'. 'What do you mean by everything?' I ask. 'Yeah, you know, that the revolution doesn't come in one day', he replies. We continue in silence, lost in our own thoughts. Later in the evening at Molodoi, we eat and wait for transport back to the camp. While eating, Nicola rests his forehead on the tabletop and starts crying: 'I was just not strong enough', he repeats. While trying to comfort him, I am also overwhelmed by a deep sadness, one that will follow me for weeks, though I will be unable to pinpoint the reason.

Forms of Action

Activists generally distinguish between 'effective' and 'symbolic' actions. The success of demonstrations, such as the one at the Sandholm retention centre, largely depends on the number of people present and the intensity of the atmosphere produced, which seem to emerge, for example, by walking in close formation, listening to incisive speeches and engaging in captivating chants. Nevertheless, demonstrations, marches and rallies are considered to be merely 'symbolic' because they aim at communicating a message or producing an image to be consumed by the public or acted upon by elected politicians and other authorities. Apart from producing an experience of sharing a cause, many activists consider demonstrations to be largely pointless as they do not in themselves bring about social change – in the end people simply go home and leave the stage to somebody else. Effective actions, on the other hand, involve acting directly on a problem; however, in order to be successful the act should accomplish a solution, if only fleetingly. The idea of effective actions is equivalent to the concept of direct action, which means that activists take matters into their own hands, acting as if the state does not exist (Graeber 2009: 204–5). The symbolic/effective distinction is frequently referred to and used in arguments in planning meetings about what form of action would be most appropriate (see Chapter 3).

In practice, the distinction between actions that are considered symbolic and those considered effective is not clear-cut. The action to shut down the retention centre at Sandholm illustrates this: on one hand the action was a symbolic action – materialized as a march to Sandholm retention centre calling attention to the unjust and racist asylum legislation of Denmark. On the other hand, it was an effective or direct action aiming at producing a solution to this problem by cutting down the fence around the retention centre. Yet, the action was spoken of in public and in the media as 'a mass action of confrontational civil disobedience', which many bystanders perceived as a contradiction in terms. Among the European public, civil disobedience is often associated with a Gandhian style of peaceful law breaking that also involves making public your intentions prior to the action and a willingness to accept arrest, and confrontation does not fit into that equation. This apparent contradiction was intended.

Direct actions may be either secret or public, but generally involve, as mentioned above, 'doing politics away from the state', and 'taking matters into one's own hands'; that is, exerting a de facto autonomy by ignoring public authorities and legislation. During direct actions you are not required to willingly submit to arrest (ibid.: 204–5). Both the G13 action to squat a new social centre in the wake of the Ungdomshuset eviction (described in Chapter 2) and Shut Down the Camp mix elements of civil disobedience and direct action. During actions such as these, people do not willingly submit to arrest, and the actions involve a high level of bodily confrontation with the police; on the other hand, activists make the date and time of the action known. The two protest events mentioned evidence the continuous attempt at renewing and adapting forms of action to the situation at hand, since both explicitly referred to and reworked the concept of action successfully employed to block the G8 summit in Heiligendamm in Germany in 2007. Both actions were part of a series of 'mass actions of civil disobedience', starting with the import of forms of action inspired by Italian Tute Bianche to Denmark in 2002, which were continually adapted, leaking sideways into one another and drawing inspiration from various sources (Krøijer 2015).

Few Scandinavians are familiar with the term 'direct action', and by employing the term 'confrontational civil disobedience' Danish activists seek to expand the grey area between violence and non-violence, while maintaining a favourable image in public. This latter point is of some importance in light of the fact that in a Danish context the media is quite deliberately used in order to mobilize participants for actions like G13, Shut Down the Camp and Reclaim Power.

Mass actions in Europe have, since the protests against the World Bank meeting in Prague in 2000 (see Juris 2008), typically been organized with different colour-coded blocs. Ideally the entire 'choreography of action' should make room for different forms of action and tactical preferences, and the colours are therefore used to create these distinctions. Viewed from a historical perspective, it is possible to discern different, relatively scripted forms, which are available to activists, but which are also continually susceptible to change. In Strasbourg, two forms of bloc can be discerned, namely the pink and the black. Each form can be understood as an aesthetic form that, by way of elaborate bodily techniques and dress, and aided by different objects, produces certain effects. If one looks closer at the forms of action, and activists' concerns over the appropriateness, persuasiveness and effectiveness of form, the activist concept of style comes into view.

The black bloc, encountered near the Europe Bridge in Strasbourg, involves the wearing of black clothing, often hoodies or black ski jackets as well as masks or bandanas to avoid identification. This mode of protesting first emerged among German squatters in the 1980s and stood for a certain kind of demonstrating. When walking together in dense formation with arms locked together and flanked by banners, individual activists are indiscernible from one another and come to appear as one (Graeber 2009: 406; Katsiaficas 2006). When employed in more free-form actions, such as during the rioting in Strasbourg, in the days following the eviction of Ungdomshuset in Copenhagen, or in Genoa (Juris 2008), the urban terrain becomes chaotic and, according to Juris, a zone of 'indistinction' (Juris 2008: 168; see also Agamben 1998: 122).[6] To a person observing the confrontations, any clear line between rule and exception breaks down in the interstice opened up by the state of exception: law maintaining and law subverting entities are hard to discern from one another in the thick of the confrontation between clubs and batons, stones and tear gas, water cannons and Molotov cocktails. According to Juris, it is paradoxical that moving through this time–space is experienced as both very terrifying and extremely liberating (Juris 2008).

Juris's description of being present in a riot resonates well not only with my own immediate experience of events, but also with the argument made in Chapter 4 about enemies that constantly slip in and out of the category. It is paradoxical that becoming subject to the force of the police or falling foul of the law can simultaneously evoke experiences of strength and autonomy. It is my conviction that the bodily confrontation between activists and the police, such as the one on the bridge in Strasbourg, is a moment of bodily intensity, and of bifurcation between two partially overlapping temporalities, namely active time and dead time.

The black bloc tactic includes vandalism of objects symbolizing capitalism, such as petrol stations, banks and storefronts, and the creation of prototypical images of revolution by way of fire, street fighting and confrontations with the police (Graeber 2009: 406–8; Juris 2005: 420–21). If it is appropriate to speak of an aesthetic in this context, 'the beautiful' involves disturbing and destroying with anger so that something new can emerge (Sullivan 2005). Seen from an activist perspective, property destruction is not violence, which is how it is often represented in mainstream media. Activists generally employ a narrow definition of violence as 'the intentional infliction of pain or harm on others', whereas the press uses a much broader definition, referring to violence as 'harm to either persons or property that is unauthorised by the proper authorities' (Coady, cited in Graeber 2009: 448). This latter definition implies that the police never – or almost never – use violence, but only authorized force. Graeber argues that activists, following a narrow definition, are strictly non-violent in the US; the picture is less clear-cut in a Danish and European context.

The pink bloc was a form of action developed at the Prague World Bank summit as an alternative to black bloc rioting. The idea of the pink bloc is to 'queer space' through rhythmic drumming, dancing and playful mockery. The Clandestine Insurgent Rebel Clown Army was 'the new thing' during the G8 protests in Gleneagles in 2005, an addition to the pink bloc. On their home page, the clowns describe themselves as deviant soldiers, who give resistance a funny face and undermine authority by holding it up to ridicule. They challenge the perceptions of and the way things are done by activists and the police, and during actions the clowns often emerge and perform in the empty space between activist and police lines. Here they march, drill and mimic the bodily postures of the police, or bend down to clean the cop's boots with their pink brushes. They typically wear a mix of military camouflage uniforms and brightly coloured skirts, hats and wigs. The clowns also hide their faces, but behind greasepaint and red noses – in their own words, 'in order to illustrate that they can be every one of us'.[7]

The form of action of the pink bloc may provide an element of comic suspense in the midst of escalating confrontation by going beyond established gender categories and entrenched notions of violence and non-violence. The clowns, like the mythical trickster figures found in anthropological literature, describe themselves as ambiguous figures that are heroes, trick players and sly deceivers (cf. Evans-Pritchard 1967; Pelton 1980; Radin 1956) who skilfully break established categories. Clowning is the form of action that most consciously plays with framing, and hence questions what kind of event it is.

The third form of action worth mentioning here is that of Tute Bianche (described in Chapter 4). The form of action of Tute Bianche, and others inspired by them, also plays with the framing and particularly with the violence/non-violence dichotomy – as in non-violent rioting, and confrontational civil disobedience. Yet, when in the street, they have a more confrontational form of action than the clowns or a normal demonstration. They push their bodies against the police line, but without hitting, kicking or throwing objects at the police. The mere pushing often results in police violence. Today, Italian Ya Basta activists continue travelling to international summits, and a large group travelled to Copenhagen to participate in the Climate Summit. They had a significant influence on the action concept of the Reclaim Power action at the Bella Centre (briefly described in the Introduction). The tactic of pushing used during the Reclaim Power action is directly inspired by Tute Bianche, while the decision not to try entering the Bella Centre conference hall, but to form a third space as an interstice between the inside and the outside in order to hold a people's assembly, was heavily influenced by the Ya Basta delegation.

At summit protests, a swarming effect is produced when the different blocs converge on the same target. Swarming is a military tactic modelled on bee swarms moving in concert without the need for a central leader and on predators hunting in packs, attacking large prey from various sides. Translated to the context of direct action, the idea is that a large number of affinity groups is trained to synchronize their actions, acting autonomously or semi-autonomously in relation to the same target. For swarming to be effective it requires intelligent 'soldiers' able to think for themselves and respond to a situation on an ongoing basis, who are also able to keep in contact through mobile communication technology.

Swarming (like trickery) can be considered an advantageous tactic for unequal encounters. While the police often have the upper hand in protest situations due to their superior number and weaponry, their monopoly on the legitimate use of violence and their better training and topographical overview, the fact that activists can react more swiftly and are not under a centralized command implies that chaotic and unexpected situations often arise.[8] The G13 action, which aimed at squatting a new social centre, and Shut Down the Camp are examples from Denmark of how activists have continued to play with swarming effects in non-summit contexts. At the Reclaim Power action during the Climate Summit in Copenhagen, the newly invented bike bloc had installed sound equipment wired to mp3 players to produce a swarming effect by way of sound (such as jungle noises and animal sounds).

Reclaim the Street, which the Hyskenstræde street party is an example of, is a form of action that grew out of the anti-roads protests in Britain in the early 1990s. Reclaim the Street is used to cover various forms of actions, such as the so-called Critical Mass bike rides, where large groups of activists ride their bikes on the road to temporarily bar cars from the city; guerrilla gardening, where a small or unoccupied plot of land in a city is transformed into a garden; or activist groups such as Space Hijackers, who through their actions draw attention to how public space is eroded by private corporations, and challenge how the spaces are used.[9] Reclaim the Street actions hence involve the temporary hijacking of a road or other public space. As opposed to the building of more permanent autonomous social centres, Reclaim the Street is, borrowing the words of anarchist writer Hakim Bey, a temporary liberation of 'an area in space, time and in imagination', whereupon it dissolves and is recreated at another time and another place (Bey 1991). John Jordan, one of the pioneers of this particular form of action, evokes the image of the carnival to describe the phenomenon: 'Reclaim the street pioneered a new, or rather resurrected a very old style of protests: the street carnival. They popularized a model of political action wherein the protest itself is a living breathing and in this case, dancing, political message' (Jordan 2002: 347). This idea of a dancing political message hints at what I want to say about the concept of style, because it overcomes the distinction between what we conventionally think of as political form and content. The act of dancing in the context of a Reclaim the Street action in itself carries the message. During a Reclaim the Street party, activists seek to transform the street from a space of consumption to a pleasure-filled space, and it is the form, the rhythm and the feel that evokes a different, yet simultaneous, interstice of time where other norms reign.

According to Jordan, a Reclaim the Street party is characterized by spontaneity, joyfulness and transformation, which are played out by turning the norms governing public space upside down (Jordan 1998, 2002). The explicit reference to the liminal or liminoid space of ritual and carnival in Jordan and other activist representations of Reclaim the Street action is difficult to ignore, yet not perfectly adequate. Looking at Victor Turner's ritual model through the lens of the Reclaim the Street party in Hyskenstræde will allow us to evaluate its analytical purchase for this kind of carnivalesque protest event.

Reclaim the Street parties usually follow a similar script, which can be found in various activist 'cookbooks'.[10] First, a network of people plans a party in secrecy; then they decide on a date and location (as well as instructions on how to get there and away), on the style of the event and on an array of practicalities such as how to transform the space – should it be done, for example, by planting trees, painting graffiti, placing armchairs or making a beach in the street? Then, the organizers need to decide on music and other entertainment, and finally, how to block the road or street. The party needs an element of suspense: participants meet up at a known meeting point and are, as in a rite of passage, led to an unfamiliar location (cf. Turner 1982: 26). This fosters anxiety and excitement, but also has the practical function of buying time and hence delaying or distracting the police. In the case of the Reclaim the Street party in Hyskenstræde, space was not only transformed through music and collective dancing, but also by painting graffiti and smashing storefronts. Many activists consider graffiti another means of transforming and establishing a conflict over public space, but the graffiti found in Hyskenstræde, for example, 'We harm with charm', went further as it also took the form of an advertisement while simultaneously twisting the logic of advertising.

A Reclaim the Street party is expected to run up against societal conventions, but also usually entails breaking the law regarding public order.[11] As a consequence, the police are expected to intervene, and in a sense it is this intervention that defines the temporality and tempo of the party, as was also the case in Hyskenstræde where the partying was particularly intense because it was expected that it would be over any moment. Depending on the style of the party, people may either leave quietly, or the party may become the beginning of a riot, as happened at a street party organized by the Left radical Action Network during the European Social Forum in Malmö in 2008. The shift of the Malmö street party from peaceful partying to vandalism and rioting was not simply a result of 'the rush of the crowd', that is, a spontaneous occurrence or something incited by a violent minority, but planned for. In Malmö the organizer's referred to this rioting as an 'after party', which was governed by other norms than those of the party itself.

At any rate, a Reclaim the Street party usually ends when the police clear the street, which the public expects them to do. Victor Turner's model of the ritual process (Turner 1982, 1995) can illuminate why the street dance in Hyskenstræde became an issue of moral concern and public outcry about police passivity, because the police did not properly close down the party; what Turner has called the phase of reintegration and redress was not properly performed. But Turner's model also has its limitations due to its focus on singular events. It fails to elucidate how the event, guided by an aesthetic, makes its relational character visible (cf. Strathern 1988: 160). What Strathern has called an aesthetic is not about abstract beauty, but concerns the appropriateness and effectiveness of a performance, which brings it much closer to Danish activists' notion of 'style'.

Revisiting Style

I have described above various forms of protesting. What the police and public commentators often overlook is that the forms of action do not refer to particular people; in other words, particular activists are not inherently black bloc, pink blocs or clowns, peaceful, troublemakers or disobedient, though individuals may have specific preferences and prior experiences. In the context of the Climate Summit in Copenhagen, various newspapers offered typologies of activists. With the help of sociologist René Karpantschof, the Danish daily newspaper *Politiken* distinguished between three kinds of activists: the peaceful, the disobedient and the militant.[12] This obviously squares nicely with the three forms of actions described above, but confuses available form with people's inner dispositions.

Contrary to mainstream sociologically inspired analysis in the media, which classifies people as different types that, depending on inner predispositions or social circumstances, may favour a certain form of action (peaceful as against violent), my participation in activism has taught me that it is the forms that are variable. I have not investigated the editorial reasoning behind this pre-summit typecasting, but there is little doubt that it conveys the impression that single persons can be identified as essentially peaceful or inherently militant. However, I have found – by following several activists through one protest event and the same activists through various protests – that forms of action and how protests develop do not reflect a person's predisposition. People may decide to shape-shift along the way, as in the case of the Freiburg clown who took off his greasepaint to engage in the black bloc in Strasbourg, or when an affinity group engaged in black bloc actions changed their clothes to walk with the peaceful demonstration during the Climate Summit in Copenhagen. Activists like Mikkel and Aske, who have never been in a riot, found that 'the time had come' to do so after the Ungdomshuset eviction in Copenhagen. While the forms of action are available to everybody, what form is considered appropriate in a given situation may vary greatly. Which form predominates in a given situation follows more complex rules than individual predispositions, which are best accessed through an attention to style.

The activist concept of style implies what, in anthropology, is called a situated ethic (judgements about right and wrong, as well as their timeliness), which does not square nicely with the law. Style illuminates the intertwining of appropriateness, effectiveness and persuasiveness of form, and is a scale used by activists to assess and pass judgement on the various forms of action.

Hitherto, the concept of style in the context of politics has been associated with the renowned work of the Birmingham School of cultural studies, and particularly Stuart Hall and Tony Jefferson's volume, *Resistance through Rituals: Youth Subcultures in Post-war Britain* (Hall and Jefferson 2006). In this book, style is defined as a pivotal characteristic of working-class youth sub-cultures juxtaposed to the parental generation and mainstream culture. The focus of the Birmingham School was on the appropriation, transformation and symbolic meaning attached to dress, music, gestures and language within the time–space defined as leisure (ibid.: 40–45), and their ideas have been employed in anthropological analyses of veganism among activists (Clark 2004; Krogstad 1986). According to this theory of style, sub-cultures hybridize styles out of the images and materials available to them from mainstream society in their effort to construct new and oppositional collective identities.[13] Due to the association of style with leisure, and the expectation of it being co-opted and reincorporated into mainstream culture, the potentiality of inducing broader societal change by way of engaging in sub-cultural lifestyles was seen as limited (Hebdige 2006: 77).

Jeffrey Juris employs this concept of sub-cultural style to account for the logic behind the black bloc form of protest in Genoa (Juris 2008: 181–82), but in my view there is much more to style than oppositional identity formation. According to most activists I have talked to, all actions have a style, which has little to do with either oppositional identity formation or an abstract Kantian sense of beauty. Activists speak explicitly about 'good meeting style' and, in connection with dumpster diving, it is considered 'good style' to clean up after oneself when dumpster diving for food; style is also used in relation to direct actions, and in Chapter 2 I quoted Aske as saying that 'style depends, to some extent, on the police'.

The Reclaim the Street action in Hyskenstræde was defined as 'open street stylee' (*sic*), in which the openness of the style implies both that there is room for all forms of action and that it is up to the participants to define what actions are considered appropriate; moreover, flirting with improvisation, spontaneity and unpredictability is not just possible but expected.

Among activists in Denmark, the styles are typically talked of as confrontational, non-violent, family friendly and, as in the case of Hyskenstræde, open or free. While these sound like an echo of the newspaper typology of activists, it is important to note that they correspond to forms and not to particular persons. Moreover, the style can be either good or bad, and thereby indicates what is considered appropriate and legitimate in a given situation. The style also tells us something about how intensity and a sense of success can be generated. For example, if the style is defined as family friendly, this implies that the demonstration/action generally stays within legal limits and, to the extent possible, avoids confrontation with the police (as in the case of the demonstration going to the Sandholm retention centre). In a demonstration defined as family friendly, intensity and success depend largely on the number of people present, but also on the 'atmosphere' generated, for example by walking in a close-knit formation or chanting.

Style is, however, not interchangeable with a fixed ethical codex, which would imply that the organizers of an action decide what is appropriate on behalf of others, and thereby place limits on the ideas and inventiveness of fellow activists – something that is never appropriate. Nevertheless, it is considered 'good style' (*god stil*) to not only adhere to the style and respect the concept of the action, but also to be able to judge when a change of form is called for. In the following, I offer a conceptualization of style, informed by activists' use of the word, as denoting the appropriateness, persuasiveness and effectiveness of form (cf. Riles 1998; Strathern 2004).

Appropriateness

The concern for appropriateness – what is suitable and timely – is intertwined with the question of violence. As previously mentioned, based on his fieldwork among North American activists, Graeber defines violence as 'the intentional infliction of pain or harm on others', humans and animals alike (Graeber 2009: 212). This largely corresponds to the understanding that I have encountered among European activists. As a rule of thumb, violence is not considered appropriate, and if it takes place it usually becomes the subject of heated internal debate. In Strasbourg we saw an example of how free-form action became mixed up with a large demonstration organized by the peace movement. The attempt of radical activists to hide behind or within the demonstration subsequently became the subject of internal critique. Before the Climate Summit in Copenhagen, the organizers of a large common demonstration were nervous about the possible participation of so-called black-bloc activists. In a court case relating to the event, it was later shown that activists from the Never Trust a Cop network were herded into the main demonstration by the police, who subsequently used this situation as justification for arresting a large section of the demonstration, which counted some 100,000 participants.

But there are also exceptions to this principle about the appropriateness of non-violence: situations where the police are considered an inhuman enemy (see Chapter 4) and where activists consider it fully legitimate to defend themselves if attacked by the police. In light of the threat of eviction at Ungdomshuset in Copenhagen, there was a common dictum among activists: 'If they attack us in court, we defend ourselves in court; if they attack us in the media, we defend ourselves in the media; if they attack us in the streets, we will defend ourselves in the street'. My interviews with activists from Ungdomshuset reveal that, after having tried to defend their house in court, through public relations and through demonstrations and humorous actions in public space, the riots and property destruction that followed the eviction were considered not only appropriate, but also a timely and legitimate response in the face of the injustice committed by the police when they evicted people from the house. There is, in other words, a concern for proportionality and symmetry in the idea of appropriateness.

In situations like Strasbourg, where the first riots were not directly caused by a police attack on the activists present in the city, but by the killing of a protestor during the G20 protests in London a few days earlier, the situation turns murky, and it becomes difficult even for many activists to distinguish between attacker and defendant. This dilemma grows over the years and from one protest to the next, which makes it difficult to interpret protests as singular events.

Yet, the employment of 'violence' (even when understood in a broad sense to include the destruction of property) is debated every time a major action is planned, and I have found that violence seldom emerges spontaneously; nor can vulgar and abusive unruliness be considered the moving force behind the destruction of private property, such as was assumed by the media in the wake of Hyskenstræde and after the Ungdomshuset eviction. Activists choosing to employ the tactic of the black bloc, destroying a cash machine or throwing a bottle at a police officer in riot uniform, are not unaware of ethical concerns, nor are they ignorant of the law, but they may be intolerant towards it. The level of dialogue maintained between activists and public authorities, elected politicians and the police also has a role to play. When dialogue is suspended, and soft power is abandoned – for example because activists will not submit to the soft power of the police (cf. Fernandez 2008) or when politicians wish to communicate to the general public that they do not 'give in to violence' – the view of the police as an abstract inhuman force tends to take over.

The form of action of the pink bloc is, in principle, always appropriate, and its effectiveness is produced by way of imaginative and serious play. Pink blocs have often maintained effective blockades for hours while dancing in the street, but the intensity of this form of action is, contrary to the black bloc, produced by mocking and subverting the police's display of force. While being a clown, an activist is supposed to materialize joy and creativity but, as the clown from Freiburg explained while we were on our way to the train station in Strasbourg, if one loses that feeling then one must take off the costume and the red nose. In other words, there are situations where even clowns may consider this form of action inappropriate, namely when police action does not leave room for a joking response. The 'kettling' of activists is a case in point. To sum up, the ethical limitations that activists place on their actions are closely tied to an ongoing analysis of the situation at hand, and not least to their position in a network of social relations.

A final matter concerning appropriateness is worth considering before turning to other aspects of style, namely the frequent equating of crowds, spontaneity and violence. The police often expect crowds to react in unpredictable ways, and crowd behaviour is largely explained in terms of processes internal to the crowd itself. The crowd is seldom perceived as homogeneous, but is divided into a violent minority and a peaceful majority. The violent minority is seen as capable of using the 'mindlessness' of ordinary people gathered, who might turn irrational and violent when they become part of the mass (Reicher 1984; Stott and Reicher 1998). Contrary to the often-cited work of Elias Canetti on the behaviour and social psychology of crowds (Canetti 1984), I have never encountered, and heard very few stories about, activists being seduced by the rush of the crowd. Instead, activists carefully reflect upon style and their own risk-taking behaviour before and during an action in combination with a concern for the most appropriate means for the situation at hand. These thoughts are not cast overboard along the way, but activists may decide, as already mentioned, that a forceful response is timely or that a change of tactic is called for. Yet, the activist concept of style does not only entail this kind of situated ethic, but also implies an attention to the persuasiveness and effectiveness of a form both vis-à-vis participating activists and in relation to a broader audience.

Persuasiveness

A concept of action presented prior to an action must be persuasive if it is to succeed in generating the participation of fellow activists. This demands a relatively clear idea as well as an inventive form, which can be communicated to others at preparation meetings, but also via posters and other kinds of call for action (for example, via activist and mainstream media). The form must not be too rigid; it should accommodate diversity, and innovation is praised. Aske explained to me on one occasion that 'a number two is always a down-turn', implying that repetitions should be avoided, and no action should be completely like a past one.[14]

Besides requiring a good cause, persuasive actions need a convincing presentation and a space for practical skills during the action. Like the ethical rules of thumb discussed above, a good action implies the ability to respond to a changing environment by improvising tactics, adapting to the context, finding a way to outwit an adversary and, in general, improving the odds. These are skills that are an absolute necessity in the concrete situation, not least in order to avoid arrest and/or injury.[15] Hence, the emphasis placed on creativity and innovation has a very practical dimension: making space for influencing the outcome of a situation.

So, for an action to be persuasive it must not only be new, but also linked to a good cause, often implying a clear identification of an injustice committed. For an anarchist, injustice takes place when someone takes control of other people's lives, that is, when people's autonomy and ability to define their own destiny, both in the individual and collective sense, is violated. This notion of injustice can be applied to the eviction of people from activist spaces, to situations where people are fenced in, or more specifically, when politicians ignore the consequences of climate change under the influence of business corporations. In this light, summit protests are highly persuasive moments because the often abstract and intangible injustices committed by corporations and world leaders become real and immediate, as also argued in Chapter 1.[16] Thus, for an action to be convincing and motivate fellow activists to participate in it, it must offer the possibility of 'establishing a conflict' with the alleged perpetrators of injustice.

Persuasiveness, the second important element in style, also has another dimension: namely of persuading the adversary to engage in the performance. The destruction of property and pushing into police lines are effective tools for provoking the superior violence of the police (whereupon they, consequently, beat up and arrest protesters). Clowning is another, parallel way of establishing a bodily exchange, but here it is the perplexity and inability of the police to handle unexpected situations that is exposed, such as when they maintain a petrified posture in response to the clowns' stupidity and foolish provocation. Either way, the skilful performance must have the effect of persuading the police to engage in bodily exchange and confrontation.

As alluded to, this bodily exchange may take various forms. I have described how the black bloc activists in the harbour area near the Europe Bridge in Strasbourg almost replicated the police by mimicking the police's tempo and bodily movements, clothing and armament: paraphrasing Michael Taussig, the copy draws on the power of the original (Taussig 1993: xiii). Obviously, the pink bloc plays into the script of cops versus protesters in a different way – the mimesis is distorted, but nonetheless has powerful effects. At any rate, the forms of action, both of the black and of the pink bloc, have persuasive effects insofar as they seduce or provoke the police to engage with them, whereby an enemy is precipitated.

Finally, the persuasiveness of protests is directed towards the general public. Though Left radical activists make a political point of ignoring the state and elected politicians, the Danish sociologist René Karpantschof has controversially argued that violent actions actually pay off. Through a statistical analysis of the connection between violent protests (in the broad sense) and media coverage, he has documented that the unrest before and after the Ungdomshuset eviction not only made it an issue of public concern, but that it moreover persuaded politicians to return to the negotiating table (Karpantschof and Mikkelsen 2009: 96). While activists disagree about the expediency of communicating with and through the mainstream media, and hard-nosed anarchists reject taking the media into account in the planning of their actions, there is little doubt that rioting and burning barricades attract media attention, and in key instances also compel the renewal of a more formal dialogue.

During the Climate Summit in Copenhagen, a peaceful march to the summit venue contained approximately 100,000 participants, but the media coverage was probably more intense than it otherwise would have been (and continued to be so in the months following the event) due to the participation of a few hundred black bloc activists. Though this group, under the name Never Trust a Cop, conveyed an image of seeking to burn down the city (achieved in part through a YouTube video),[17] they (only) ended up throwing a few stones at Copenhagen's stock exchange and outside the Ministry of Foreign Affairs after having been being herded into the large peaceful march by the police. However, this incident was intensively covered by the media, along with the spectacular arrest of a whole section of demonstrators. In the end, the judge did not accept the police's argument that being clad in black was a display of violent intent, and something which could justify the arrests.[18] So, even though the organizers of the demonstration regretted the participation of the alleged black bloc, there is little doubt that they often enhance the visibility of protests and causes that may otherwise go unnoticed.

The clowns attract almost as much media attention as the black bloc. In Strasbourg, approximately fifty clowns from England, Germany, Spain and France held a press conference, attended by about twice as many journalists. They mostly spoke gibberish, interrupted by violent crying about not having been invited to the official party. Then they announced some silly plan about how to attend the summit anyway. In the public eye the clowns often counterbalance the black bloc, but that neither means that they are less serious about their endeavours, nor that they are less able to stage a performative confrontation.

The point here is that activists initiate a public debate about democracy and how society handles political dissent by a variety of means. In fact, and contrary to many activists' stated intentions about ignoring and rejecting mainstream media, activists are destined to spend a significant amount of time in documenting, and drawing public attention to, incidents of police repression, if not before then after major protest events.

As a small digression from the issue of style, I find it important to highlight that activists' emphasis on the persuasive effects of spectacular and public protests are – in addition to a generalized distaste for vanguardism, internal hierarchies and the weighting of creativity – important factors that prevent Left radical activists in Northern Europe from being attracted to illegal forms of actions, such as those of urban guerrillas that have haunted Europe in recent history. Left radical activists live through periods of public visibility and invisibility, but an attention to style, and to persuasiveness in particular, reveal that the enmity between activists and the police is tied to particular events. By paying attention to style it is possible to get a good idea about what is both in store and at stake for activists.

Effectiveness

The last element in the concept of style concerns the effectiveness of form. As previously mentioned, activists distinguish between effective and symbolic actions. Obviously, symbolic actions such as a demonstration can also have effects, depending on the extent to which elected politicians are incited to make policy changes. However, if we use Austin's typology of speech acts in relation to the symbolic/effective division, the conceptual reach of the effectiveness of form may become clearer. In this light, demonstrations could be classified as perlocutionary (speech) acts that may initiate a series of consequences, but where the enunciation, or in this case the performance, and the consequences are temporally distinct. An effective action, on the other hand, can be considered a kind of illocutionary act, which is saying something and doing something simultaneously. In other words, effective actions are supposed to produce effects without any lapse of time (cf. Butler 1997: 17).

I believe that this points to something essential about the magic of Left radical politics: first, that form and content cannot be distinguished from one another – what we usually think of as political intentions or the content of a message are embodied within and evoked by a skilful form (epitomized in the activist notion of 'good style'); second, this evocation takes place simultaneously.

Performances in general are not performed to have a meaning, but to produce effects (Hobart 1986; Kapferer 2005; Keane 2006; Strathern 2004: 80–81). This also holds for protest performances. The most interesting and powerful effects are not necessarily the consequences intended by subjects, nor do the effects necessarily correspond to activist-stated success criteria prior to an action (such as closing down a retention centre), but are inherent in and elicited by a skilful form. The concept of style that I have drawn out so far elucidates how what we conventionally think of as political form and content are joined together. The form *is* the message, and the concept of style is the scale or measure for the form's appropriateness, persuasiveness and effectiveness.

In the remainder of this chapter I turn to the particular kind of effect that skilful performances (that is, actions with a 'good style') have on the body and on time. I argue that a good style temporarily evokes a different bodily point of view. This radicalizing endeavour also calls for a return to the nature of the collective body in order to talk about a 'bodily seeing' along the lines of Amerindian perspectivism theorized by Viveiros de Castro (1992, 1998, 2004).

On the Ritual Process and Bodily Affect

There is little doubt that protesting and engaging in bodily confrontation with the police gives rise to what we usually think of as strong emotions. In the ethnographic description of the dance in Hyskenstræde, I have described how the loud music, the temporary nature of the event and the suspension of normal relations of control exerted over a public space produced an outburst of joy among participants. Similarly, I have described how being 'kettled' in Strasbourg evoked not only anxiety and fear, but also a sense of mutual solidarity, control and (bodily) strength. In a similar vein, a well-facilitated meeting is often accompanied by an experience of equality and genuine democracy.

An obvious model for understanding these emotions is that of the ritual process, as argued by people close to the alterglobalization movement (Jordan 2002; Juris 2008). Victor Turner's work on ritual and performance is of particular relevance here. As mentioned in the Introduction, based on Van Gennep's theory of rites of passage, Turner's model of the ritual process divides time into phases of separation, transition – a state of social limbo or liminality out of secular time – and reincorporation. According to Turner, it is characteristic of the liminal and liminoid phase that strong feelings are evoked (Turner 1982: 29–32; 1987: 34; cf. Mitchell 2006: 384; Sjørslev 2007: 15–16). Protests, and moments of bodily confrontation in particular, can be associated with the liminal or liminoid phase of rituals, and equated with the reversal of order and disorder, rule and exception, inherent to this phase in rituals (Turner 1982: 52–55; Juris 2008: 331 n.25). Nevertheless, I believe that Juris's attention to the generation of emotions during a protest event, and his argument that protests involve the embodiment of utopian ideals (Juris 2008: 9), overemphasizes the expressive qualities of protest performances, by seeing them as containers for underlying perceptions and values, instead of probing into their world-making effects.

It follows that from an anthropological perspective, the ritual reversal entailed in protesting can either be understood as a Gluckman-like ritual of rebellion, that is, a social safety valve necessary for the restoration and maintenance of social order (Gluckman 1963), or as a reflexive and subjunctive moment á la Victor Turner (Turner 1982). In earlier work, Turner stressed the integrative function of ritual, in agreement with Gluckman, and in so doing he also reproduced Emile Durkheim's basic thesis about the function of symbols in rituals, namely that rituals first and foremost reaffirm the sentiments upon which a group is based (Durkheim 1954: 216).[19] Turner formulated this in the concept of communitas (Turner 1982: 44). Later, Turner came to highlight the transformative or potential quality of the liminal/liminoid that, as he put it, 'can generate and store a plurality of alternative models for living, from utopias to programs' (ibid.: 33; cf. Kapferer 2006: 137).

While Victor Turner's ritual model might be apposite for describing and understanding single events, it runs up against problems when series of overlapping events are at stake (see Palmer and Jankowiak 1996), or when employed to explain situations of chronic crisis (Vigh

2008), not least because the ritual model suffers from an ontology of linear time; the ritual is described as a unified and linear process around which order and disorder, rule and exception, the everyday and the festive are temporally reversed. Yet, Turner's allusion to the existence of other immanent models or worlds that may emerge during a ritual or performance goes to the heart of what I believe is also at stake here.

If we return for a moment to the street dance in Hyskenstræde, activists did not characterize the ludic play (Turner 1982) in Hyskenstræde as a moment of disorder, but a temporary restoration of (cosmological) order, reclaiming public space from corporate control. As described in Chapter 1, the capitalist world is perceived by activists as being in a state of perpetual crisis: it is a fundamentally unjust and disorderly world offering no point of transcendence. Activists can establish interstices of what I have called active time when opening up self-governed social spaces or consuming vegan food, or via bodily confrontations with the police. These interstices are always accompanied by a latent danger of sliding back into undifferentiated dead time.

To turn the ritual model on its head, to establish a reverse symmetry, would therefore at first glance seem more appropriate for coming to grips with activists' forms of action. In this light, the bodily confrontations during an action, which activists themselves talk of as the single most important criterion for judging the successfulness of a protest event,[20] can be perceived as a moment of reversal that, for the moment, restores rule and order or, in other words, a genuine sociality characterized by solidarity, autonomy and equality among people.

Yet I do not find this model of explanation wholly satisfying. First, turning the ritual model upside down, as Juris also implicitly does by arguing that protests involve the embodiment of utopian ideals (Juris 2008: 9), does not solve the problem of the ontology of linear time underlying the model. Second, a reversal of the model still hinges on the constructivist assumption that it is the point of view (the subject) that creates the object (see Viveiros de Castro 2004: 467) or, in other words, that the emotional effects are simply a consequence of activists perceiving the event differently from, for example, the police.

I am reluctant to understand the ritual, and thus the protests, as a social construction of personal feelings, as is common in the anthropology of emotions (Lutz and White 1986; Wulff 2007). Instead, I have found that the key to understanding protest events is bodily affect, and that this affect is intimately linked to the evocation of a different point of view.[21] In the following I shall therefore offer an alternative way of thinking about the times of protest and political action – entailing the peculiar oscillation between moments of active time and dead time – which builds on Brian Massumi's concept of affect (Massumi 1987, 2002) and Viveiros de Castro's Amerindian perspectivism (Viveiros de Castro 1998). The argument concerns the nature of the collective body, and how the body engenders time.

To make this point I need to revisit some key ethnographic passages. I began this book with a description of the Reclaim Power action during the Climate Summit in Copenhagen in 2009. Immediately preceding the activists' collective push against the police line and the fence around the Bella Centre, Iza, an experienced activist trainer who was standing on the sound truck, made everybody repeat her words:

> IZA: First we will take three steps to the left.
> EVERYBODY: First we will take three steps to the left.
> IZA: Then we will count down from ten.
> EVERYBODY: Then we will count down from ten.
> IZA: Then we will push and push until we can get over the fence.
> EVERYBODY: Then we will push and push until we can get over the fence.[22]

At that time, I believed that making the people standing nearest repeat her words in such a way that people came to repeat them in waves throughout the crowd, was her way of ensuring that all the people assembled were able to hear what she said (creating a 'people's microphone'); later, I thought it was an exercise to make people feel confident about collective illegal endeavour. Now I am inclined to believe that her words, and the fact that everybody repeated them, generated bodily synchronization or a sense of belonging to the same time.[23] The activists proceeded in accordance with her and their words, but in not managing to cross the fence, a tight pack of people was produced between the sound truck, the police and the fence. Aske, who later described the experience of pushing against the police line as that of 'one big body acting together', confirms my understanding of the emergence of a synchronic body in moments of confrontation.[24]

Becoming a collective or synchronic body is frequent at protests, but may take a variety of forms, such as when activists walk in tight blocs with their arms locked together during a demonstration, dressed in similar black clothes and thereby becoming indiscernible from one another, or when free-form actions, such as the riots in Strasbourg, create a swarming effect, which exemplifies synchronization between dispersed elements. In these contexts, however, the synchronization need not involve all the persons present. Here, the words of Little Emma after the chaotic attempt at swarming the fence during Shut Down the Camp come to mind, namely that to stick together in a bloc made her feel strong and 'lemming-like', and that she was 'not the least bit scared of the police', and contrasts with the insecurity she associated with free-form actions.

An outside force may produce a similar effect; a collective body often emerges in situations in which bodies are confined in narrow spaces (as in Hyskenstræde or inside a dumpster) or become physically compressed. This was particularly salient when several hundred activists were 'kettled' by the police on the Grand Pont in Strasbourg. I have described how the physical compression of protesters at the bridge assembled a collective body, breathing as one, with the movement of one part instantly impinging on the rest, and the rhythm of the samba band becoming the collective pulse. The effect of this is an experience of absorption and increased bodily intensity and force.

Brian Massumi (1987) offers a Deleuzian concept of affect. He argues that affect is 'prepersonal intensity corresponding to the passage from one experiential state of the body to another and implying an augmentation or diminution of the body's capacity to act' (ibid.: xvi); hence, affect is an experience of intensity, or perhaps more precisely a moment of unformed potentiality that cannot be captured in language (Massumi 2002: 30). Among activists, this sense of intensity is cast in a bodily idiom and experienced as strength. In the context of the so-called G13 action to seize a new Ungdomshus at Grøndalsvænge Allé 13 (briefly described in Chapter 2), the 25-year-old Vigga described the experience in the following way:

> It was really cool to break through the fence and get onto the site, but it did not compare with the victories on the way there: to pass the police line, and the incredible strength and force in 'now we walk in chains together', and 'we stick together', and 'we do not give a damn that the police are here' ... If I sometimes feel powerless then there is an enormous strength in taking back the street and setting the agenda ... If I have to think of one moment where I felt that way strongly, then it was when we were on our way to Grøndalsvænge with a yellow bloc and managed to get around the police line; or the situation that emerged in Nørrebro the night after Ungeren [slang for Ungdomshuset] was evicted.

What Vigga's characterization of the action allows us to capture is how important moments are often talked about in a bodily idiom, namely moments when bodily strength is experienced or felt as lacking. Strength is, in short, an experience of bodily intensity and force, an increased capacity to act, which among activists is explicitly associated with being part of a collective body of protesters and 'absorbed by action'. This can be seen in opposition to other moments, such as when Nicola and I were feeling followed and watched by the police on our night-time drive through Strasbourg, or when he cried from exhaustion and 'lack of strength' the evening after the protests.

In my view, this enables us to grasp not only the contradiction between being immobilized by the 'kettle' and the increased sense of power and strength that this induced, but also the particular relationship between body and time at stake in these situations. The moment on the bridge in Strasbourg, for example, caused a change in the experiential state of the body in terms of form and vitality. In Strasbourg and during the Reclaim Power action in Copenhagen, the actions revealed that the collective body is neither an expression of communitas nor of affective solidarity, but a matter of bodily affect (Massumi 2002; see also Krøijer 2010, 2014). In attending to the synchronization of the collective body, the ontology of linear time underlying the ritual process must be dissolved. It is not the subject (inside or outside the ritual or action) that obtains different perceptions of the same linear time, or who experiences a 'moments outside time' (Day et al. 1999: 2), but different ontologies of time that come into existence by virtue of the affected body/bodies. The techniques of the body and the intensity of the situation allow for the oscillation between what I think of as different coexistent bodily perspectives. Bodily confrontation is therefore key to understanding the logic of Left radical protesting due to its particular effect on time. In this light, the antinomy between the present and the future, underlying the ritual model and the concept of prefiguration alike, must be reconsidered.

The Temporal Perspective of a Collective Body

In the case of the 'kettle', the compressed bodies were put together as one composite entity and became, to use the words of Viveiros de Castro, the site of a 'differentiating perspective' (Viveiros de Castro 1998: 482).

In his work on Amerindian cosmology, Viveiros de Castro redefines the categories of nature and culture and criticizes the use of Western naturalism, which is founded on the idea of a shared nature and multiple cultures, to describe non-Western cosmologies. Based on his study of the way humans, animals and spirits see each other among the Araweté in Brazil, Viveiros de Castro argues that all these categories share an anthropomorphic essence (culture), but that they show themselves in different 'clothes', that is, different bodily appearances (natures). In so doing, Western multiculturalism is replaced with Amazonian multinaturalism, implying a spiritual unity and a corporeal diversity. The result is a cosmology of multiple bodily viewpoints. As pointed out earlier, the existence of multiple points of view does not mean that the same world is being apprehended from different angles, but that 'all beings see the world the same way – what changes is the world they see' (ibid.: 477).

Obviously, an activist cosmology is different from that of indigenous Amazonians, but the bodily ability to take a certain point of view is analogous. In both contexts it is the body that makes the difference, and among activists it is the body that enables the oscillation between active time and dead time. If we transpose Amazonian multinaturalism to Western thinking about time, it should be possible to reconsider the antinomy between the present and the future (and between immanence and transcendence), which are inherent in much thinking about social change. As argued previously, it is often taken for granted that the ontology of time is a linear, fluid time; that is, there is just one shared clock that we may in turn perceive differently (Gell 1992; Hodges 2008). What my ethnography suggests is that time, under some circumstances, is not one flow from the past through the present to the future, but that it is non-chronological and that multiple times are simultaneous or coexistent (see also Foucault 1986: 24–26; Hodges 2008: 409; Tonkin 1992: 72–75).

In a short article, Michel Foucault (1986) describes the present epoch as one of the simultaneity of spaces. He talks of heterotopias as real places, but also as counter-sites or effectively enacted utopias that have the property of standing in relation to all other spaces 'in such a way as to suspect, neutralize or invert the set of relations that they happen to designate, mirror or reflect' (ibid.: 24). According to Foucault, it is a principle of the heterotopia that it juxtaposes several spaces in a single real place (the example being the Persian carpets that are reproductions of gardens, and gardens as the rug on to which the whole world is enacted). Moreover, Foucault argues, heterotopias are linked to 'slices in time', that is, to heterochronicity (ibid.: 26), which implies the emergence of several simultaneous times, or perhaps more precisely in the present context, several simultaneous modes of engendering time via bodily figuration.

So, it is Foucault's attention to heterochronicity (simultaneous times) together with Viveiros de Castro's perspectives that are important in order to make sense of Left radical protesting. Rather than being several simultaneous views from somewhere, as in the case of Amerindian perspectivism (Viveiros de Castro 1992, 1998), we are as much talking of several simultaneous views from 'somewhen' (Da Col 2007) tied to the event of the confrontation and the temporality of the collective body/ies. Like the different natures that shamans and spirits may assume in Amazonian societies, activists can, by way of bodily alterity, acquire different temporal perspectives. The absorption into common action, and particularly the becoming of a collective body, give rise to a different temporal perspective. In the case of street protests, it is the bodily confrontation between activists and the police (in its various forms) that works as the point of transition between different bodily points of view. The bodily confrontation is of decisive importance because it has an effect on time: it is the body that splits time when it is confronted with an obstacle (say, the police) and brings activists 'out of sync' with the world around them.

The life of an activist oscillates between multiple temporal modes of being, namely between what activists characterize respectively as dead time and active time, which both hinge on the body. Both active time and dead time are complex and multifaceted experiences, but active time is prevalent in situations – such as the one on the bridge in Strasbourg or when harvesting thrown-out food in a supermarket container – when activists come to exist in a state of differentiated or precipitated synchrony. In this context, what we conventionally talk of as experiences or feelings of solidarity, equality, strength and freedom are characteristics of this precipitated active time. Obviously, active time is experienced differently in situations such as riots, demonstrations, a dumpster dive or a well facilitated meeting, but what they have in common is a state of bodily vitality and absorption in common action. It is a skilful performance with 'good style' that makes the temporal (bodily) perspective appear. This temporal perspective does not follow any neat division between the everyday and the festive, but is a figuration of time that can emerge in all realms of life.

The moments of active time such as the emergence of a collective body of protesters are qualitatively different from several other moments during the situations described in the previous pages, where people describe themselves as apathetic or inactive due to paranoia, sadness or burn out, or when giving in to over-consumption and indifference. The experience of apathy was most clearly exemplified by Aske, who not only associated apathy with the period before getting taken up by activism, but also with the long period of 'depression' he suffered after the police violently disrupted the occupation of a church in Copenhagen, which had been squatted in collaboration with rejected Iraqi asylum seekers. The bodily perspective of dead time also emerges, unspectacularly, when activists describe themselves as indiscernible from the rest of the population because they have 'dropped out' of activism and given in to consumption and passivity; or it takes an unsettling turn when activists find they are being followed by police cars while cycling through the streets of Copenhagen prior to the Climate Summit or when they are put into solitary confinement after an arrest. Obviously, the experience of being singled out for prosecution or held in solitary confinement is different from the experience of being unable to perform according to the high social standards of daily life, but what they share is a requirement of bodily endurance and strength.

In the perspectivist model of time presented here what we conventionally think of as the present and the future are replaced by active time and dead time, which become coexisting bodily perspectives or simultaneous times.

Closing Remarks

I have found that an attention to style, bodily confrontation and time is decisive for understanding the forms politics takes among Left radical activists. Not unlike people's attraction to the magic of shamans (cf. Taussig 2006), there is something inherently magical and deeply fascinating about the 'as if' politics involved in cutting down a fence around a retention centre for refugees – 'as if' it would effectively solve the problem and change the condition of the detained refugees – or in shutting down a meeting of heads of state 'as if' it would fundamentally change the course of global capitalism. While the participants know that the magic is fraudulent, direct action also magnifies the demand for more. Taussig quotes Marcel Mauss's classic text on the techniques of the body by stating that 'underlying all our mystical states are corporal techniques, biological methods of entering into communication with God' (Taussig 2006: 121; cf. Mauss 1992: 475). In Mauss' words, certain bodily actions have 'a moral, ritual and cosmological effectiveness' (Mauss 1992: 460).

I have argued that activist experiences of a skilful protest performance are epitomized in the notion of style. Style is not a feature of sub-cultural identity, but encompasses concerns about appropriateness (that is, judging when a particular form of action is ethically appropriate), persuasiveness (which mainly refers to the form's ability to persuade fellow activists and the police to engage in bodily confrontation) and, finally, its effectiveness. A skilful performance, a protest with 'good style', has an effect on time.

In the above, I have described several forms of actions, and shown how activists make a fundamental distinction between symbolic and effective actions. Effective actions are, not unlike illocutionary speech acts, characterized by simultaneously saying something and doing something; via techniques of the body they produce an effect without a lapse in time. In the context of political action, this also implies that form and content cannot be distinguished from one another: intentions are, so to speak, embedded in and made apparent by a skilful form. This implies that intentions do not tie up neatly with individual activists, but are evoked by material forms and by the appearance of collective bodies. In sum, scrutiny of the ethical underpinning of Left radical protest events must go through an attention to style simply because the ethical and political content is immanent to form, and not the property of individual activists. The ethical is, so to speak, materialized in the collective body of protesters during an action or demonstration, and this is what the concept of style conveys.

The political performance of Left radical activists is, in other words, about making something appear (Strathern 1988), and what appears in the moment of confrontation is a collective body, which eclipses not only the relationship between activists and the police, but also groups and individuals, which are often depicted as the building blocks in theories about social movements (cf. Melucci 1996; Eschle 2011). It is the 'one big body acting together' or a collective body that takes 'singular' form through the confrontation. From the perspective of the collective body, cosmology is not an underlying system of thought that orients political action, but a momentary order – a world that falls into place (cf. Willerslev and Pedersen 2010) – in the moment of confrontation with the police. In this light, it is not so paradoxical that engaging in the chaotic space of a protest event is often experienced as liberating.

The collective body is a particular temporal perspective, which implies what I have called a 'figuration of the future', insofar as the body of protesters becomes an intentional entity that gives bodily or determinate form to the indeterminate. The collective body is one such determinate form or figuration among others, but it has a privileged relation to movement, action and the generation of affect. I do not think of these figurations as prefigurations, foreshadowing a future to come (Maeckelbergh 2009, 2011). Rather, the future only exists as latent (active) time (cf. Grosz 2005: 110; Miyazaki 2004: 70), and it is the performative confrontation with 'good style' that makes it appear.

Acknowledgements

Some of the ethnographic passages included in this chapter first appeared in articles published in *Social Analysis*, 54, 3 (2010) and in Anne Line Dalsgård, Martin Demant Frederiksen, Lotte Meinert and Susanne Højlund (eds), *Time Objectified: Ethnographies of Youth and Temporality* (Temple University Press, 2014).

Notes

1. This approach is inspired by what Holbraad and others have called 'the recursive move', which refers to allowing 'the contingency of ethnographic alterity to transmute itself to the level of analysis' (Holbraad 2012: 264). This is also at the heart of what Viveiros de Castro calls ontological self-determination (Viveiros de Castro, cited in Carrithers et al. 2010: 152–53)
2. Among these authors, Ekman (1991) is the only one who studies carnival and political protests in a Scandinavian context (more specifically, rural Sweden). She shares with Cohen an interest in how political strategies melt into cultural movements. She analyses annual summer festivals and a local carnival, and finds that egalitarianism prevails over hierarchy, spontaneity over routine, freedom over restrictions and communitas over structure (ibid.: 110–18; see also Cohen 1980; Turner 1982). This, she argues, breaks down barriers between social groups and classes, and fosters local belonging.
3. One of the key functions performed by selected activists during a demonstration is that of being a runner. Runners take care of communication between different parts of a demonstration, such as the front banner and the sound truck, when mobile communication is either impossible due to background noise or undesirable due to police interception of mobile phone communications. Runners enable different parts of a demonstration to sustain a discussion about tactical matters.
4. A spokes-council is an assembly of affinity groups working by consensus (Graeber 2002: 70–71). As described in the Introduction, affinity groups are small groups of activists who know and trust each other, but they can also be formed on a more ad hoc basis around specific goals. People within the affinity group take decisions about what kinds of actions they will participate in and using what means. Moreover, they look after each other during and after confrontations with the police. Each group sends a delegate to spokes-council meetings, which are held several times throughout an action or blockade to reach consensus on tactical issues.
5. A *banlieue* is a residential area on the outer edge of a city. In France the word *banlieue* is more frequently used to describe areas of low-income apartment blocks and social housing.
6. Agamben (1998: 122) talks of a zone of indistinction in the context of his arguments about the role of the camp in modern societies. The camp is not a physical entity, but the space created when the state of exception becomes the rule. This space of anomie is a zone of indistinction, a threshold between inside and outside where 'the force of law without law' is at stake (ibid.: 181; Agamben 2005: 39–40). In the zone of indistinction, there is no clear borderline between killable bare life (*zoé*) and the political life of the citizen (*bios*).
7. See the Clandestine Insurgent Rebel Clown Army website: www.clownarmy.org. Last accessed 12 October 2010.
8. How a situation plays out is obviously not only defined by the tactical balance between activists and the police, nor does it depend fully on the materials and equipment available, but is influenced by a number of other contextual factors, not least fundamental human rights and the freedom of demonstration (in Denmark stipulated in the Constitution § 79), which frame the event in a certain way and sanction the legitimate use of force by the police. Moreover, as in most situations of conflict and war, there is a public concern with the proportionality of force (a theme that in itself merits anthropological attention), and excessive use of force is often sanctioned

by public opinion. Finally, the public debate about the legitimacy of a given cause sometimes works to the same end.
9. See the Space Hijackers website: www.spacehijackers.co.uk/. Last accessed 15 December 2014.
10. An activist 'cookbook' is a guide which tells fellow activists how to organize a particular kind of action. See e.g. the homepage of Reclaim the Street, London, for a guide on how to organize a Reclaim the Street action: http://rts.gn.apc.org/. Last accessed 13 December 2014.
11. In Denmark, chapter 15 of the Criminal Code is the specific section concerned with crimes against public order and peace (*forbrydelse mod den offentlige orden og fred*).
12. 'Tre typer aktivister indtager Københavns gader', *Politiken*, 10 December 2009. In a similar vein, a left-wing political paper offered five archetypes developed by an alleged expert in climate activism ('Fem typer demonstrerer for klimaet', *Dagbladet Information*, 25 November 2009). He distinguished between the 'comfort demonstrator' (*hyggedemonstranten*), who comes along for a good time; the climate conscious demonstrator who demonstrates to show their discontent and put pressure on the politicians; the creative protester who is in opposition to the system, but always peaceful and likes juggling and dressing up; the confrontational protester, employing confrontational civil disobedience; and finally the violent protester. While the typology is a caricature and meant in a humorous vein, it is nevertheless built on the assumption that people have essential characteristics, and are hence innately violent or peaceful.
13. All of its shortcomings notwithstanding, particularly the description of sub-cultures as homogeneous and bounded entities, one of the major contributions of the Birmingham School was to demonstrate that sub-cultures were not as distinct as conventionally imagined, but actually similar to the culture of the parental generation.
14. Past actions should always push new actions along. They connect 'sidewards', as Massumi (2002: 16–18) puts it, setting things in motion in unexpected directions (Krøijer 2015). Inventiveness and potentiality is crucial for upholding the expectation that radical change will be possible in the face of the all encompassing nature of capitalism.
15. These skills are, as previously mentioned, are difficult to teach without engaging in actions. Young and inexperienced activists are expected to get arrested at least a couple of times while learning how to read and engage with the police. Good activists are hence expected to have been arrested, at some point, but should not expose themselves to unnecessary arrest (this is often referred to as 'committing suicide', that is, a wilful sacrifice without any larger effect).
16. David Graeber has argued that the persuasive effect also acts at a different, subtler plane. Property destruction (as encountered in Hyskenstræde, and on a much larger scale in Strasbourg) is also about demonstrating how fragile 'the system' really is. As opposed to the puppets (described in Chapter 3) that are made up of perishable and transient materials, capitalism seems permanent and monumental. However, the smashing of a storefront window quite literally shatters this illusion (Graeber 2009: 490).
17. See *COP 15: War on Capitalism*. Retrieved 21 March 2011 from: www.youtube.com/watch?v=DWEzLoUgXw0. In my view, and as argued in Chapter 1, this video distributed did not primarily convey the intention of actually burning down the city; rather, it sought to convince the audience of a particular threat and a common enemy (namely, capitalism as well as the COP process and the police who were shielding it).

18. The police undertook a pincer movement that led to the mass arrest of almost 1,000 protesters approximately 1 kilometre further along the route of the demonstration. Several of those arrested subsequently pressed charges for unwarranted arrest and for inhuman treatment. The police have argued in court that the arrests were legitimate, with references to aerial photos of the section of demonstrators showing that the majority were black clad (as if this was in itself a sign of having committed an illegal act), which entailed that they could be considered as 'a collective threat' (*en trussel under ét*). The police lost the case. With few exceptions, the arrests were judged to be unwarranted, and the police were criticized for 'not having performed the required sorting' (separation). Moreover, having people seated for many hours in the cold street was judged to be 'inhumane treatment'. For the ruling, see: http://www.domstol.dk/KobenhavnsByret/nyheder/domsresumeer/Pages/DomiCOP15sag.aspx. Last accessed 8 January 2015. The police appealed the ruling to the High Court (Landsretten). In January 2012 the court found that arrest of the 'black bloc' was justified, but the court also ruled on compensation for unwarranted arrest to a large group of protestors. See: http://www.domstol.dk/oestrelandsret/nyheder/domsresumeer/Pages/ErstatningtildefrihedsberoevedeunderklimatopmoedetCOP15.aspx. Last accessed 8 January 2015.
19. Durkheim focused explicitly on the forms of religious life. According to Durkheim, however, the true function of the rites performed by Australian clans was not, as they themselves understood it, to increase their totem species, but to produce socially useful effects. According to Durkheim, during the rite, the Australians experience a strong enthusiasm, and as a consequence are 'transported to another level of reality', which makes them feel outside and above normal moral life (Durkheim 1954: 216, 226).
20. As this might be a politically controversial claim, it is important to underline that confrontation is not synonymous with violence. Confrontations may take a variety of forms, as described above, or they may simply involve a confrontation of values, as exemplified by dumpster diving.
21. The words 'feeling and emotion' are often used interchangeably. Following Massumi, I take feeling to be personal and biographical, whereas emotions are social (for example, collective expressions of feelings, or the social construction of feelings). Affects are pre-personal and non-conscious experiences of (bodily) intensity.
22. This quoted from memory (see Krøijer 2015).
23. David Graeber has described a similar call-and-response pattern during A16 (protest against the World Bank/IMF in Washington on 16 April 2000), but in the context of a spokes-council meeting. He sees it as a way to ensure that the speaker is 'keenly aware of the gravity of what they were saying', and 'cuts out the extraneous' (that is, heightens the focus of participants); but he also emphasizes that the repetition 'somehow makes the entire process a collective one' (Graeber 2009: 484), so that chanting is a collective dissolution of individuality and authorship (ibid.: 485).
24. At the Reclaim Power action I was not part of this body myself, merely due to the fact that I had decided to stay out of the worst clashes with the police, but the bodily effect is not unfamiliar.

Conclusion

The Collective Body as a Theory of Politics

In the summer of 2010, the former leader of the Danish opposition and current prime minister, Helle Thorning-Schmidt of the Social Democratic Party, ran into a political storm when it was publicly revealed that she had chosen to enrol her daughter in a renowned private school in Copenhagen. Eight years earlier, Thorning-Schmidt had pointed out that 'a dangerous undermining of the quality of the state-run public school' was underway produced by so-called resourceful parents who removed their children from schools, which were arguably an important meeting place for children from different economic and cultural backgrounds (see Aurvig Brøndum et al. 2002). During the controversy following the public exposure, political commentators pointed out the alleged contradiction that prominent leaders of a party known for defending the Danish welfare state and celebrating the social solidarity produced by the free-of-charge Danish Folkeskole (state-run public school) chose to place their own children in private schools. In the debate, which in the following months also came to involve her and her husband, the British diplomat and Labour candidate Stephen Kinnock, and his tax affairs, she was repeatedly referred to as 'Gucci-Helle with the expensive look'. This was taken as an expression of her alienation from the working-class constituency of the party and her de facto acceptance of increasing social inequality.[1] Thorning-Schmidt defended herself by arguing that, for the Social Democrats, fighting for better future public schooling was a key issue, but also argued that her personal choice on behalf of her children in no way contradicted this. Despite this, and the fact that her husband was acquitted of accusations of tax fraud, years later the couple are still not considered to live in satisfactory accordance with the political project of their party.

How does this debate relate to the arguments put forward here? The public debate about the prime minister's actions clearly underlines the expectation that political leaders should embody their own political ideals. At a more abstract level, the case speaks to the relationship between politics and time. While Thorning-Schmidt maintained that politics is a matter of actors setting and pursuing goals in the future, a large section of the public demanded a prefigurative politics of her, namely that her private choices should anticipate or foreshadow the future in making it a model for her present private life. Thorning-Schmidt's troubles show that even in mainstream politics, forms of action and material objects (such as an expensive Gucci bag) may have effects of their own, and that goals do not have a simple, linear relationship with the reasons behind an act. But if politics do not hinge on individual aspirations for the future, what then?

In this book I have described some of the most important forms politics takes among Left radical activists in Northern Europe: the experiments with self-management and egalitarian modes of being together in social centres; the daily re-collection, preparation and consumption of vegan and non-industrially produced food; and the planning, training for and many-sided performance of protest actions. Here I wish to extend my argument to consider its analytical purchase for an understanding of the recent wave of global protest and for public politics more generally.

I have offered a way to think about politics, and Left radical activism in particular, which is not dependant on the constitutive power of the individual, but addresses the relationship between form and time in a new way. The argument presented is twofold. The first insight concerns how form engenders intentions when it comes to Left radical politics. Rather than expecting people to live and act in accordance with pre-defined values or goals, I have argued that form is prior to intention and impels effects of its own. This contradicts the common contention in approaches to social movements and political actions, which rely on the idea that politics is the concerted activity of individual and collective actors pursuing predefined goals (Melucci 1996: 8, 387; Verdery 2004: 303). The second insight is that Left radical politics and protesting is neither simply a celebration of community nor does it primarily revolve around reaffirmations of collective identity. I have argued that it is necessary to take the nature of time into account, and particularly the particular way in which activists relate to an emerging future, in order to understand the raison d'être of Left radical politics.

In fact, much of the existing literature on the radical Left, the global justice movement and the recent wave of global protests is (in one way or another) concerned with their relationship to 'the future' (Graeber 2002; Juris 2008; Maeckelbergh 2009, 2011; Razsa and Kurnik 2012). I have criticized the assumption that Left radical politics should be characterized as prefigurative, which entail that activists are said to make a model of the future in their present political practices (that is, what Helle Thorning-Schmidt failed to do). The weakness in the notion of prefiguration is its dependence on a deduction from a future point or goal, whereby political activities become a progressive realization of future possibilities. As others have pointed out, activist practices are far more creative and no one knows in advance what form struggles can take (Razsa and Kurnik 2012: 252). In addition, willingly or not, activists refrain from formulating anticipatory imaginings or pictures of an ideal society, as has characterized previous generations on the Left; instead, they leave the contours of the future open and indeterminate. This fact often renders the politics of activists unintelligible to those around them, who expect political actors to formulate – as Helle Thorning-Schmidt and other 'normal' politicians do – ideological positions and goals for the future. Among activists, the relationship with the future is far from straightforward; it is indeterminate, a void, and consequently it does not make a lot of sense directing oneself towards it. Instead, focus is on real and immediate change during both daily life and extraordinary events, which both come to mirror and leak into one another. In this light, I have defined political practices as 'figurations' in order to grasp how the indeterminate sometimes acquires determinate form.

To fully appreciate this, one needs to accept the ontology of non-linear time inherent in activist practices, which means that the future is not a future point in time, but a co-present bodily perspective. Transposing Viveiros de Castro's Amerindian perspectivism (Viveiros de Castro 1998) to the collective body of protesters has enabled me to grasp the perspectivist nature of activist time. The collective body that often emerges during confrontations between activists and the police in itself makes up an activist 'theory of politics', which I have sought to imitate as an anthropological argument. The collective body in the 'kettle' in Strasbourg and during the intense pushing of the fence during the Reclaim Power action in Copenhagen are expressions of a momentary co-presence of what we normally think of as opposites – action and inaction, the individual and the social, the present and the future.

Left radical politics must be comprehended from a relational perspective, which in this context implies that form is primary (Sjørslev 1999) to the intentions of any single individual. Activists' acute attention to, debates about and experimentation with forms of protesting, organizing and finding ways to live their life is one way this is evidenced. The creative renovation of forms of actions is a key element in activist politics. Along the way, activists sometimes become absorbed by common action, which I have thought of here as an interstice of active time in a situation where capitalism is experienced as a pervading circumstance of life. From a YouTube video for a summit protest, I extracted the notion of 'dead time' and combined this with activists' personal experience of apathy, exhaustion and burn out, which involve a sense of life coming to a standstill. Active time and dead time are not opposites, pairs or dichotomies that cut a whole into parts (cf. Strathern 2009: 4), but represent, rather, a capacity to take on different bodily viewpoints.

The fieldwork for the present book was carried out during the last year of a global economic boom and the first years after its ensuing financial meltdown. Surprisingly, the revolutionary anticipation, the expectation to be able to change the system in its totality, remained relatively low throughout. The view of capitalism as a disordered whole was relatively constant, now with a more accentuated critique of the greed and excesses of the banks and financial speculators. Activists still described themselves as caught in a world characterized not only by extreme individuality and greed, but also of lurking indifference, apathy and resignation. What was new was the force with which activists, in a more or less close alliance with those groups most affected by the economic crisis, could renovate forms of action and open up comprehensive interstices of autonomy in public space. Taken together, this implies that the activists I have been involved with have no expectation of a single revolutionary moment that will transform the world in its totality. This cosmology of capitalism is, however, not simply the precondition for the form politics takes among Left radical activists but, as argued here, as much an effect of the orchestrated confrontations that occur during political actions.

What is characteristic of Left radical politics is that what we conventionally think of as form and content or message are inseparable, which is captured in the activist concept of style. The present work has hence departed from the Birmingham School's understanding of style as tied to the expression of an oppositional youth culture through clothing, language and leisure activities (Clark 2004; Hall and Jefferson 2006; Krogstad 1986) by offering a new concept of style that imitates activists' use of the notion (see Holbraad 2004; Viveiros de Castro 2003). In this book we have encountered activists' comments and opinions regarding style in connection with the facilitation of meetings, the proper way to dumpster dive and, not least, how a protest can obtain the correct, most persuasive form. This new concept of style works as a scale for comparing and passing judgment on a form's ethical appropriateness, as well as its persuasiveness and effectiveness, for a situation at hand.

Against this background, one may return to reconsider the much-debated issues of violence and vandalism in the context of protest actions. Violence, narrowly defined as personal injury, and vandalism are questions of style, insofar as activists may consider these forms of action respectively 'good style' or 'bad style' depending on various situational factors. In relation to the Ungdomshuset eviction, the injustices committed, the suspension of dialogue and the experience of being attacked by an unpredictable enemy made violence and vandalism seem like the only appropriate and timely responses. The established viewpoint that injury to human beings should be avoided was temporarily suspended, which was made possible by transposing the police from the category of human beings to the category of material objects. While some activists recognize that violence has aesthetic persuasiveness resulting in both the police and politicians becoming engaged in the performance, its employment also has large costs when people are singled out for prosecution, or the conflict is escalated.

Activists' taxonomy of forms of protesting is more elaborate and nuanced than appears to be the norm among ordinary citizens in Northern Europe. In recent times, activists have developed an array of other forms of protesting and direct action, such as clowning, confrontational civil disobedience and occupations, which are often as effective, but Ungdomshuset proves to be a limit case, in the sense of illustrating the exception to the norm about non-violence. It is the notion of style that produces comparability between the forms by drawing attention to both the ethic and aesthetic choices involved. It is my conviction that it is only by paying attention to style that one can approach the dynamics of protesting.

This intertwining of aesthetics and politics is in no way limited to Left radical politics. Probably, spectacular performances like those encountered during summit protests have always been an integral part of politics among political leaders and dissidents alike. One may well argue that it is a characteristic of all politics, as has been pointed out in several fields of study, including anthropology (Kapferer 2005; Riles 1998; Yurchak 2003). In political debate among the Danish public, the attention to form is significant, though it is particularly the use of spin doctors that has been debated and cast into doubt. Spin doctors are experts hired to turn or twist a message or a political point of view in a specific direction to render it more acceptable, even appealing, to voters, or enable a politician to (re)gain a favourable position (Carlsen et al. 1999: 48; Esser et al. 2000: 214). The debate over the use of spin doctors generally represents them as people who distort an open public debate, who violate the message, whose political 'spinning' contradicts elected politicians' right to design their own politics. Yet, if we approach this debate from the viewpoint of my own findings in the context of Left radical politics, we see that the appropriate form engenders politics, for example by persuading others to engage in a debate. In a similar vein, one may rethink the debate about Helle Thorning-Schmidt's choice of school and personal accessories, leading to the conclusion that rather than her handbag or school choice misrepresenting her viewpoint, these items and choices in fact generate her politics. The message is neither caused by nor implanted in form, but inherent in it.

My analysis of material objects, such as over-size bolt cutters and giant puppets, has made clear that objects can cause events in their vicinity (Gell 1998; Keane 2006). Activists use various means to fabricate objects and talk of abstract forms as actors, while individual intentions are conspicuously absent. The police, on the other hand, seek to abduct individual human agency from material objects (black clothes, bolt cutters), and it is in this context that the myth of hard-core activists orchestrating the actions of their fellow activists proliferates, which has led to the prosecution of individual activists for organizing or inciting others to violence. Both the police's methods of investigation, and the Danish and broader European juridical system, requires the identification of individual perpetrators and intentional law-breakers. That this is difficult to accomplish has, in my view, less to do with activists' security measures (being as they are rather rudimentary) than the fact that intentions are not the property of individuals but, at best, an after effect.

Left radical activism claims to be a particular kind of body politics, and it is in relationship to the collective body that the way form engenders politics is best exemplified. This politics of the body is distinct from Foucault's concept of bio-power, which describes how plans and programmes of the modern state are implanted en masse in the population through ethical and political interventions (concerned, for example, with hygiene or the making of life) or through disciplining single bodies to obtain subjugation and population control (Foucault 1979: 80–88; Rose 1999: 23, 104). This difference rests on the fact that the relationship between intention and form is reversed, and because my concern has been with the materiality of the body, not with its discursive production (cf. Povinelli 2011). Activist bodies are material and affective entities, yet simultaneously highly unstable and transformational. I have described how the body becomes a political entity or container through eating habits, where the preference for 'raw' and 'rotten' food (Lévi-Strauss 1997) makes the body distinguishable from all other entities. Besides being a bodily expression, this politics is also highly moral, with historical connections to both Puritanism and middle-class bohemians' critique of civilisation, with all their detailed directions on how to live one's daily life (Korsgaard 2004; Schmidt and Kristensen 1986). Like activism in general, activists describe eating as a process of absorption: the body absorbs the norms and political connotations of the food, so the body gains the ability to chart the frontiers of capitalism as long as it is filled with non-capitalist food. It is the materiality that acts, or at least has effects of its own: the body is politic, not that upon which meaning is inscribed.

If anything characterizes Left radical activists, it is their commitment to take action, which often plays out as frenzied activity. In the present context, activism is a state of vigorous (bodily) action, and absorption in common action is the single defining characteristic of being an activist. I have described incidents of 'absorption' among others in the context of action training; the participants, by way of different techniques of the body – for example learning how to endure tear gas, walking with one's arms locked as part of a blockade or swarming a police line to break through it – achieve a bodily belonging to the same time.

The concept of active time grew out of this concern for absorption in vital common action, and it has been used to describe a state of bodily affect, a real and concrete sense of potentiality, which many activists refer to in connection to direct actions, and which are described with words such as strength, freedom and solidarity. This focus on common action makes the Left radical scene open to newcomers who are not asked by others to account for their political views, but to engage themselves in some practical activity such as helping out during a concert, cutting vegetables for a soup kitchen or arranging an action. On the other hand, the ability to take part in such activities also determines when people 'burn out' or 'drop out' of activism. As Strathern puts it, the binary can be thought of as a kind of 'licence' where 'a moment of relation is created through divergence' (Strathern 2009). That time has different qualities depending on the bodily point of view in the confrontation has been a significant insight that has emerged from studying protest events.

Activism's different qualities of time are not completely unfamiliar to some (vocal) activists – for example, those of the Clandestine Insurgent Rebel Clown Army: 'We are insurgent because we have risen up from nowhere and are everywhere … Because whenever we fall over we rise up again and again and again, knowing that nothing is lost for history, that nothing is final. Because history doesn't move in straight lines but surges like water, sometimes swirling, sometimes dripping, flowing, flooding'.[2] Though the clowns also draw on the metaphor of time as flow, they also point to the experience of time as having different textures and modalities. In theoretical terms, I have phrased this as co-present temporal perspectives, that is, different coexisting textures of active time and dead time. Activists' lives oscillate between these temporal modes, with all their internal variation, but with various forms of bodily confrontation working as the point of bifurcation, such as what happens when becoming absorbed by a collective body of protesters. In the Introduction I asked what the collective body is an appearance of. It is, as I see it, exactly the appearance of a relationship between dead time and active time (or what we conventionally think of as the present and the future).

The importance of the confrontation cannot therefore be underestimated. Confrontation does not necessarily imply violence; rather, it implies that the body 'works as the medium', as the activist dictum goes, through which everything falls into place. Confrontation and the collective body thus *are* the cosmology of Left radical activism. What do I mean by this? At a very concrete level, it implies that one need not know more about Left radical politics, its ideological programme or political goal, than what is to be learnt from participating in a successful demonstration or action. What I have described as bodily sensations of active time and dead time, or the political cosmology of capitalism, follows from this moment of confrontation during direct actions or the sense of strength in an encampment. Consequently, the logic of confrontation also plays out across what we normally associate with either everyday life or special events; it repeats itself in all the activities and conflicts that this kind of politics revolves around.

Given this defining role of the body in Left radical politics – as another expression of the intertwining of what we conventionally think of as form and content – a broader investigation of the body in politics would be a useful road to pursue; it is, however, outside the scope of the present work. The question remains, of cause, if the 'theory of politics' with its attention to the politics of the body and other 'mediated manifestations of intentionality' is of any broader relevance. To make a brief approximation at an answer, I want to consider one historical situation where mainstream and Left radical politics encountered each other in a very tangible way, as well as examine the politics practised during the new wave of protests.

In March 2003, two activists from Globale Rødder sneaked into the Danish Parliament, where they poured red paint on the former prime minister, Anders Fogh Rasmussen, as a protest against Danish participation in the invasion of Iraq. Fogh Rasmussen, who was appointed secretary general of NATO during its sixtieth-anniversary summit in 2009, has become known among the Danish public for his determination, bodily self-control, his fixed stare and formal appearance in the media. On various occasions he has been depicted on his morning run in an impeccable outfit, definitively not as a *folkelig* figure (that is, popular, and also similar and appealing to the ordinary citizen). Fogh Rasmussen's statesman-like appearance was taken as being in close concordance with the content of his politics. What was interesting about the incident, when the activists encountered Fogh Rasmussen in the blue-carpeted hallway and poured red paint over his head and shoulders so that it dripped from his attractive suit while yelling 'You have blood on your hands!', was his marching off down the hallway, relatively calmly, yet as if most of the joints in his body had stiffened. The blood not only stood for Iraqi blood (though it also clearly did so); the artificial blood, in accordance with the argument presented here, also became absorbed by and transformed his body. The former prime minister's body stiffened in an alteration between movement and non-movement, somehow comparable to a group of protesters being 'kettled' on a bridge. Enacting in this way both the impotence of the war on terror and a stern determinacy to continue to participate in the war at all costs, the former prime minister was foreshadowing the sturdy ineptitude of the Danish 'activist foreign policy', and maybe even his own appointment as NATO's secretary general in 2009.

In December 2011, *Time Magazine* chose 'the protester' as the 'person of the year'. Echoing the butterfly metaphor first employed to explain chaos theory, the magazine wrote: 'No one could have known that when a Tunisian fruit vendor set himself on fire in a public square, it would incite protests that would topple dictators and start a global wave of dissent'[3] – referring to the recent wave of global protests, from the Arab Spring beginning in December 2010 through the Indignados of Spain in May 2011, to the Occupy Movement in the US in September the same year, and the ongoing European resistance to the consequences of speculative capitalism and to the politicians' austerity measures.

While the new protests were neither incidental nor without precedent, they marked a creative reinvention of forms of protesting and democratic decision making, elements of which had been discussed in social forums, and practised in the global justice movement as well as in Left radical self-governed spaces for a long time. What the Spanish Indignados and the Occupy movement so convincingly did was to turn these practices inside-out, thereby making the previously invisible practices of direct democracy the visible centre of the protest.

When the Indignados occupied the Plaza del Sol in the centre of Madrid on 15 May 2011, just before the Spanish elections, they were inspired by the uprisings in Tunis and the occupation of Tahrir Square in Cairo, but their action also resonated with ongoing discussions during the G8/G20 protest planning in France and smaller experiments with people's assemblies in public space, such as the one on climate change during the Climate Summit described here. The Indignados carried forward and reactualized the summit protests and the long debates about the direct democracy of the social forum in demanding and exercising *democracia real, ya!* (real democracy, now!) in the public square of the city. In so doing, the protest of the gathered activists consisted in embodying, or seeking to embody, an alternative to representative democracy. Even before the encampments in Spain were dismantled, others sprung up in Syntagma Square in Athens, where people were protesting against the government's response to the country's debt crisis. Like the protests of the global justice movement, these events speak to and spill into one another, pushing along new reinventions of form (Krøijer 2015). The European encampments were part of the background to the Occupy Wall Street encampment in Zuccotti Park in New York City, where the words of left-wing and activist celebrities were 'consumed' through the 'people's microphone', and the repetition of words enabled their absorption into the collective body of the those who were camped there.

In attending to the circulation of forms, one easily overlooks how different protests and the conditions of participants are unequally shaped by the economic crisis. The Occupy movement spread throughout the US, and 951 cities took part in a global day of action on 15 October 2011, but the protests did not take hold everywhere to the same extent (Della Porta and Andretta 2013: 24). In Europe, a split between northern and southern European countries is clearly visible; frustration and indignation have been pronounced in many southern European countries, undoubtedly associated with the real impact of the economic crisis on people's daily life, and perhaps also with the state's lack of ability or willingness to bolster its population against the effects of the crisis. The reasons behind the regional differences will need further investigation for more nuanced insights. In many northern European countries, the tendency has been for activists to withdraw to the activities in and around social centres in order to experiment, for example, with alternative forms of barter economy and sustainable production. Shortly after the G8 meeting in Genoa in 2001, critical voices began to emerge against the practice of 'summit hopping', the practice of travelling from one summit to the next to protest, arguing in favour of placing much more emphasis on local autonomist struggles, and thereby extending disobedience 'to all aspects of life'. Both the activities around social centres as well as the occupation of public squares by the Indignados and Occupy strands can be understood as such attempts, expanding the struggle by opening up new interstices of autonomy. The duration of these interstices is different from that produced during a week of summit protesting, but the public attention drawn, endurance demanded and intensity produced by those leaping to the (virtual) centre of global financial capitalism by encamping in front of their physical headquarters has been at least as great. The attention to newness and reinvention of form – both within the movement and among its observers – has been a constant from the time of the global justice movement. But the concern with newness often entails an inattention to the continuity at stake for example in setting up interim camps, organizing media outreach, legal assistance and action training, or establishing decision-making procedures.

The persuasive slogan 'We are the 99 per cent', pointing to all those not enjoying the inordinate influence and wealth of the wealthiest 1 per cent, glosses over the fact that the participants in the encampments – as was the case of the global justice movement and the Left radical scene more generally – has been said to fail to represent the diversity of the group (Juris 2012). The majority of the participants in Occupy are young, well-educated, white people from a middle-class background, sometimes joined by contingents of homeless people (ibid.: 265). Like in the alterglobalization movement and in social centres, Occupy also struggled with the issue of how to perform appropriate 'spaciousness' and create an alliance between the bohemian middle class and those more directly affected by the economic crisis (Graeber 2009; Juris 2012).

What a view from afar may easily overlook was how different forms of direct democracy coexisted in the encampments and among various branches of the Occupy movement, such as between the principle of the autonomous organizing of so-called workshops (which entailed that the people directly involved in organizing them would make their own decisions) and the modified consensus practised in the large assemblies of Occupy Wall Street (Razsa and Kurnik 2012: 247). Both of these forms of decision-making have been part of Left radical or anarchist-inspired organizational spaces, such as Ungdomshuset and the summit protest preparations, for a long time, but the principles of decision-making and room for internal diversity continue to foster internal debate and are likely to do so also in the future.

The new wave of global protests also represents a reinvention of movement and forms of political action, where encamped protesters come to embody the hope for something different; as evidenced here it is also, however, a continuation of established political practices and associated dilemmas, for example about inclusion, spaciousness and forms of decision making. When the Indignados and Occupy movement took to the streets, they were also quickly met by public demand for clear political alternatives, a demand that the public also routinely raised against the global justice movement and the political actions of Left radical activists more broadly. In fact now, as before, the movement is criticized both for its lack of demands, which is said to leave the public confused, and for its 'unrealistic' and impossible demands. Against this, we see the politics of the collective body of protesters, sitting, standing and moving through public space in its endeavour to give determinate form to the indeterminate or, as Judith Butler put it during her speech to those encamped at Zuccotti Park, to demand the impossible.[4]

Notes

1. See 'Gucci-Helle nu med Rolex-ur', *Fyens Stiftstidende*, 24 June 2010; 'Kammerat Helle', *Berlingske Tidende*, 2 July 2010; 'Er ferie-Lene og Gucci-Helle vor tids hekse?' *Ekstra Bladet*, 16 August 2010.
2. Retrieved 10 November 2010 from: www.clownarmy.org/about/about.html.
3. 'Person of the Year 2011: The Protester', *Time*, 14 December 2011.
4. For a transcript of Butler's speech via The People's Microphone at Zuccotti Park see http://occupywsp.tumblr.com/page/4. Last accessed 6 August 2014.

REFERENCES

Agamben, G. 1998. *Homo Sacer: Sovereign Power and Bare Life*. Stanford, CA: Stanford University Press.
——— 2005. *State of Exception*. Chicago: University of Chicago Press.
Alvarez, S., E. Dagnino and A Escobar (eds). 1998. *Cultures of Politics/Politics of Cultures: Revisioning Latin American Social Movements*. Boulder, CO: Westview Press.
Anderson, S. 2008. *Civil Sociality: Children, Sport and Cultural Policy in Denmark*. Charlotte, NC: Information Age Publishing.
Appadurai, A. 1996. *Modernity at Large: Cultural Dimensions of Globalization*. Minneapolis: University of Minnesota Press.
Arendt, H. 1958. *The Human Condition*. Chicago: University of Chicago Press.
Aurvig Brøndum, T., et al. 2002. *Forsvar for fællesskabet*. Copenhagen: Fremad.
Basso, K. 1988. 'Speaking with Names: Language and Landscape among the Western Apache'. *Cultural Anthropology* 3(2): 99–130.
Bateson, G. 1972. *Steps to an Ecology of Mind*. New York: Ballantine Books.
Bey, H. 1991. *TAZ: The Temporary Autonomous Zone, Ontological Anarchy, Poetic Terrorism*. Brooklyn, NY: Automedia.
Bloch, M. 1977. 'The Past and the Present in the Present'. *Man* 12: 278–92.
Bourdieu, P. 1977. *Outline of a Theory of Practice*. Cambridge: Cambridge University Press.
Bruun M., G. Jacobsen and S. Krøijer. 2011. 'Introduction: The Concern for Sociality – Practicing Equality and Hierarchy in Denmark'. *Social Analysis* 55(2): 1–19.
Bui, R. 2001. 'Tute Bianche: The Practical Side of Myth-making (in Catastrophic Times)'. Retrieved 7 February 2008 from: www.wumingfoundation.com/english/giap/giapdigest11.html.
Bulmer, M. 1982. 'Introduction'. In M. Bulmer (ed.), *Social Research Ethics: An Examination of the Merits of Covert Participant Observation*. London: Macmillan, pp. 3–12.

Bunyan, T. 2008. 'The Shape of Things to Come – EU Future Report', Statewatch Report. Retrieved 20 March 2011 from: www.statewatch.org/future-group.htm.

Burridge, K. 1960. *Mambu: A Melanesian Millennium*. London: Methuen.

Butler, C.T., and K. McHenry. 2010. *Food Not Bombs*. Tucson: Sharp Press.

Butler, J. 1997. 'Introduction: On Linguistic Vulnerability'. In *Excitable Speech: A Politics of the Performative*. New York: Routledge, pp.1–42.

——— 1999 [1990]. *Gender Trouble: Feminism and the Subversion of Identity*. New York: Routledge.

Buzan, B., O. Wæver and J. Wilde. 1998. *Security: A New Framework for Analysis*. London: Lynne Rienner.

Candea, M. 2007. 'Arbitrary Locations: In Defense of the Bounded Field-site'. *Journal of the Royal Anthropological Institute* 13: 167–84.

——— 2010. 'Other Worlds Close to Home: Ethological Methodology as a Holding in Abeyance'. Unpublished paper delivered at the EASA Biennial Conference, 24–27 August, Maynooth, Ireland.

Canetti, E. 1984 [1960]. *Crowds and Power*. New York: Farrar, Straus and Giroux.

Carlsen, E.M., P. Kjær and O.K. Pedersen. 1999. *Magt og Fortælling: hvad er politisk journalistik?* Aarhus: Ajour.

Carrithers, M., et al. 2010. 'Ontology Is Just Another Word for Culture: Motion Tabled at the 2008 Meeting of the Group for Debates in Anthropological Theory, University of Manchester'. *Critique of Anthropology* 30(2): 152–200.

Castañeda, Ernesto. 2012. 'The Indignados of Spain: A Precedent to Occupy Wall Street'. *Social Movement Studies* 11(3-4): 309–19.

Castoriadis, C. 1987. *The Imaginary Institution of Society*. Cambridge, MA: MIT Press.

——— 1991. 'Power, Politics, Autonomy'. In *Philosophy, Politics, Autonomy: Essays in Political Philosophy*. New York: Oxford University Press, pp.143–74.

CEU. 2006. 'Security Handbook for the Use of Police Authorities and Services at International Events'. Council of European Union, EU doc. no.15226/1/06. Retrieved 7 March 2011 from: www.statewatch.org/news/2007/jan/eu-sec-handbook-int-events.pdf.

——— 2009. 'The Stockholm Programme – An Open and Secure Europe Serving and Protecting the Citizens'. Council of European Union, EU doc no. 16484/09. Retrieved 7 March 2011 from: www.statewatch.org/news/2009/nov/eu-draft-stockholm-programme-23-11-09-16484-09.pdf.

Christensen, T.W. 2009.'Forrest eller bagerst i demo'en'. *Norsk Antropologisk Tidsskrift* 20(4): 236–50.

Clark, D. 2004. 'The Raw and the Rotten: Punk Cuisine'. *Ethnology* 43(1): 19–31.

Clarke, J. 2006 [1975]. 'Style'. In Stuart Hall and Tony Jefferson (eds), *Resistance through Rituals: Youth subcultures in post-war Britain*. London: Routledge, pp.147–61.

Clarke, J., et al. 2006 [1975]. 'Subcultures, Culture, Class'. In Stuart Hall and Tony Jefferson (eds), *Resistance through Rituals: Youth Subcultures in Post-war Britain*. London: Routledge, pp.1–59.

Cohen, A. 1980. 'Drama and Politics in the Development of a London Carnival'. *Man* 15(1): 65–87.
Copenhagen Municipality. 1999. 'Referat af møde i Borgerrepræsentationen', May and November 1999. Retrieved 20 November 2009 from: www.kk.dk/politikogindflydelse/ByensStyre/Borgerrepræsentationen/referater/referater1999.aspx.
——— 2009. 'Tryghedsindeks for København 2009'. Retrieved 7 March 2011 from http://www.kk.dk/Nyheder/2009/August/~/media/1220E16F49224C3CA3EAE27C13D04D6E.ashx.
Critchley, S. 2007. *Infinitely Demanding: Ethics of Commitment, Politics of Resistance.* London: Verso.
Crone, M. 2010. *Dynamikker i ekstremistiske miljøer*. DIIS Working Paper. Copenhagen: Danish Institute for International Studies.
Da Col, G. 2007. 'The View from Somewhen: Events, Bodies and the Perspective of Fortune around Khawa Karpo, a Tibetan Sacred Mountain in Yunnan Province'. *Inner Asia* 9(2): 215–35.
Day, S., E. Papataxiarches and M. Stewart. 1999. 'Consider the Lilies of the Field'. In S. Day, E. Papataxiarches and M. Steward (eds), *Lilies of the Field: Marginal People Who Live for the Moment*. Boulder, CO: Westview Press, pp.1–24.
De Angelis, M. 2006. 'The World Social Forum: Challenging Empires. Book Review'. *Development* 49(2): 125–28.
De Jong, W., M. Shaw and N. Stammers. 2005. *Global Activism, Global Media.* London: Pluto Press.
Deleuze, G. 1994. *Difference and Repetition*. New York: Columbia University Press.
Della Porta, D. 2006. *Globalization from Below: Transnational Activists and Protest Networks*. Minneapolis: University of Minnesota Press.
——— 2007. *The Global Justice Movement: Cross-national and Transnational Perspectives*. Boulder, CO: Paradigm Publishers.
——— 2008. 'Research on Social Movements and Political Violence'. *Qualitative Sociology* 31(3): 221–30.
Della Porta, D., and M. Andretta. 2013. 'Protesting for Justice and Democracy: Italian Indignados?' *Contemporary Italian Politics* 5(1): 23–37.
Della Porta, D., and H. Reiter (eds.). 1999. *Policing Protest: The Control of Mass Demonstration in Western Democracies*. Minneapolis: The University of Minnesota Press.
Derrida, J. 1994. *Specters of Marx: The State of the Debt, the Work of Mourning, and the New International*. London: Routledge.
Descola, P. 1992. 'Society of Nature and the Nature of Society'. In A. Kuper (ed.), *Conceptualizing Society*. London: Routledge, pp.107–26.
De Soosa Santos, B. 2006. *The Rise of the Global Left: The World Social Forum and Beyond*. London: Zed Books.
Dumont, L. 1970. *Homo Hierarchicus: The Caste System and its Implications*. Chicago: University of Chicago Press.
Durkheim, E. 1954 [1912]. *The Elementary Forms of Religious Life*. New York: Free Press.

Eagleton, T. 1991. *Ideology: An Introduction*. London: Verso.
Ekman, A.-K. 1991. *Community, Carnival and Campaign: Expressions of Belonging in a Swedish Region*. Stockholm: Stockholm Studies in Social Anthropology.
Epstein, B. 1991. *Political Protest and Cultural Revolution: Non-violent Direct Action in the 1970s and 1980s*. Berkeley: University of California Press.
────── 2001. 'Anarchism and the Anti-globalization Movement'. *Monthly Review* 54(4): 1–14.
Eschle, C. 2005. 'Skeleton Women: Feminism and the Antiglobalisation Movement'. *Signs* 30(3): 1741–1769.
────── 2011. '(Anti-)globalization and Resistance Identities'. In A. Elliott (ed.), *Routledge Handbook of Identity Studies*. London: Routledge, pp.364–79.
Esser, F., C. Reinemann and D. Fan. 2000. 'Spin Doctoring in British and German Elections Campaigns'. *SAGE* 15(2): 209–39.
Evans-Prichard, E.E. 1940. *The Nuer*. Oxford: Clarendon Press.
────── 1967. *The Zande Trickster*. Oxford: Clarendon Press.
Fabian, J. 1983. *Time and the Other: How Anthropology Makes its Object*. New York: Columbia University Press.
Fernandez, L.A. 2008. *Policing Dissent: Social Control and the Anti-globalization Movement*. New Brunswick, NJ: Rutgers University Press.
Fiddes, N. 1997. 'Declining Meat: Past, Present … and Future Imperfect?' In P. Caplan (ed.), *Food, Health and Identity*. London: Routledge, pp.252–67.
Fock, N. 1963. *Waiwai: Religion and Society of an Amazonian Tribe*. Copenhagen: National Museum.
Foucault, M. 1977. *Discipline and Punish: The Birth of the Clinic*. New York: Pantheon Books.
────── 1979. *The History of Sexuality*, Vol. 1: *An Introduction*. London: Allen Lane.
────── 1982. 'The Subject and Power'. In H. Dreyfus and P. Rabinow (eds), *Beyond Structuralism and Hermeneutics*. Chicago: University of Chicago Press, pp.208–26.
────── 1986. 'Of Other Spaces'. *Diacritics* 16: 22–37.
Franks, B. 2003. 'The Direct Action Ethic from 59 Upwards'. *Anarchist Studies* 11(1): 13–41.
Frykman, J. 1993. 'Nationella ord och handlingar'. In *Försvenskningen av Sverige: det nationellas förvandlingar*. Stockholm: Bokförlaget Natur och Kultur, pp.120–203.
Frykman, J., and O. Löfgren. 2008 [1979]. *Culture Builders: A Historical Anthropology of Middle-class Life*. New Brunswick, NJ: Rutgers University Press.
Fukuyama, F. 1992. *The End of History and the Last Man*. New York: Free Press.
Future Group. 2008. 'Freedom, Security, Privacy – European Home Affairs in an Open World'. Report of the High Level Advisory Group on the Future of European Home Affairs Policy. Retrieved 7 March 2011 from http://www.statewatch.org/news/2008/jul/eu-futures-jha-report.pdf.
Gaonkar, D.P., and E.A. Povinelli. 2003. 'Technologies of Public Forms: Circulation, Transfiguration, Recognition'. *Public Culture* 15(3): 385–97.

Gell, A. 1992. *The Anthropology of Time: Cultural Constructions of Temporal Maps and Images*. Oxford: Berg.

——— 1998. *Art and Agency: An Anthropological Theory*. Oxford: Oxford University Press.1999. 'Strathernograms, or the Semiotics of Mixed Metaphors'. In *The Art of Anthropology: Essays and Diagrams*. London: Athlone Press, pp.29–75.

——— 2002. 'Closure and Multiplication: An Essay on Polynesian Cosmology and Ritual'. In M. Lambek (ed.), *A Reader in the Anthropology of Religion*. Malden, MA: Blackwell, pp.290–305.

Gibson-Graham, J.K. 2006 [1996]. *The End of Capitalism (As We Knew It): A Feminist Critique of Political Economy*. Minneapolis: University of Minnesota Press.

Gluckman, M. 1963. *Order and Rebellion in Tribal Africa*. London: Cohen and West.

Goffman, E. 1959. *The Presentation of Self in Everyday Life*. New York: Doubleday.

Graeber, D. 2002. 'The New Anarchists'. *New Left Review* 13: 61–73.

——— 2009. *Direct Action: An Ethnography*. Edinburgh: AK Press.

Grosz, E. 2005. *Time Travels: Feminism, Nature, Power*. Durham, NC: Duke University Press.

Gullestad, M. 1984. *Kitchen-table Society: A Case Study from the Family Life and Friendships of Young Working-class Mothers in Urban Norway*. Oslo: Universitetsforlaget.

——— 1991. 'The Transformation of the Norwegian Notion of Everyday Life'. *American Ethnologist* 18(3): 480–99.

——— 1992. *The Art of Social Relations: Essays on Culture, Social Action and Everyday Life in Modern Norway*. Oslo: Scandinavian University Press.

——— 2001. 'Likhetens grenser'. In Marianne E. Lien, H. Lidén and H. Vike (eds), *Likhetens paradokser: Antropologiske undersøkelser i det moderne Norge*. Oslo: Universitetsforlaget, pp.32–62.

——— 2002. *Det norske sett med nye øyne*. Oslo: Universitetsforlaget/Scandinavian University Press.

——— 2006. *Plausible Prejudice: Everyday Experiences and Social Images of Nation, Culture and Race*. Oslo: Universitetsforlaget/Scandinavian University Press.

Guyer, J.I. 2007. 'Prophecy and the Near Future: Thoughts on Macroeconomic, Evangelical, and Punctuated Time'. *American Ethnologist* 34(3): 409–21.

Hall, S., and T. Jefferson (eds). 2006. *Resistance through Rituals: Youth Subcultures in Post-war Britain*. London: Routledge.

Hammersley, M., and P. Atkinson. 1995. *Ethnography: Principles in Practice*. London: Routledge.

Handelman, D. 2008. 'Afterword: Returning to Cosmology – Thoughts on the Positioning of Belief'. *Social Analysis* 52(1): 181–95.

Hansen, H. 2008. *69*. Copenhagen: Bastard Books.

Hardt, M., and A. Negri. 2000. *Empire*. Cambridge, MA: Harvard University Press.

——— 2004. *Multitude: War and Democracy in the Age of Empire*. New York: Penguin.

Hebdige, D. 2006 [1975]. 'The Meaning of Mod'. In S. Hall and T. Jefferson (eds), *Resistance through Rituals: Youth Subcultures in Post-war Britain*. London: Routledge, pp.71–79.

Heinemann, T. 1995. *Uro - 25 års gadekamp*. Copenhagen: Tiderne Skifter.
Henare, A., M. Holbraad and S. Wastell. 2007. 'Introduction: Thinking through Things'. In A. Henare, M. Holbraad and S. Wastell (eds), *Thinking Through Things: Theorizing Artefacts Ethnographically*. London: Routledge, pp.1–31.
Hill, J.D. 1988. *Rethinking History and Myth: Indigenous South American Perspectives on the Past*. Urbana: University of Illinois Press.
Hobart, A. 1986. *Balinese Shadow Play Figures*. London: British Museum.
Hodges, M. 2008. 'Rethinking Time's Arrow: Bergson, Deleuze and the Anthropology of Time'. *Anthropological Theory* 8(4): 399–429.
Hodkinson, S., and P. Chatterton. 2006. 'Autonomy in the City? Reflections on the Social Centres Movement in the UK'. *City* 10(3): 305–15.
Holbraad, M. 2004. 'Defining Anthropological Truth'. Paper delivered at the 'Truth Conference', 24 September, Cambridge.
——— 2012. *Truth in Motion: The Recursive Anthropology of Cuban Divination*. Chicago: University of Chicago Press.
Holbraad, M., and M.A. Pedersen. 2013. 'Introduction: Times of Security'. In M. Holbraad and M.A. Pedersen (eds), *Times of Security: Ethnographies of Fear, Protest and the Future*. London: Routledge, pp.1–28.
Jackson, M. 2002. *The Politics of Storytelling: Violence, Transgression and Intersubjectivity*. Copenhagen: Museum Tusculanum Press.
——— 2005. *Existential Anthropology: Events, Exigencies and Effects*. Oxford: Berghahn Books.
Jenkins, R. 2011. *Being Danish: Paradoxes of Identity in Everyday Life*. Copenhagen: Museum Tusculanum Press.
Jiménez, A.C. 2003. 'On Space as a Capacity'. *Journal of the Royal Anthropological Institute* 9(1): 137–53.
——— 2007. 'Introduction: Re-institutionalisations'. In A.C. Jiménez (ed.), *The Anthropology of Organisations*. Aldershot: Ashgate/Dartmouth, pp.1–32.
Jöhncke, S. 2011. 'Integrating Denmark: The Welfare State as National(ist) Accomplishment'. In K.F. Olwig and K. Paerregaard (eds), *The Question of Integration: Immigration, Exclusion and the Danish Welfare State*. Newcastle-upon-Tyne: Cambridge Scholars Publishing, pp.30–54.
Jordan, J. 1998. 'The Art of Necessity: The Subversive Imagination of Anti-road Protest and Reclaim the Streets'. In G. McKay (ed.), *DiY Culture: Party and Protest in Nineties Britain*. London: Verso, pp.129–51.
——— 2002. 'The Art of Necessity: The Subversive Imagination of Anti-road Protest and Reclaim the Streets'. In S. Duncombe (ed.), *Cultural Resistance: A Reader*. London: Verso, pp. 347–57.
——— 2005. 'Notes Whilst Walking on "How to Break the Heart of Empire"'. Retrieved 20 March 2011 from: http://eipcp.net/transversal/1007/jordan/en.
Juris, J.S. 2005. 'Violence Performed and Imagined: Militant Action, the Black Bloc and the Mass Media in Genoa'. *Critique of Anthropology* 25(4): 413–32.
——— 2008. *Networking Futures: The Movements against Corporate Globalization*. Durham, NC: Duke University Press.
——— 2009. *Militant Anthropology*.

———— 2012. 'Reflections on #Occupy Everywhere: Social Media, Public Space, and Emerging Logics of Aggregation'. *American Ethnologist* 39(2): 259–79.

Kapferer, B. 1998. *Legends of People; Myth of State: Violence, Intolerance, and Political Culture in Sri Lanka and Australia*. Washington: Smithsonian Institution Press.

———— 2005. 'Sorcery and the Beautiful: A Discourse on the Aesthetic of Ritual'. In A. Hobart and B. Kapferer (eds), *Aesthetics in Performance: Formations of Symbolic Constructions and Experience*. Oxford: Berghahn Books, pp.129–60.

———— 2006. 'Situations, Crisis and the Anthropology of the Concrete: The Contribution of Max Gluckman'. In T.M.S. Evens and D. Handleman (eds), *The Manchester School: Practice and Ethnographic Praxis in Anthropology*. New York: Berghan Books, pp.118–56.

Karker, A. 2007. *Jagtvej 69: Historien om et hus*. Copenhagen: Lindhardt and Ringhof.

Karpantschof, R., and M. Lindblom (eds). 2009. *Kampen om Ungdomshuset: Studier i et oprør.* Copenhagen: Frydlund and Monsun.

Karpantschof, R., and F. Mikkelsen. 2002. 'Fra slumstormere til autonome – husbesættelse, ungdom og social protest i Danmark 1965–2000'. In F. Mikkelsen (ed.), *Bevægelser i demokrati: Foreninger og kollektive aktioner i Danmark*. Copenhagen: Hans Reizels Forlag.

———— 2009. 'Kampen om byens rum: Ungdomshuset, Christiania og husbesættelser i København 1965–2008', and 'Ungdomshusoprøret 2006–2008.' In R. Karpantschof and M. Lindblom (eds), *Kampen om Ungdomshuset: Studier i et oprør.* Copenhagen: Frydlund and Monsun, pp.19–102.

Katsiaficas, G. 2006. *The Subversion of Politics: European Autonomous Social Movements and the Decolonization of Everyday Life*. Oakland, CA: AK Press.

Keane, W. 2006. 'Signs are Not the Garb of Meaning: On the Social Analysis of Material Things'. In D. Miller (ed.), *Materiality*. Durham, NC: Duke University Press, pp.182–205.

Klein, N. 2008. *The Shock Doctrine*. London: Penguin.

Københavns Politi. 2007. 'Redegørelse vedrørende Københavns Politis virksomhed 2007'. Retrieved 20 November 2009 from www.politi.dk/koebenhavn/da/lokalnyt/presse/beretninger/redegørelse_2007.htm.

Korsgaard, O. 1998. *The Struggle for Enlightenment: Danish Adult Education during 500 Years*. Copenhagen: Gyldendal.

———— 2001. *Poetisk demokrati: om personlig dannelse og samfundsdannelse*. Copenhagen: Gads Forlag.

———— 2004. *Kampen om folket: et dannelsesperspektiv på dansk historie gennem 500 år*. Copenhagen: Gyldendal.

Krogstad, A. 1986. 'Punk Symbols on a Concrete Background: From External Provocation to Internal Moralism'. *Tidsskrift for Samfunnsforskning* 27: 499–527.

Krøijer, S. 2003. 'The Company and the Trickster: A Study of Secoya Storytelling as a Mode of Government'. M.A. diss. Copenhagen: Department of Anthropology, University of Copenhagen.

———— 2008. 'Direkte aktion: utopisk nutid blandt venstre-radikale unge'. *Jordens Folk* 4: 56–62.

——— 2010. 'Figurations of the Future: On the Form and Temporality of Protests among Left Radical Activists in Europe'. *Social Analysis* 54(3): 139–52.

——— 2011. 'Fremtiden i skraldespanden: temporær perspektivisme blandt venstre-radikale aktivister'. *Tidsskriftet Antropologi* 63: 49–67.

——— 2013. 'Security Is a Collective Body: Intersecting Temporalities of Security around the Climate Summit in Copenhagen'. In M. Holbraad and M.A. Pedersen (eds), *Times of Security: Ethnographies of Fear, Protest and the Future*. New York: Routledge, pp.33–56.

——— 2014. 'Aske's Dead Time: An Exploration of the Qualities of Time among Left Radical Activists in Denmark'. In A.L. Dalsgård et al. (eds), *Ethnographies of Youth and Temporality: Time Objectified*. Philadelphia: Temple University Press, pp.57–80.

——— 2015. 'Revolution is the Way You Eat: Exemplification among Left Radical Activists and in Anthropology'. *Journal of the Royal Anthropological Institute*, forthcoming.

Krøijer, S., and I. Sjørslev. 2011. 'Autonomy and the Spaciousness of the Social: The Conflict between Ungdomshuset and Faderhuset in Denmark'. *Social Analysis* 55(2): 84–105.

KUC. 1997. 'Midlertidig aftale om benyttelse af Jagtvej 69'. Copenhagen: Københavns Ungdomscenter.

Lacey, A. 2005. 'Spaces of Justice: The Social Divine of Global Anti-capital Activists' Sites of Resistance'. *Canadian Review of Sociology and Anthropology* 42(4): 403–20.

——— 2005. 'Networked Communities. Social Centres and Activist Spaces in Contemporary Britain'. *Space and Culture* 8(3): 286–301.

Latour, B 2004. 'Whose Cosmos, Which Cosmopolitics? Comments on the Peace Terms of Ulrich Beck'. *Common Knowledge* 10(3): 450–62.

——— 1999. 'Do You Believe in Reality? News from the Trenches of Social Science Wars'. In *Pandora's Hope: Essays on the Reality of Science Studies*. Cambridge, MA: Harvard University Press, pp.1–23.

Leach, E.R. 1985 [1965]. 'Two Essays Concerning the Symbolic Representation of Time'. In W. Lessa and E.Z.Vogt (eds), *Reader in Comparative Religion: An Anthropological Approach*. New York: Harper and Row, pp.170–202.

Leite, J.C., et al. 2007. *World Social Forum – Et globalt alternativ til nyliberalismen*. Copenhagen: Frydenlund.

Lévi-Strauss, C. 1997. 'The Culinary Triangle'. In C. Counihan and P. van Esterik (eds), *Food and Culture: A Reader*. London: Routledge, pp.36–43.

Lien, M.E., H. Lidén and H. Vike. 2001. 'Likhetens virkeligheter'. In M.E. Lien, H. Lidén and H. Vike (eds), *Likhetens paradokser: Antropologiske undersøkelser i det moderne Norge*. Oslo: Universitetsforlaget, pp.11–31.

Lock, M. 1993. 'Cultivating the Body: Epistemologies of Bodily Practice and Knowledge'. *Annual Review of Anthropology* 22: 133–55.

Lutz, C., and G. White. 1986. 'The Anthropology of Emotions'. *Annual Review of Anthropology* 15: 405–36.

McKay, G. (ed.). 1998. *DIY Culture: Party and Protest in Nineties Britain*. London: Verso.

Maeckelbergh, M. 2009. *The Will of the Many: How the Alterglobalization Movement is Changing the Face of Democracy*. New York: Pluto Press.
——— 2011. 'Doing is Believing: Prefiguration as Strategic Practice in the Alterglobalization Movement'. *Social Movement Studies* 10(1): 1–20.
Marcus, G.E. 1995. 'Ethnography in/of the World System: The Emergence of Multi-sited Ethnography'. *Annual Review of Anthropology* 24: 95–117.
Marx, K., and F. Engels. 2002 [1848]. *The Communist Manifesto*. London: Penguin.
Massumi, B. 1987. 'Notes on the Translation and Acknowledgements'. In G. Deleuze and F. Guattari, *A Thousand Plateaus: Capitalism and Schizophrenia*. Minneapolis: University of Minnesota Press, pp.xvi–xx.
——— 2002. *Parables of the Virtual: Movement, Affect, Sensation*. Durham, NC: Duke University Press.
Mauss, M. 1992 [1934]. 'Techniques of the Body'. In J. Crary and S. Kwinter (eds), *Incorporations*. New York: Zone Books, pp.455–77.
Melucci, A. 1996. *Challenging Codes: Collective Action in the Information Age*. Cambridge: Cambridge University Press.
——— 2003 [1995]. 'The Process of Collective Identity'. In H. Johnston and B. Klandersman (eds), *Social Movements and Culture*. Oxford: Routledge, pp.41–63.
Mikkelsen, F. and R. Karpantschof. 2001. 'Youth as a Political Movement. Development of the Squatters and Autonomous Movement in Copenhagen 1981–1995'. *International Journal of Urban and Regional Research* 25(3): 609–28.
Mitchell, J.P. 2006. 'Performance'. In C. Tilley et al. (eds), *Handbook of Material Culture*. London: Sage, pp.384–401.
Miyazaki, H. 2004. *The Method of Hope: Anthropology, Philosophy, and Fijian Knowledge*. Stanford, CA: Stanford University Press.
Munn, N.D. 1992. 'The Cultural Anthropology of Time: A Critical Essay'. *Annual Review of Anthropology* 21: 931–23.
Nielsen, A.S. 2009. 'Farvefjernsyn i sort/hvid: TV-Avisen Extra og Ungdomshusets rydning'. In R. Karpantschof and M. Lindblom (eds), *Kampen om Ungdomshuset: Studier i et oprør*. Copenhagen: Frydlund and Monsun, pp.155–76.
Olwig, K.F. 2000. 'Generations in the Making: The Role of Children'. Paper presented at the EASA Biennial Conference, 26–29 July, Krakow.
Olwig, K.F., and E. Gulløv. 2003. 'Towards an Anthropology of Children and Place'. In K.F. Olwig and E. Gulløv (eds), *Children's Places: Cross-cultural Perspectives*. London: Routledge, pp.1–20.
Olwig, K., and K. Paerregaard. 2011. 'Introduction: "Strangers" in the Nation'. In K. Olwig and K. Paerregaard (eds), *The Question of Integration: Immigration, Exclusion and the Danish Welfare State*. Newcastle-upon-Tyne: Cambridge Scholars Publishing, pp.1–28.
Osterweil, M. 2004. 'The Dynamics of Open Space: A Cultural-political Approach to Reinventing the Political'. *International Social Science Journal* 56(4): 495–506.
——— 2005. 'Place-based Globalism: Theorizing the Global Justice Movement'. *Development* 48(2): 23–28.

Overing, J. 1988. 'Personal Autonomy and the Domestication of the Self in Piaroa Society'. In G. Jahoda and I.M. Lewis (eds), *Acquiring Culture: Cross Cultural Studies in Child Development*. London: Croom Helm, pp.169–92.

Palmer, G.B., and W.R. Jankowiak. 1996. 'Performance and Imagination: An Anthropology of the Spectacular and the Mundane'. *Cultural Anthropology* 11(2): 225–58.

Pelton, R. 1980. *The Trickster in West Africa: A Study of Mythic Irony and Sacred Delight*. Berkeley: University of California Press.

Ponniah, T., and W. Fisher. 2003. *Another World is Possible: Popular Alternatives to Globalisation at the World Social Forum*. London: Zed Books.

Povinelli, E. 2006. *Empire of Love: Toward a Theory of Intimacy, Genealogy and Carnality*. Durham NC: Duke University Press.

——— 2011. *The Economies of Abandonment: Social Belonging and Endurance in Late Liberalism*. Durham NC: Duke University Press.

Radin, P. 1956. The *Trickster: A Study in American Indian Mythology*. London. Routledge and Kegan Paul.

Rasmussen, M.B. 2008. 'On the Youth House Protests and the Situation in Denmark'. *Journal of Aesthetics and Protest* 35: 121–26.

Razsa, M. 2013. 'Beyond "Riot Porn": Protest Video and the Production of Unruly Subjects'. *Ethnos* 79(4): 496–524.

Razsa, M., and A. Kurnik. 2012. 'The Occupy Movement in Žižek's Hometown: Direct Democracy and a Politics of Becoming'. *American Ethnologist* 39(2): 238–58.

Reicher, S.D. 1984. 'The St Pauls Riot: An Explanation of the Limits of Crowd Action in Terms of a Social Identity Model'. *European Journal of Social Psychology* 14: 1–21.

Riles, A. 1998. 'Infinity within the Brackets'. *American Ethnologist* 25(3): 378–98.

Rival, L. 1999. 'Prey at the Centre: Resistance and Marginality'. In S. Day, E. Papataxiarchis and M. Stewart (eds), *Lilies of the Field: Marginal People Who Live for the Moment*. Boulder, CO: Westview Press, pp.61–80.

Robbins, J. 2001. 'Secrecy and the Sense of an Ending: Narrative, Time and Everyday Millenarianism in Papua New Guinea and in Christian Fundamentalism'. *Comparative Studies in Society and History* 43(3): 525–51.

——— 2007a. 'Causality, Ethics and the Near Future'. *American Ethnologist* 34(3): 433–36.

——— 2007b. 'Continuity Thinking and the Problem of Christian Culture: Belief, Time, and the Anthropology of Christianity'. *Current Anthropology* 48(1): 5–37.

Robinson, C.M. 2008. 'Order in Chaos: Security Culture as Anarchist Resistance to the Terrorist Label'. *Deviant Behaviour* 29: 225–52.

Rose, N. 1999. *Powers of Freedom: Reframing Political Thought*. Cambridge: Cambridge University Press.

Rubow, C. 2000. *Hverdagens teologi: Folkereligiøsitet i danske verdener*. Copenhagen: Forlaget ANIS.

Rupert, M. 2005. 'In the Belly of the Beast: Resisting Globalisation and War in a Neo-imperial Moment'. In C. Eschle (ed.), *Critical Theories, International*

Relations, and 'The Anti-globalisation Movement': The Politics of Global Resistance. London: Routledge, pp.36–52.

Sahlins, M. 1996. 'The Sadness of Sweetness: The Native Anthropology of Western Cosmology'. Current Anthropology 37(3): 395–428.

Scheper-Hughes, N. 1995. 'The Primacy of the Ethical: Propositions for a Militant Anthropology'. Current Anthropology 36(3): 409–40.

――― 2004. 'Parts Unknown: Undercover Ethnography of the Organ-Trafficking Underworld'. Ethnography 5(1): 29–73.

Schieffelin, E.L. 1985. 'Performance and the Cultural Construction of Reality'. American Ethnologist 12(4): 707–24.

――― 1997. 'Problematizing Performance'. In F. Hughes-Freeland (ed.), Ritual, Performance, Media. London: Routledge, pp.194–207.

Schmidt, L.-H., and J.E. Kristensen. 1986. Lys, luft og renlighed – den moderne socialhygiejnes fødsel. Copenhagen: Akademisk Forlag.

Schmitt, C. 2006. 'The Concept of the Political'. In The Concept of the Political. Chicago: University of Chicago Press, pp.19–79.

Schrempp, G. 1992. Magical Arrows: The Maori, the Greeks, and the Folklore of the Universe. Madison: University of Wisconsin Press, pp.3–16.

Schwartzman, H.B. 1987. 'The Significance of Meetings in an American Mental Health Care Centre'. American Ethnologist 14(2): 271–94.

Scott, J. C.1985. Weapons of the Weak: Everyday Forms of Peasant Resistance. New Haven: Yale University Press.

Sen, J. 2004a. 'How Open? The Forum as Logo, the Forum as Religion: Scepticism of the Intellect, Optimism of the Will'. In J. Sen et al. (eds), The World Social Forum: Challenging Empires. New Delhi: Viveka Foundation, pp.210–27.

――― 2004b. 'A Tale of Two Charters'. In J. Sen et al. (eds), The World Social Forum: Challenging Empires. New Delhi: Viveka Foundation, pp.72–76.

Singer, P. 1975. Animal Liberation: A New Ethics for our Treatment of Animals. New York: Review/Random House.

Sjørslev, I. 1995. 'Det metodiske forløb: Kunst og håndværk i den antropologiske proces'. Tidsskriftet Antropologi 31: 177–84.

――― 1999. 'Form is Primary: A Conversation with Niels Fock'. Folk 40: 23–56.

――― 2007a. 'Ritual, performance og socialitet'. In I. Sjørslev (ed.), Scener for samvær: Ritualer, performance og socialitet. Aarhus: Aarhus Universitetsforlag, pp.16–18.

――― 2007b. 'Ting og person: Bidrag til socialitetsteknologi'. In I Sjørslev (ed.), Scener for samvær: Ritualer, performance og socialitet. Aarhus: Aarhus Universitetsforlag, pp.179–202.

Skrædderdal, G. 2006. 'Fra jord til bord og tilbage: Om amerikanske homesteaders bestræbelser på at blive ét med naturen'. M.A. diss. Copenhagen: Copenhagen University.

Sneath, D., M. Holbraad and M.A. Pedersen. 2009. 'Technologies of the Imagination'. Ethnos 74(1): 5–30.

Starn, O. 1992. 'I Dreamed of Foxes and Hawks: Reflections on Peasant Protest, New Social Movements, and the Rondas Campesinas of Northern Peru'. In A. Escobar and S. Alvarez (eds), *The Making of Social Movements in Latin America: Identity, Strategy and Democracy*, Boulder, CO: Westview Press, pp.89–111.

Stott, C., and S. Reicher. 1998. 'Crowd Action as Intergroup Process: Introducing the Police Perspective'. *European Journal of Social Psychology* 28: 509–29.

Strathern, M. 1988. *The Gender of the Gift*. Berkeley: University of California Press.

—— 1996. 'Cutting the Network'. *Journal of the Royal Anthropological Institute* 2(3): 517–35.

—— 2004 [1991]. *Partial Connections*. Lanham, MD: Rowman Altamira Press.

—— 2009. 'Binary License'. Paper presented at the colloquium 'Comparative Relativism', 3–4 September, University of Copenhagen.

Sullivan, S. 2005. 'We are Heartbroken and Furious! Violence and the (Anti-)globalisation Movement(s)'. In C. Eschle and B. Maiguascha (eds), *Critical Theories, International Relations and 'the Anti-Globalisation Movement': The Politics of Global Resistance*. London: Routledge, pp.174–94.

Taussig. M. 1993. *Mimesis and Alterity: A Particular History of the Senses*. New York: Routledge.

—— 2006. 'Viscerality, Faith, and Scepticism: Another Theory of Magic'. In *Walter Benjamin's Grave*. Chicago: University of Chicago Press, pp.121–56.

Tavory, I. 2007. 'Towards a Phenomenology of Synchronization: A Study in Communion'. Paper presented at the annual meeting of the American Sociological Association, 11 August, New York.

Tonkin, E. 1992. *Narrating our Pasts: The Social Construction of Oral History*. Cambridge: Cambridge University Press.

Tornatore, L., et al., 'Letter from Climate Prisoners in Denmark', 2010. Retrieved 7 March 2011 from: www.climate-justice-action.org/news/2010/01/01/letter-from-our-friends-in-prison/.

Turner, V. 1982. *From Ritual to Theatre: The Human Seriousness of Play*. New York: PAJ Publications.

—— 1987. *The Anthropology of Performance*. New York: PAJ Publications.

—— 1995 [1969]. *The Ritual Process: Structure and Anti-structure*. New York: Aldine de Gruyter.

US and FBZB. 1982. 'Vilkår for etablering og drift af et ungdomshus', Signed contract between activists from Ungdomshuset and the Municipality of Copenhagen, 26 March. Copenhagen: Ungdomsudvalgets Sekretariat and Forhandlingsgruppen for BZ Brigaden.

Veber, H. 1997. 'Ritualiseret tale i hovedløse samfund: Etablering af magt og offentlighed i hovedløse samfund'. *Tidsskrift for Antropologi* 35/36: 267–80.

Verdery, K. 2004. 'Dead Bodies Animate the Study of Politics'. In C.G. Antonious and M. Robben (eds), *Death, Mourning, and Burial: A Cross-cultural Reader*. Malden, MA: Blackwell, pp.303–10.

Vigh, H. 2008. 'Crisis and Chronicity: Anthropological Perspectives on Continuous Conflict and Decline'. *Ethnos* 72(1): 5–25.

Vilaça, A. 2005. 'Chronically Unstable Bodies: Reflections on Amazonian Corporalities'. *Journal of the Royal Anthropological Institute* 11(3): 445–64.

Vittrup, K. 2002. *Operation*. Copenhagen: Københavns Politi.

Viveiros de Castro, E. 1992. *From the Enemy's Point of View: Humanity and Divinity in an Amazonian Society*. Chicago: University of Chicago Press.

——— 1998. 'Cosmological Deixis and Amerindian Perspectivism'. *Journal of the Royal Anthropological Institute* 4(3): 469–88.

——— 2003. 'AND'. Speech delivered at the 5th Decennial Conference of the Association of Social Anthropologists of Great Britain and the Commonwealth, 14 July, Manchester.

——— 2004. 'Exchanging Perspectives: The Transformation of Objects into Subjects in Amerindian Ontologies'. *Common Knowledge* 10(3): 463–84.

Wagner, R. 1991. 'The Fractal Person'. In M. Godelier and M. Strathern (eds), *Big Men and Great Men: Personifications of Power in Melanesia*. Cambridge: Cambridge University Press, pp.159–73.

Wainwright, H. 2004. 'Foreword: The Forum as Jazz'. In J. Sen et al. (eds), *The World Social Forum: Challenging Empires*. New Delhi: Viveka Foundation, pp.xvii–xx.

Whitaker, C. 2004. 'The WSF as Open Space'. In J. Sen et al (eds), *The World Social Forum: Challenging Empires*. New Delhi: Viveka Foundation, pp.111–20.

Whyte, S.R., E. Alber and S. van der Geest. 2008. 'Generational Connections and Conflicts in Africa: An Introduction'. In E. Alber, S. van der Geest and S.R. Whyte (eds), *Generations in Africa: Connections and Conflicts*. Münster: LIT Verlag, pp.1–23.

Willerslev, R., and M.A. Pedersen. 2010. 'Proportional Holism: Joking Cosmos into the Right Shape in North Asia'. In T. Otto and N. Bubandt (eds), *Experiments in Holism: Theory and Practice in Contemporary Anthropology*. Oxford: Wiley-Blackwell.

Williams, M.C. 2003. 'Words, Images, Enemies: Securitization and International Politics'. *International Study Quarterly* 47: 511–31.

Wolputte, S. van. 2004. 'Hang On to Your Self: Of Bodies, Embodiment, and Selves'. *Annual Review of Anthropology* 33: 251–69.

Wulff, H. 2007. 'Introduction: The Cultural Study of Emotions, Mood and Meaning'. In H. Wulff (ed.), *The Emotions: A Cultural Reader*. Oxford: Berg Publishers, pp.1–18.

Wæver, O. 1995. 'Securitization and Desecuritization'. In R. Lipschutz (ed.), *On Security*. New York: Columbia University Press, pp.46–86.

Yurchak, A. 2003. "Soviet Hegemony of Form: Everything Was Forever, Until It Was No More'. *Comparative Studies in Society and History* 45(3): 480–510.

INDEX

abduction, 103, 124–25, 135n1, 136n13
of intentionality, 103, 140, 147–48
absorption,
activism as engagement and, 3, 4–5, 11, 53, 88–9, 93, 198, 200–1, 213–14
eating and, 213
action,
call for, 37, 55, 107, 156, 191–92 (*see also* YouTube videos)
choreography of, 14, 101–3, 105, 107, 116, 181
codex, 132, 188 (*see also* style)
concept of, 114, 180, 191
conference, 102, 105, 107–8, 112–15, 122
direct, 4, 6, 17, 26, 29–30, 39, 53, 54–55, 59–60, 85–86, 121, 133, 155, 157, 165–73, 180–203
effective and symbolic, 29, 114–15, 179–80, 193–94
forms of, 3, 5–6, 12–15, 16–17, 25–26, 60, 96, 146, 157, 165–73, 179–86
free-form, 134, 172, 181, 188, 197
planning, 18–19, 32, 83, 101–16, 122, 123, 131–34

and success, 1, 3, 15, 40, 48–49, 55, 77, 79, 80, 81–82, 114, 115, 131, 132, 133, 157, 172–73, 179–80, 188, 194, 196, 214
training, 31, 95n21, 103, 110, 114, 115, 116, 126, 127–31, 183, 213, 217 (*see also* police: training)
Action Network, 17, 18, 46–47, 104, 185
active time, 3, 6, 27, 32, 33, 82, 83, 88–89, 91, 92–93, 166, 168, 182, 196, 200–203, 210, 213–14
activism,
as absorption in common action, 3, 4–5, 11, 53, 88–89, 93, 198, 200–201, 213–14 (*see also* active time)
and 'drop out', 19, 97, 213 (*see also* burn out)
initial involvement in, 7, 10–11, 16, 53, 85, 89
activist,
becoming an, 10–11, 130 (*see also* activism: as absorption)
organization, 6–7, 10–11, 39, 45, 51, 53, 54, 85, 95n18 (*see also* affinity groups, self-organization)

activist (*cont.*)
  left radical, 3, 4–5, 6–7, 10, 11, 25, 39, 41–42, 48, 51, 54, 57–58, 59, 78, 83, 92, 130, 136n9, 143–44, 158, 161n17, 192, 193, 202–3 (*see also* anarchist)
actor-network theory, 7
aesthetic, 30, 35n11, 167, 181, 182, 186, 211 (*see also* style)
affect, 20, 31, 194–99, 203, 206n21 (*see also* strength, bodily: perspective)
affinity group, 10–11, 20, 79, 97, 110, 115, 118, 122, 126–27, 129, 131–34, 156, 170, 183, 186, 204n4
  during actions, 133, 156, 168, 170, 172, 177, 183, 186
  flexibility of, 133–34
agent provocateur, 136n6, 160n2, 161n12–13
alterglobalization movement, 4, 13, 23, 26, 33n2, 34n3, 42, 119–20, 123, 135, 136n8, 138, 158, 195, 217 (*see also* global justice movement)
Amazon, 65, 120, 139, 156, 157, 199–201
Amerindian perspectivism, 3, 27, 33, 144, 167, 194, 197, 199–200, 209
anarchism, 26, 39, 54, 58, 87, 129, 184, 191
anarchist, 4, 10, 11, 37, 39, 42, 58, 78, 83, 107, 161n15
Anarchist Federation, 10, 13, 78, 109, 161n13
Animal Liberation Front (ALF), 85–86, 88, 95n18
animal rights, 85–87, 95n20
'Another World is Possible', 4, 32, 40 (*see also* European Social Forum)
Anti-Fascist Action (AFA), 46
apathy, 53–54, 56, 60, 89, 91, 155, 201, 210 (*see also* dead time)
appearance, 20, 30, 33, 164, 203, 214, 215

  bodily, 33, 116, 150, 156, 199, 203, 215
  performative, 28, 30, 156
appropriateness, 5, 30, 33, 108, 167, 181, 186, 187, 188–90, 194, 202, 211 (*see also* style)
Arab Spring, 215
Araweté, 33, 139, 144, 156, 199
Assembly of Social Movements, 42, 44, 49–51
Assistens Kirkegård, 10
ATTAC, 42, 44, 60n4
autological subject, 68, 81–82 (*see also* autonomy)
Autonomia Operaia, 39, 92
autonome (autonomist activists), 4, 92
autonomism, 4, 10, 11, 39, 157–58, 217
autonomous,
  forum at the ESF, 17–18
  space, 10, 11, 34n5, 92 (*see also* self-managed social centre)
autonomy, 4, 11, 67–68, 91–93, 165, 191
  and 'finding one-self', 67, 80–81, 92
  common activity and collective, 32, 66, 68, 82
  individual, 67–68, 80–81, 93
  spaciousness and spatial, 10, 73–74, 92, 93
  time and interstices of, 68, 74, 91–93, 96, 180, 196, 210, 217

Babels, 50
Baden-Baden, 108, 109, 145, 151–52, 160n8
banlieue, 178, 204n5
barricade, 8, 38, 55, 74, 110, 114, 128, 152, 192
Bateson, Gregory, 29
becoming active, 32, 82, 88 (*see also* activism, absorption)
Bella Centre (Copenhagen), 2, 13, 102, 147, 149, 152, 183, 197
Berlin, 3, 19, 21–22, 96–100, 104
  Wall, 54, 96

big data, 142
biometric data, 160n6
Birmingham School, 28, 166, 187, 205n13, 210 (*see also* style)
Blågårdsgade and Blågårds Plads (Copenhagen), 8–9
bloc,
  bike, 2, 14, 33n1, 149, 184
  black, 13, 33n1, 71–72, 87, 103, 109, 110, 139, 142, 148–49, 157, 166, 172, 173–74, 176, 178, 181–82, 186, 187, 189–90, 192–93, 206n18
  color-codes of, 14, 33n1, 79, 110, 181
  grey, 76
  lemming-like quality of, 171, 197–98
  pink, 33n1, 175–76, 178, 181, 182–83 (*see also* clowns)
  yellow queer-feminist, 79, 131–32, 171, 198
blockade,
  agency of blockading points, 114, 122
  of G8 in Heiligendamm (Germany), 14, 114, 127–28, 142
  of NATO, 21, 107–12, 113–16, 127, 174–75, 176
  tactics and training, 80, 111–12, 113–15, 127–29, 130, 142, 190, 204n4, 213
body,
  and affect, 20, 31, 194–99, 196–97, 203, 206n21 (*see also* affect)
  collective, 1–2, 3, 27, 30–31, 168, 177, 194, 197–99, 200–1, 203, 207
  as engendering time, 31–32, 56, 167–68, 197, 200, 212–14
  materiality of the, 30–31, 36n22, 57, 66, 100, 144, 190, 212
  as medium, 133, 157, 214
  as site of politics, 19, 32, 212–13, 214–15
  techniques of the, 27, 127, 129–31, 165–66, 181, 199

  transformability of, 33, 129–30, 139–40, 153, 156–57, 202, 213
bodily confrontation, 3, 30–32, 159, 166, 168, 180, 182, 194–96, 199, 201, 202, 214
  exchange, 31, 191–92
  intensity, 17, 166, 182, 198, 206n21
  perspective, 3, 27–28, 136n11, 156, 199, 201–2, 209
  synchronization, 31, 33, 127, 129–31, 197, 199
bolt cutter, 2, 102, 103, 123–25, 169, 212
Britain, 13, 49, 60n5, 115, 184, 187
burn out, 1, 19, 54, 91, 178 201, 210, 213 (*see also* dead time)
Butler, Judith, 28, 29–30, 100, 139, 194, 218
Byggeren, 10
BZ, 34n8 (*see also* squatters)

Café Under Construction, 9
call for action, 37, 55, 104, 107, 156, 191–92 (*see also* YouTube videos)
camouflage, 158–59, 161n17, 182
  camp, 6, 22, 34n3, 93, 105, 106, 107, 108, 110, 112, 115–16, 122, 127–30, 134, 145, 151, 155, 173–74, 177, 178, 204n6, 214, 217 (*see also* Shut Down the Camp)
  encampment, 214, 216, 217
  internal organization of, 93, 112, 129, 116, 122, 129, 154–55
  or village, 112
capitalism, 4, 25, 37–40, 41–42, 45, 51–60, 61n11, 80–81, 163, 166, 205n14, 210–11, 215, 217
  animal production and eating, 64, 65, 85–86, 210–11
  cosmology of, 5, 25, 37–39, 51–55, 56–60, 61n13, 80, 144, 182, 202, 205n14, 205n16–17, 210–11, 214
  and crisis, 37, 44–45, 49, 52
  financial, 215, 217
carnival, 167, 184–85, 204n2

CEPOL (the European Police College), 141–42
change, 4, 17, 25, 47, 53, 134, 153, 167, 186, 200, 202, 209, 210
  and indeterminacy, 25, 134
  radical, 3, 4, 25, 32, 38, 41, 66, 205n14
  role, 148, 149–50, 159, 186
  of scale, 12
  theory of, 46, 54, 61n13, 178
chant, 2, 29, 152, 153, 179, 188, 206n23 (*see also* oho chant)
choreography of action, 14, 101–3, 105, 107, 116, 181
Christiania (Copenhagen). *See* Freetown Christiania
citizen, 73, 82, 95n21, 143, 149
  as potential threats, 101, 142–43, 160n6, 178, 204n6, 211, 215
  youth as, 69–70, 75–76, 82
civil disobedience, 21, 57, 78, 103, 123, 157, 180–81, 211 (*see also* direct action)
  mass actions of confrontational, 13, 34n3, 79–80, 117, 168, 180–81, 183, 205n12, 211
Clandestine Insurgent Rebel Clown Army, 60n5, 128, 182, 213–14 (*see also* clowns and clowning)
Climate Justice Action (CJA), 1, 52, 59, 117, 123
Climate Summit(Copenhagen), 1–3, 9, 14, 18, 22, 29, 37–38, 52, 54, 56–57, 62, 101, 103, 106, 116, 117, 123–25, 135, 138, 139, 145–51, 155–56, 183, 184, 185, 186, 189, 192–93, 197, 201, 216
clinamen, 58, 61n15
clowns and clowning, 2, 33n1, 48, 128, 175, 177–78, 182–83, 186, 190, 191–92, 193, 211, 213–14
collective body, 1–2, 3, 27, 30–31, 168, 177, 194, 197–99, 200–201, 203, 207
  as theory of politics, 207, 209–10
concussion grenade, 127, 128, 131, 178

confrontation, 1–3, 9, 14, 15, 26, 30–32, 55, 59, 66, 99, 110, 128, 133, 144, 145, 149, 157, 167–68, 172, 173, 177, 178, 180, 181–83, 192, 196–97, 199, 200, 201, 202, 203, 214
  bodily, 3, 30–32, 72, 74, 159, 166, 168, 180, 182, 194–96, 199, 201, 202, 214
  fences as site of, 1, 2, 14, 102, 114, 131–32, 133, 135n4, 145, 152, 168, 170–72, 180, 197, 198, 202
  moment of, 2, 33, 168, 203, 214
consensus,
  decision-making, 83, 85, 95n16, 111, 118, 128, 129, 134, 136n7
  democracy, 27, 53, 119. See also direct democracy
  and hand signals, 105, 117
  leadership and facilitation of, 2, 111, 122–23, 195, 201
convergence centre, 9, 21, 104, 106, 108, 125–26, 147, 155, 174
  police raiding of, 147, 151, 161n10
co-operative shops and housing, 7, 9, 13, 53, 55, 131
COP 15. *See* climate summit
Copenhagen, 1, 3, 7–10, 12–14, 15–16, 18, 19, 32, 34n5, 35n9–10, 37, 50, 51–54, 57, 62, 66, 67–80, 101–2, 124, 125, 131–32, 138, 144–45, 146, 147–48, 151, 152, 155, 160n9, 162–64, 172, 192–93, 197, 201, 207
Copenhagen School in IR, 139, 159
cosmology, 5, 33, 38, 58–59, 61n9, 144, 166, 199–200, 214
  as emergent effect, 59, 166, 203, 210
  of capitalism, 5, 25, 37–39, 51–55, 56–60, 61n13, 80, 144, 182, 202, 205n14, 205n16–17, 210–11, 214
  political, 5, 32, 38–39, 60n2, 144, 214
cosmos, 38, 58–59

Critical Mass, 13, 184
crowd, 14, 47, 74, 148, 150, 152, 159, 172, 185, 190, 197 (*see also* collective body)
  control, 9, 142, 144, 150
  and violence, 185, 190

Danish Social Forum, 16, 17, 34n3, 43
dead time, 6, 24, 27, 32, 33, 39, 51, 53–54, 56, 83, 89–91, 155, 166, 168, 182, 196, 200, 201–2, 210, 214
De Danske Statsbaner (DSB), 169
Deleuze, Gilles, 61n15
demonstration, 6, 7, 13, 15, 18, 20, 30, 40, 48, 50, 55, 76, 78, 91, 97, 103, 107, 116–17, 123–26, 138, 157, 171–72, 176, 178, 179, 193, 197, 201, 203, 214
  black bloc, 13, 71, 72, 73–74, 87, 109, 110, 173, 188–89, 193, 197
  family friendly, 132, 168, 186, 188–89
  internal organization of, 79, 108–9, 131–33, 169–70, 204n3
  police and demonstrations, 138, 144, 147, 148–50, 160n7, 206n18
Denmark, 3, 4, 7, 11, 13, 16, 20, 36n16, 61n13, 68, 70, 72, 75, 77, 78, 81–82, 98, 101, 127, 132, 145, 180, 184, 188, 204n8, 205n11
depression, 91, 201 (*see also* dead time)
Det Fri Gymnasium (the Free Gymnasium), 8, 34n7, 53, 85
direct action, 4, 6, 17, 26, 29–30, 39, 53, 54–55, 59–60, 85–86, 121, 133, 155, 157, 165–73, 180–203
direct democracy, 4, 39, 215–16, 217 (*see also* consensus decision-making)
Disobedient, 121, 186 (*see also* Tute Bianche)
Disobedienti. *See* Tute Bianche
distributed personhood, 102–3, 120, 122, 123–24, 126, 134, 135, 136n14–15, 153

diversity, 6, 40, 41, 117, 118, 129, 191, 199, 217
  of tactics, 14, 48, 107, 165, 173 (*see also* tactics)
Do-It-Yourself (DIY), 6, 19, 34n4
domination, 21, 83–84, 117
dropping out, 19, 97, 213
dumpster diving, 62–66, 201, 211
Durkheim, Émilie, 28, 31, 36n19, 130, 195, 206n19

Eastern Europe, 43, 44
effectiveness, 5, 29, 33, 167, 181, 186, 187, 188, 190, 193–94, 202, 211 (*see also* style)
egalitarianism, 11, 60n2, 65, 70, 73, 81, 87, 204n2, 208
embodiment, 27, 91, 118, 195, 196 (*see also* body)
Empire, 6, 57–58, 61n14
endurance, 2, 7, 79, 82, 93, 100n1, 202, 217
enemy, 33, 139–40, 153–54, 155, 156, 159, 189, 192, 205n17, 211 (*see also* enmity)
  within, 140–44
Enhedslisten. *See* Red-Green Alliance
enmity, 139
  among the Araweté, 33, 139, 144, 156–57
  between activists and the police, 33, 139, 140, 158–59, 193
  and the body, 156–57, 159
  in securitization theory, 139–40, 159
  symmetry in, 140, 156, 158–59
  temporality and transformability of, 139, 140, 153, 156, 159, 193
equality, 4, 19, 20, 26, 65, 93, 95n19, 195, 196, 201
ethics, 22, 23–24, 108, 212
  situated, 133, 167, 187, 188, 189–90, 191, 202, 203, 211 (*see also* appropriateness)
EU, 33n2, 50, 135, 139, 142–43, 158, 159, 160n2–6
  Security Handbook, 20, 47, 140–42

EU (*cont.*)
  summit in Copenhagen (Denmark) in 2002, 13, 34n3, 78, 146, 150, 161n13
  summit in Göteborg (Sweden) in 2001, 13, 47–48
EuroMayDay, 16, 34n3, 35n13
Europe Bridge, 106, 175–76, 178, 181, 192
European
  peace movement, 102, 105, 173, 176
  Preparatory Assembly (EPA), 17, 35n14, 42–45, 50
  security architecture and policies around major events, 21, 97, 98, 139, 140–41, 142–43, 145, 150, 158, 159
  Social Forum (ESF), 4, 5, 17, 18, 21, 27, 32, 38, 39, 42–50, 51, 54, 60, 61n7–8, 103, 118–19, 136n9, 169, 177, 185
Europol, 141, 160n3
EU-SEC, 141
event, 9, 11, 12, 15, 19, 29–30, 40–41, 42, 43, 44, 46, 102, 120, 123, 126, 140, 165–66, 167, 183, 185, 186, 189, 194–97, 200–201, 203, 209, 213, 214, 216
  dated, 40, 42, 44, 50–53, 57, 58, 59, 103
  enmity as an, 140, 143, 153, 159, 181–82, 193
  time and, 167–68, 195–97, 200–201, 213
  See also European security architecture around major events

Faderhuset (the Father House), 34n6, 67, 68–69, 71, 73, 75, 76–77, 94n8
Fighters and Lovers, 78
figuration of the future, 3, 6, 11, 15, 25–26, 27, 32, 33, 103, 120, 122–23, 124, 134–35, 157, 167–68, 200, 201, 203, 209

'finding oneself' (finde sig selv), 67–68, 70, 80–81, 81–82, 92 (*see also* autonomy)
fire, 37, 38, 74, 75, 77, 113, 128, 129, 136n15, 154, 161n10, 163, 176, 178, 182, 215
Fogh Rasmussen, Anders (former Danish Prime Minister, Head of NATO), 214–15
Folkets Hus (People's House), 9–10, 164, 172
Folkets Park (People's Park), 9–10, 44, 49, 60n6
Initiativet (People's Park Initiative), 10, 88
foraging, 65 (*see also* dumpster diving)
form, 3, 5, 14–15, 27, 30, 99–100, 120, 193–94, 202–3, 208 (*see also* style)
  of action, 3, 5, 12, 13, 14–15, 17, 30, 40, 51, 55, 60, 100, 117, 146, 166, 179–86, 202–3, 208–9
  of activist meetings, 27, 116–120, 121
  appropriate and persuasive, 6, 121, 167, 181, 186–93, 211–12
  of being together, living and organizing, 10–11, 19, 60, 61n13, 68, 70, 71, 82–85, 92–93, 98, 99, 133–34, 136n7
  and content, 5–6, 20, 30, 167, 184, 194, 202–3, 210–11, 214
  determinate, 3, 12, 26, 32, 33, 102–3, 123, 126, 203, 209
  enmity and bodily, 144, 148–50, 153–54, 156, 159. *See also* enmity
  intentions taking a, 6, 17, 100, 103, 120, 121–23, 134–35
  non-human, 32, 102, 123–24, 136n15, 153
  as object, 5, 12–15, 30
  the primacy of, 5, 25, 209, 120, 209
  renewal and reinvention of, 12, 14, 26, 60, 157–58, 186, 210, 215–18
  skillful, 121, 134, 194, 202
  and time, 3, 6, 32, 45, 51, 82, 92, 120, 202–3, 208–9

Foucault, Michel, 58, 94n10, 200
framing, 29–30, 71–72, 183
France, 60n4, 105–106, 107, 108–9, 145, 175, 193, 204n5, 216 (*see also* Strasbourg)
Free Gymnasium (det Fri Gymnasium), 8, 34n7, 53, 85
Freetown Christiania, 7, 8, 9, 34n5, 35n9, 52, 55, 62, 78, 117, 155
front banner, 131, 132, 133, 168, 169–70, 204n3
Front of Socialist Youth, 9, 53, 54, 61n10, 95n17, 170
future, 2, 3, 27–28 (*see also* figuration of the future)
   activist ideas about, 1, 6, 38, 41, 45, 51, 52, 55, 56, 59–60, 80, 91, 100, 118–20, 122, 124, 134–35, 209
   as bodily perspective, 3, 27–28, 136n11, 156, 199, 201–2, 209
   indeterminate character of, 3, 32, 124, 209
   near, 25, 32, 38, 41, 45, 50–51, 58, 59, 102, 103, 126, 134
Future Group, 142–43, 160n6

G8 summit and protests, 33n2, 50, 135n4, 141, 216
   in Genoa, 97, 140, 145, 146, 147, 157, 158, 181, 187, 216
   in Gleneagles, 27, 118, 182
   in Heiligendamm, 14, 55, 79, 97, 100, 106, 107, 114, 142, 180
G13, 34n3, 79–80, 131, 132, 163, 169, 171–72, 180, 181, 184, 198
G20 summit in London, 106, 173, 189
Gadeterapeuterne (Street Therapists), 91
Gell, Alfred, 30, 32, 36n21, 102–3, 123–24, 134, 135n1, 136n14, 140, 200, 212
generation, 20, 32, 48, 52, 67, 68, 70, 75, 80–82, 85, 92, 187, 205n13 (*see also* youth)
Genoa. *See* G8

gentrification, 9, 18, 92, 98, 162, 106, 107, 108, 116, 145, 151, 175, 180, 193
Germany, 14, 55, 79, 98
Gleneagles. *See* G8
Globale Rødder, 6, 7, 13, 15–16, 34n3, 78, 131, 158, 169, 214
Globalisering Underifrån, 158
Global justice movement, 34n2, 38, 40, 61n11, 119, 209, 215, 216, 217, 218 (*see also* alterglobalization movement)
Göteborg, 13, 47–48, 146
Graeber, David, 10, 13, 23, 26, 39, 52, 59, 93, 95n16, 119, 122, 123–24, 125–26, 136n7, 136n12, 147, 161n12, 180, 181, 182, 188, 204n4, 205n16, 206n23
graffiti, 10, 48, 68, 88, 136n15, 163, 178, 185
Grand Pont (Strasbourg), 176–77, 198
Grannies for Asylum (bedsteforældre for asyl), 170
Grøndalsvænge allé, 79, 198 (*see also* G13)
'Ground 69', 76, 78
grupos de afinidad, 10 (*see also* affinity group)
guerrilla gardening, 13, 15, 184
Guyer, Jane, 25, 38, 50–51, 58

hand signals, 105, 117 (*see also* consensus decision-making)
Hardt, Michael, 6, 40, 57–58, 61n11, 61n14–15, 157
Heiligendamm. *See* G8
hierarchy, 87, 95n19, 156, 204n2
Holbraad, Martin, 24, 144, 204n1
holism, 5, 12, 24–25, 38, 166, 210
home, 18–19, 46, 65, 66, 69, 82, 97–99, 122, 147
horizontal relations, 117
horizontality, 26, 42, 117, 118, 120, 129, 165
   and reinvention of form, 11–12
Human A/S Under Foundation, 71 (*see also* Faderhuset)

Hyskenstræde, 162–64, 168, 169, 184–85, 187, 188, 189, 194, 196, 198, 205n16

identity, 4, 13, 15, 22, 24–25, 70, 86, 106, 119
  check by police, 125, 128, 145, 175
  collective or common, 4, 25, 106, 119, 136n8, 208
  and new social movement theory, 24–25, 119
  oppositional, 28, 86, 166, 187, 202
  transient and reinvention of, 6–7, 13, 15, 22
ideology, 5, 38–39, 136n7, 136n11, 209
IMF (International Monetary Fund), 33n2, 206n23
immanence, 26, 28, 61n11, 88, 100n1, 116, 196, 200, 203
indeterminacy, 25–26, 122, 134–35, 137n17
Indignados, 4, 215, 216, 217, 218
individualism,
  egalitarian, 60n1, 80–81
individuality, 17, 25, 32, 35n12, 42, 68, 70, 81, 206n23, 210
Indymedia, 106, 113, 135n2
inequality, 55, 207 (*see also* equality)
infiltration, 2, 108, 116, 136n6, 150–51, 154–55, 157 (*see also* surveillance, undercover police)
injustice, 55, 71, 91, 144, 189, 191, 211
intensity, 17, 30, 31, 108, 147, 166, 179, 182, 185, 188, 190, 198–99, 206n21, 217 (*see also* affect, potentiality)
intentionality, 5, 118, 120, 123, 125 (*see also* intentions)
  mediated manifestations of, 6, 123, 214
intentions, 6, 102–3, 120, 126, 134–35
  abducting intentions from objects and things, 102–3, 126, 135, 135n1

  distribution of, 32, 102–3, 120, 122, 123, 125, 126, 134
  as immanent to forms and things, 6, 15, 17, 98, 99, 100n1, 117, 121, 123, 135, 194, 195, 208, 212
  individual, 6, 35n12, 101–2, 120, 134, 144, 148, 154, 159, 203, 210
  intentional agent and abeyance of agency, 4, 89, 103, 111, 131, 144, 147, 156, 158, 212
  synchronization of, 127–31, 134, 135
internal distance, 10, 55, 57, 59, 61n13, 92
International Permanent Observatory on Security during Major Events (IPO), 141
International Forum, 9
interstice, 5, 39, 55, 58–59, 61n11, 61n13, 181, 183, 217
  of active time, 5, 59, 92, 129, 184, 196, 210 (*see also* active time)
  of autonomy, 55, 68, 74, 91–93, 96, 180, 196, 210, 217
Interventionistiche Linke (IL), 106, 110, 112, 114, 115, 173

Jagtvej 69, 68–69, 76, 78
Jordan, John, 13, 167, 184–85, 195
Juris, Jeffrey, 4, 5, 7, 23–24, 26–27, 40, 134, 135n2, 136n7, 138, 157–58, 165–67, 181, 187, 195, 196, 217

Kafax, 10
Kapferer, Bruce, 28, 29, 60n2, 194, 195, 211
Karpantschof, René, 8, 9, 20, 74, 75, 94n6, 186, 192
'kende sin plads' (know one's place), 67, 81–82
kettle(ing), 176–78, 195, 198, 199, 209, 215
Kiev (Ukraine), 43–45, 50
'klare sig selv' (managing on one's own), 70, 81
Klein, Naomi, 52
Kollund, 13

Kreutzberg, 96
Krogstad, Anne, 86–87
Kværs, 13

Law on Popular Enlightenment (Folkeoplysningsloven), 73
left radical activists, 3, 4–5, 6–7, 10, 11, 25, 39, 41–42, 48, 51, 54, 57–58, 59, 78, 83, 92, 130, 136n9, 143–44, 158, 161n17, 192, 193, 202–3
Lévi-Strauss, Claude, 64, 213
liminality, 27, 28, 168, 184, 195 (see also ritual)
liminoid, 28, 167, 184, 195 (see also performance)
listserv, 21, 56, 104
London, 106, 118, 119, 173, 177, 189
Lund, 46

Maastricht Treaty, 9
Maeckelbergh, Marianne, 4, 6, 23, 25, 27, 33, 36n18, 41, 51, 61n7, 95n16, 103, 118–20, 125, 134–35, 136n8–11, 203, 209
Malmö, 4, 17–18, 21, 32, 38, 42–44, 46, 48–50, 60n6, 103, 104, 119, 158, 175, 177, 185
marionettes, 124 (see also puppets)
Marxist left, 6, 17, 38, 41, 49, 50–51, 59, 117
Massumi, Brian, 12, 25, 31, 197, 198, 199, 205n14, 206n21
material turn, 30
Mauss, Marcel, 31, 129, 165, 202
media, 5, 8, 16, 18, 26, 36n16, 37, 104, 111, 112, 140, 147, 150, 181, 186, 189, 191–93, 215, 217
  activist media, 55, 104, 106, 113, 129, 135n2, 155, 191 (see also Indymedia)
  coverage of protests, 5, 37, 74, 80, 132, 150, 157, 163–64, 172, 178, 180, 182, 186, 189–90, 192–93
  and persuasiveness, 79, 181, 192–93

meeting, 1–2, 6, 18–19, 21–22, 40, 71, 83, 102–3, 116–23, 131–35, 201, 210
  affinity group, 131–34, 168
  consensus decision-making during, 71, 117–18, 122, 134, 136n7
  domination during, 83–84, 117, 136n7
  and distribution of intentions, 32–33, 35n12, 103, 120–23, 125, 134
  facilitation of, 2, 22, 116–18, 121, 136n7, 195, 201
  form of, 59, 66, 116–20, 120–23, 125, 134
  'good meeting style' (god møde stil), 83–84, 187, 201, 210
  Monday, 71, 77–78, 83, 85, 89–90
  as prefiguration, 33, 103, 118–21, 122–23, 125, 135
  preparation and planning, 16, 17, 21, 35n12, 43–45, 49–50, 59, 62, 96, 97, 102, 103–16, 155–56
  See also spokes-council
Melucci, Alberto, 4, 24–25, 204 (see also movement)
middle-class, 9, 26, 53, 63, 69, 213, 217
militancy, 13, 72, 93, 116, 117, 178, 186
militant anthropology, 23–24
mimetic disguise, 158
mimicry, 124, 154, 175, 182, 192
Miyazaki, Hirokazu, 3, 25, 134, 137n17, 203
Molodoi, 105, 115, 174, 175, 179
Monday meeting (mandagsmøde). See meeting
moral, 36n19, 51, 63, 70, 86–87, 185, 202, 206n19, 213. See also ethic
movement, 1–2, 4–5, 18, 23, 24–28, 39, 40, 42, 44, 51, 77, 118–20, 157–58, 203, 215–18
  being, 2, 25, 177, 203
  bodily, 69–70, 159, 175, 177, 178, 203, 215

movement (*cont.*)
　European peace, 102, 105, 107, 109, 113, 173, 178, 188, 192, 198
　of movements, 33n2, 136n8
　new social, 4–5, 24–25, 119, 136n8, 136n10, 203, 208
　See also alterglobalization movement, Occupy, squatters
Movement for More Opera Houses, 72
Movement for More Youth Houses, 78
multinaturalism, 199–200 (*see also* Amerindian perspectivism)
multitude, 58, 61n14
Municipality of Copenhagen, 16, 18, 35n10, 69

naming, 99–100, 158, 161n17
NATO summit in 2009, 18, 20–21, 50, 55, 93, 96, 102, 104, 106–8, 109, 113, 127, 129, 135n4, 139, 145, 154, 160n8, 166, 174–76, 215
near future. *See* future
Negri, Antonio, 6, 39, 49, 57–58, 61n11, 61n15, 92, 157
neoliberalism, 40, 42, 50, 52. *See also* capitalism
Never Trust a Cop, 37, 117, 189, 192
new social movement, 4–5, 24–25, 119, 136n8, 136n10, 203, 208
non-violence, 13, 114, 181, 183, 189, 211 (*see also* civil disobedience)
normalization, 8, 35n9, 73, 77, 78, 94n10
Nørrebro, 7–10, 35n10, 53–54, 67, 69, 72, 74, 79, 85, 102, 155, 164, 198
　Beboeraktion (Nørrebro tenants' action group), 8
Northern Europe, 4, 51, 88, 98, 193, 208, 211, 216
No to War (Nej til Krig), 113

Occupy, 4, 60, 215–18
oho chant, 120–21
ontological self-determination, 24, 204n1
ontology, 25, 26, 27, 29, 30, 33, 167, 196, 199–200, 209

Openhagen, 18
openness, 2, 6, 25, 27, 34n8, 40, 41–42, 56, 71, 77, 95n18, 134, 155, 187, 209
　as theory of change, 46
Optøj, 78
order and disorder, 38, 57, 58–59, 63, 126, 167, 179, 196, 210
Øresundsbroen, 13, 15, 35n12
otherwise, the, 31

Palais de la Musique et des Congrès (Strasbourg), 175
paranoia, 23, 33, 155, 161n15, 201
Parents against Police Brutality, 76, 91
Paris Commune, the, 58
people's assembly, 1, 183
people's microphone, 197, 216, 218n4
People's Park. *See* Folkets Park
pepper spray, 127, 152
performance,
　as appearance, 30, 203
　as organizing time and space, 32, 166
　protest, 18, 60, 165–66, 203, 208, 211
　skillful, 123, 126, 166, 186, 192, 194, 201, 202–3
　theory, 19, 26, 28–32, 167, 194–96
performative,
　appearance, 28–30, 156, 203
　confrontation, 166, 191, 193, 196, 203
　effectiveness, 29, 186, 194, 195
　enmity, 153
　unpredictability, 150, 156
perspectivism. *See* Amerindian perspectivism
persuasiveness, 5, 30, 33, 167, 181, 187, 188, 191–94, 202, 211 (*see also* style)
PGP (Pretty Good Privacy), 112, 136n5
Pippi Longstocking (Pippi Langstrømpe), 98–99
Piratgruppen (The Pirate Group), 16, 34n3

Index

'plads til alle'. *See* room for all, spaciousness
Plaza del Sol, 216
police, 1–2, 20
   and activist intentions, 101–2, 121, 123, 134–35, 143, 147–49, 158, 193, 212
   actions against puppets, 103, 123, 125–26
   attack, 78, 127–28, 131, 155, 189
   confrontation with the, 1–2, 3, 7–10, 14, 15, 26, 30, 33, 47, 55, 59, 67, 69, 72, 74, 79, 99, 110, 133, 136n16, 166, 167, 172, 174–75, 176–77, 178, 180, 182, 183, 185, 188, 192, 194, 196, 197–98, 201–3, 209
   dialogue, 146–47, 148–49, 161n11
   human/non-human nature of, 33, 127–28, 152–153, 179, 189, 190, 211
   infiltration and surveillance, 18, 33, 57, 97, 104, 108, 115, 148, 150, 154, 201, 204n3
   and media, 9, 75, 80, 125, 147, 150, 185, 193, 204n8
   nicknames, 153
   operational tactics of, 9, 20, 78, 97, 107, 116, 126, 135n4, 138–39, 140–42, 144–50, 160n7–9, 169–70, 173, 206n18
   plain-clothes, 145, 149–50, 161n12, 172
   raids of camps and convergence centres, 125, 147, 151, 156, 161n10, 174
   repression and violence, 9, 21, 47–48, 52, 76, 77, 91, 97,99, 134, 152, 157–58, 160n1, 176, 182, 183, 193, 204n8
   and style, 74, 187
   training, 128–29, 141–42, 145, 158, 183
   transformability, invisibility and role changing of, 20, 33, 57, 138–39, 140, 146, 149–50, 152–54, 156, 159
   undercover, 22, 35n15, 36n16, 116, 136n6, 160n2, 161n13
political action, 3, 5, 19, 31, 184, 196–97, 202–3, 208, 217
politics,
   body, 32, 212–13
   as elicited by form, 20, 166, 194
   form and content distinction in, 5–6, 20, 30, 167, 184, 194, 202–3, 210–11, 214
   identity, 24–25, 86, 119, 136n8
   as immanent to action, 61n11, 88, 100n1, 116, 203, 208, 212–13 (*see also* absorption)
   at an internal distance of the state ,10, 55, 57, 59, 61n13, 79, 92
   as mediated manifestation of intentionality, 6, 123, 214
   prefigurative, 118, 208 (*see also* prefiguration)
   public, 69, 76, 82, 208
   theory of, 209, 214
Porto Alegre, 16, 40
potentiality, 31, 99, 143, 187, 198, 205n14, 213
Povinelli, Elizabeth, 31, 32, 36n22, 68, 76, 81, 82, 92–93, 100n1, 154, 212
power, 7, 12, 24, 25, 26, 36n22, 55, 57, 61n9, 95n19, 124, 126, 136n12, 156, 177, 190, 192, 194, 198–99, 208, 212
Prague, 13, 26, 136n16
prefiguration, 27, 32, 103, 118–20, 122–23, 135, 167, 199, 203, 209
Preum Treaty, 160n6
preventive arrest and detention, 57, 146, 160n2
proactive protection, 142, 159
process, 17, 25, 27, 28–29, 41, 43, 45–46, 60, 81–82, 118–20, 135, 136n9
property destruction, 136n12, 163, 178, 182, 189, 191, 205n16

protest, 18, 19–20, 26–27, 29–30, 31–32, 33n1–2, 50, 55, 68, 100, 102–3, 126, 140, 141, 156, 157–58, 165–68, 183–85, 186, 189, 191, 192, 194–96, 201, 202, 203, 204n2, 208–9, 211, 213, 215–17
public,
   appearance, 33, 164, 193, 203
   debate, 5, 13, 23, 32, 48, 67, 68, 70–71, 72, 75, 79–80, 91–92, 94n8, 139, 143, 157, 167, 179, 180–81, 185, 186, 189, 190, 192–93, 204n8, 208, 211–12, 218 (*see also* media)
   order, 101, 140, 141–42, 146, 159, 175, 185, 205n11
   politics, 69, 76, 82, 208, 217
   private partnership, 141
   space, 4, 18, 19, 22, 33, 60, 69, 70–71, 75–76, 79, 82, 88, 94n6, 95n21, 148, 162, 164, 184–85, 189, 196, 210, 215–16
   young people in, 69–70
punk, 10, 64, 76, 83, 86, 88, 89–90, 91, 96, 110
puppet, 15, 123–25, 129, 134, 136n12, 147, 212
   and abduction of agency, 123, 125–26, 134–35
   agency and intentionality, 15, 32, 102, 120, 123–25, 126, 134, 136n15, 212
   animal, 123–24
   as sacred objects, 123–24, 205n16
Pusher Street, 8, 35n9

Queen Louise's Bridge (Dronning Louises bro), 7, 72

radical,
   assembly, 21, 48
   change, 3, 4, 25, 32, 38, 41, 61n13, 66, 205n14
   See also left radical
radicalization, 4, 79, 93, 194
rebel, 85, 95n17

rebellion, 51, 58, 59, 91, 94n14, 195
Reclaim Power, 1, 29, 30, 33n1, 52, 55, 59, 101, 117, 125, 149, 152, 181, 183, 184, 197, 199, 209
Reclaim the Streets, 13, 15, 18, 47, 162–64, 184–86, 187–88, 205n10
Red-Green Alliance (Enhedslisten), 61n10, 69, 94n1, 95n17
red zone, 107, 128, 135n4, 145, 146, 147, 157, 159, 174
   and pink zone, 128
relation,
   enmity as a social, 159
   social, 7, 15, 30–31, 55, 56, 84, 88, 91, 93, 123, 126, 130, 140, 190
repression. *See* police repression
Résistance des Deux Rives, 106, 116
Revolt Network, 96–97, 102, 104, 106, 109
revolution, 6, 41, 45, 51, 55, 58, 59, 66, 84, 179, 182, 210
riot, 2, 13, 19, 29, 37, 67, 74–75, 76, 78–79, 94n6, 117, 129, 142, 145, 173, 178, 181–82, 185, 186, 189, 192, 197, 201
   non-violent rioting, 2, 107, 157, 183
   'riot porn', 55 (*see also* Youtube)
ritual, 26, 28–29, 35n11, 65, 86, 100, 102, 121, 125, 130, 165, 167, 171, 178, 184–86, 187, 194–96, 199, 202
   time, 100, 199
Robbins, Joel, 3, 25, 38, 51, 100, 136n9
room for all (plads til alle), 70, 73, 76, 84, 91, 187 (*see also* spaciousness)
Rosengård, 44, 49
Rostock, 14, 142, 145
rummelighed. *See* spaciousness
rupture, 39, 51, 58–59, 66, 84
Ryesgade, 7

safety index, 35n10
Sandholm, 131, 168–70, 179, 180, 188
scale, 12, 167, 187, 194, 211
   self-scaling figure, 12, 136n11

Index **245**

Schengen agreement, 106, 135n3, 145, 160n2
securitization, 138, 159
 inverse securitizing move, 144, 156
 symmetry in, 156, 158–59
 theory, 139–40, 141, 159
security, 139–40
 and big data, 142–43
 culture, 19, 21, 95, 121–22, 135, 151, 154, 157–58, 161n15, 212
 and intentions, 121–22, 152, 159
 around major events, 20,21, 33,47, 97, 98, 138–39, 140–43, 145–46
 spatial security, 135n4, 145–46, 154, 155
 times of, 33, 139, 143, 158–59
 via the production of insecurity, 20, 126, 138, 146, 150, 152
 See also European Security Architecture, EU Security Handbook
self-determination, 24, 204n1
self-managed social centre, 8, 9, 46, 48, 53, 67, 68, 73, 80, 174
 playground, 97–98 (*see also* Byggeren)
 space during ESF, 48
self-organization, 39, 40–41, 45, 60, 83, 134
shape-shifting, 154, 156, 178
Shut Down the Camp, 14, 18, 19, 103, 165, 168–73, 180, 181, 184, 197
situated ethic. *See* ethic: situated
social centre. *See* self-managed social centre
Social Democratic Party, 60n6, 207–8
Social Forum. *See* European Social Forum or World Social Forum
Socialist Workers Party (SWP), 49, 51
Socialistisk Ungdomsfront (Front of Socialist Youth), 9, 53, 54, 61n10, 95n17, 170
Solvognen, 14
sound truck, 1, 163, 169, 170, 171, 172, 197, 204n3
soup kitchen, 3, 10, 48, 65, 83, 88, 104, 129, 213

space,
 autonomous and self-managed, 7, 8–9, 10, 11, 27, 34n5, 46, 48, 67, 68, 70, 71, 73, 78, 81, 83, 92–93, 104, 158, 184, 191, 196, 200, 215, 217
 free, 47, 48–49, 73, 84, 92, 184, 191, 200, 203
 open, 41, 42, 44, 77
 reclaiming, 162, 165, 184, 185. *See also* reclaim the street
 third, 183
 See also public space
Space Hijackers, 184
spaciousness (rummelighed), 4, 67, 70–72, 73, 76–77, 78, 84–85, 93, 94n7, 217, 218
Spanish Civil War, 10
speech act, 29–30, 100, 139, 194–95, 202
Spidsroden, 9
spoke, 118
spokes-council, 129, 173, 175, 176, 177–78, 204n4, 206n23
squatters, 4, 7–8, 12, 14, 34n6, 72, 74, 83, 86, 87, 153, 157, 181 (*see also* BZ)
state, the, 35n9, 39, 57, 59, 61n13, 72, 73, 77, 82, 85, 90, 92, 131, 143, 180, 192, 207, 212, 216
Stengade, 9, 88
Stockholm Programme, the, 143
Strasbourg, 3, 4, 18, 19, 20, 21, 50, 93, 96, 97, 100, 103–17, 121, 127, 130, 135n4, 139, 144, 145–46, 147, 151–52, 154–55, 166, 173–79, 181, 182, 186, 188, 189, 190, 192, 193, 195, 197, 198, 199, 201, 209
Strathern, Marilyn, 7, 11, 12, 25, 3–31, 36n20, 120, 125, 157, 167, 186, 188, 194, 203, 210, 213
strength, 18, 40, 45, 56, 66, 72, 80, 107, 108, 146, 160n7, 171, 177, 182, 195, 198–99, 201, 202, 213, 214

style, 5–6, 12, 29, 31, 33, 74, 80, 110, 126, 132, 157, 162, 165, 166–68, 178, 181, 184, 185, 186–94, 202–3, 210–11
  bad style, 65, 211
  Birmingham School and, 166, 187, 210
  good style, 33, 83, 90, 168, 187, 188, 194, 201, 202, 203, 211
subcultural studies. *See* Birmingham school
sub-culture, 86, 87, 187, 205n13
surveillance. *See* police: surveillance
swarming, 2, 79, 128, 183–84, 197, 213
Sweden, 3, 4, 13, 38, 42, 46, 47, 49, 60n6, 98, 116, 143, 158, 204n2
symbol, 14–15, 24, 28–29, 75, 86–87, 106, 115, 157, 166, 179, 187, 195
synchronization, 31, 33, 127, 129–31, 135, 183, 197, 199, 201
Syntagma Square, 216

tactic, 2, 5, 16, 23, 54, 58, 109, 114–15, 122, 124, 126, 131, 133–34, 157, 158, 168, 179, 182, 183, 189, 190, 191, 204n3–4, 204n8
  diversity of, 13–14, 33n1, 48, 71, 79–80, 106–7, 110, 114, 117, 165, 173, 181
  of focusing on the gaps, 106, 114, 127–28
  police, 9, 20, 74, 140, 144–50, 152, 160n1, 160n9
Tahrir Square, 216
targets, 55, 104, 110–11, 116, 118, 121, 122, 140, 155, 156, 173, 178, 183
tear gas, 5, 9, 74, 78, 79, 80, 127, 128, 129, 146, 169, 170, 171, 172, 174, 175, 176, 178, 181, 213
techniques of the body, 27, 127, 129, 130–31, 165, 166, 181, 199, 202, 213
theory of politics, 207, 209, 214
Thorning-Schmidt, Helle, 207–8, 209, 212

threat, 20, 57, 77, 92, 125, 131, 139–40, 141–44, 145, 146, 147, 154, 155, 156, 159, 175, 205n17, 206n18
time, 3, 5, 6, 11, 12, 15, 17, 18, 23, 25–26, 27, 30, 31, 32, 38, 41, 47, 64, 66, 82, 92, 97–98, 100, 102, 119, 129, 131, 135, 138, 143, 167–68, 181–82, 184, 187, 188–89, 190, 194, 196–203, 208, 213–14
  active, 3, 6, 27, 32, 33, 67, 82, 83–91, 92–93, 100, 166, 168, 182, 196, 200–201, 210, 213–14
  as bodily perspective, 3, 31, 56, 92, 130, 136n11, 150, 159, 167, 194, 197, 199–202, 213
  bracketed, 82
  dead, 6, 24, 27, 32, 33, 39, 51–56, 89–91, 155, 166, 182, 196, 200–201, 210, 214
  discontinuous, 38, 41, 45, 49, 50–51, 58, 59, 74, 119, 209
  as flow, flux and process, 119, 135, 136n9, 167, 195
  linear time, 3, 27–28, 29, 33, 100, 119, 167, 196, 199, 200
  ontology of, 27, 29, 32, 166, 200
  perspectivist model of, 3, 27, 32, 165, 167–68, 201–3, 209
transformability, 33, 139, 140, 153, 156
troublemaker, 8, 34n3, 67, 69, 91, 94n14, 139, 148–49, 150, 152, 160n7, 178, 186
Turner, Victor, 26–27, 28–29, 31, 167, 184–86, 195–96, 204n2
Tute Bianche, 13, 34n3, 157–58, 161n16, 180, 183
twinkling, 105, 108, 109, 117, 121, 126 (*see also* hand signals)

Undoing the City, 18, 162, 164
Ungdomshuset, 3, 7, 8, 9, 10, 13, 14, 16–17, 18, 20, 32, 34n6, 48, 53–54, 67–95, 146, 153, 155, 158, 160n9, 162, 169, 180, 181, 186, 189, 192, 198, 211, 217

United Nations Interregional Crime and Justice Research Institute (UNICRI), 141
uniforms , 9, 148, 150, 153, 182
unpredictability, 20, 33, 138, 140, 149–52, 156, 188
Utkanten, 17, 21, 46, 47, 48–49, 158
utopia, 26–27, 28, 39, 161n17, 195, 196, 200

veganism, 4, 48, 62, 63, 66, 83, 85–86, 87, 88, 89, 93, 110, 111, 115, 157, 187, 196, 208
violence, 13, 72, 76, 77, 79, 94n7, 101, 125, 127, 140, 146, 148, 152, 153, 155, 161n12–13, 167, 181, 182, 183, 188–90, 191, 206n20, 211, 212
vitality, 3, 88, 199, 201 (*see also* activism, active time)
Viveiros de Castro, Eduardo, 3, 24, 27, 31, 33, 139, 140, 144, 156–57, 159, 167, 194, 196–97, 199–200, 204n1, 209, 210

volt sorcery, 124, 136n14 (*see also* Alfred Gell)

warrior bike, 14, 125, 147, 149
White Overalls. *See* Tute Bianche
World Bank, 14, 33n2, 136n16, 140, 165, 181, 182, 206n23
World Economic Forum (WEF), 40
World Social Forum (WSF), 4, 16, 40–41
World Trade Organization (WTO), 4, 14, 33n2, 135n2

Ya Basta, 2, 157, 158, 161n16, 183
youth, 5, 8, 28, 32, 34n6, 54, 64, 67–68, 69–70, 75–77, 80–82, 91–92, 94n14, 97, 98, 140, 146, 166, 187, 205n15, 210
Youth House. *See* Ungdomshuset
YouTube videos, 20, 32, 37–38, 39, 55, 56–57, 192, 210

Zapatista, 13, 161n16
Zuccotti Park, 216, 218

www.ingramcontent.com/pod-product-compliance
Lightning Source LLC
Chambersburg PA
CBHW070918030426
42336CB00014BA/2458